Papa

A JOURNEY BACK

STORIES OF FAMILY, FRIENDS & LIFE

JERRY IL'GIOVINE JR.

bambino
PUBLISHING

Cover design by Clare Il'Giovine

For more on PAPA A JOURNEY BACK
visit www.bambinopublishing.weebly.com

ISBN: 978-1-7354071-1-1

For my Sweet Judi and the rest of our beautiful family
– past, present, and future...
~ Con Amore

We influence the universe without ever speaking a word, teaching and learning life lessons through subtle vibrations.
~ *Proverbial Wisdom*

Papa

CONTENTS

PREFACE

Va bene! When I retired in December of 2014, it was time to leave Corporate America's daily grind behind me. Let them keep their daily schedules, monthly deadlines, and yearly objectives. I've had my share of those distractions. It was time to focus on the things I value most in this world.

I began by reflecting on my happy yet unassuming past. Admittedly, I'm not a wealthy or famous man, nor am I poor or friendless. I've done well by some, and arguably not so well by others. No buildings or parks bear my name. And I've never held high public office or had my name etched in the Guinness Book of World Records.

So why would an ordinary Joe like me even bother to write about anything? My reasoning might surprise you. It is simple and straightforward, and what inspired me to sit down at a keyboard and bang away.

It has everything to do with enjoying history, all kinds of history, but especially family history. I have since I was old enough to ask questions.

My family ancestry is relatively common by American standards. Cultivated in Europe, my roots sprouted limbs reaching over an ocean to the United States through the first half of the twentieth century. Mine specifically stretched across from southern Italy to settle in Ohio. But who were these daring people, really? They were so much more than the tidbits I picked up here and there; tiny snippets passed down from one generation to the next. Lifetimes reduced to names, dates, and photos in a scrapbook. I wondered about their everyday circumstances, their passions, personal observations, and pet peeves. If I could only go back and see for myself since they left so little of that behind.

This kind of wishful thinking motivated me to leave a more prominent trail of breadcrumbs for future generations to follow back, at least the ones that share this ancestral curiosity of mine. I aim to bestow something much more personal to them, something that may breathe a little life into the scrapbooks they will inherit. I realized I could answer some of their questions concerning *my* everyday circumstances, passions, personal observations, and pet peeves. It's a tie that binds. **Descendants are really the intended audience**, though I'm sure most everyone will relate, not to the actual events necessarily, but to the emotions they evoke.

Once I began to reflect on what I could share with my present and future kin, it quickly became apparent. An unassuming life doesn't mean an ordinary or insignificant one at all. As I journeyed back in time for a closer look, I found days filled with plenty of material that sparked the kind of universal emotions we all share.

Ultimately, when it comes to recollections, we remember our feelings above all, more so than the tangible details that fade with time. This project gave me a chance to relive many of those heartfelt moments. My conclusion? It's a wonderful life. And the thought of my subtle vibrations rippling through the universe into the future is a pretty damn exciting prospect.

Jerry Il'Giovine Jr. – a.k.a. Papa

TO THE READER

Each story is a bite-size, stand-alone piece. These trips back in time, along with some good old-fashion imagination, allowed me to recreate the aura of an event, locale, or conversation, meaning I used artistic license. This includes fictional and composite characters, places, and dialogues to help capture, condense, and convey the narrative.

Names of people, places, and things may be altered to keep everyone happy and protected. If any sound recognizable, I still may have tweaked some identifying characteristics with no harm intended, or it is strictly coincidental. If at times, it sounds like lecturing or gloating, I very well could be, but it's all in the name of a papa sharing his family pride or imparting life lessons learned with his children.

This project never started out as a linear autobiography. It was about reminiscing memorable times in no particular order and then writing them down as self-contained stories. One of the consequences of writing this way resulted in some repetition of information. So if you pardon the redundancy, I prefer it to read more like an overlapping collage of adventures.

Finally, you can brush up on your Italian words and slang phrases using the glossary in the back of the book.

SOCRATES CAVE

THE FOUR OF US RUMBLED OVER the Lorain-Carnegie Bridge in a souped-up Ford Fairlane. It was early spring in 1970 as we headed toward a new destination just across downtown Cleveland. The bridge spanned the infamous Cuyahoga, the river that made national headlines by catching fire the year before. The massive steel and concrete structure also connected two very polarized areas of town, our near west side to the unfamiliar east side. And it didn't really matter which side of the river you came from back in those days. Social mores and fear of the unknown allowed for very little need or desire to use the bridge, regardless of how close you lived to it. This would become a trek into uncharted territory in more ways than one.

We were *racks*, the local term for greasers. More importantly to us, we were *Rocco Boys* – members of a much larger, what I'll call a *street fraternity* of mostly Italian teenagers banded together in an ethnic area of town known as Clark-Fulton. The name Rocco Boys originated from our neighborhood parish Saint Rocco, literally built by the Italians in the community brick by brick. It was a proud, close-knit, and safe neighborhood assuming you were respectful of it. God help you if you weren't.

The evening air was warm, so all the windows were rolled down. Paul was driving, Tom rode shotgun, and I was in the back seat with Leo. I was just seventeen and the only minor in the car. Paul looked at me from the rearview mirror.

"Jerry, you gotta way in, right?"

"Yeah, I'm good," I said to the eyes in the mirror.

A college bar had recently opened in an old industrial area on the east side of town. The state university and community college were both nearby. Tom heard it was worth checking out despite having to cross the river and ignoring the fact college was not on anyone's radar. I had no idea what I was about to get myself into at the time.

"There it is," Tom said, smacking Paul's arm and pointing, "Socrates Cave."

"I don't see any spots on the street," Paul replied as we drove past the nightclub.

"Then turn around and go back to that lot on the corner," Tom said as we continued down the road. "Just make a damn U-turn right here."

"Take it easy, *chooch*," Paul fired back. "I got this."

We left the car parked in the gravel lot and walked up

the street toward the sound of a muted percussion that grew louder as we approached the old brick building. I opened the heavy door to a blast of loud, crisp music, and the four of us entered single-file.

We found ourselves at the end of a long line in a dimly lit foyer, standing behind three young women who stopped speaking the moment they noticed us. But I swear they began a whole new conversation without uttering a single word by staring at each other and giggling. The intermittent glances toward us suggested we were the topic of discussion. I glanced over their heads toward the front of the line to see what was delaying us. A rather large bouncer perched on a barstool was checking IDs with a penlight.

Since this was a planned visit, I was carrying my friend Gabriel's draft card. It identified my age as eighteen. I pulled it out of my wallet and flashed it at Paul. He nodded and smirked. Military drafts were in session during this Vietnam era, and draft cards were mandatory identification for all young males eighteen and over.

The excitement intensified as we approached the guarded entryway. I stretched my neck a few times to peer into the bar. Using a borrowed ID was a first for me, so when I made it to the head of the line, I probably should've been nervous handing Gabe's card to the big man, but I wasn't. There was no photo on a draft card, and I matched the physical characteristics exactly; height, weight, hair, and eye color. I thought the worst that could happen should my ruse be discovered was a soft *bounce* out the door.

He fixed the light to the card, and studied it for what seemed to be an excessive amount of time, then without moving his head, shifted his squinty eyes up toward me. His pause created an adrenaline rush, and both my heart and mind began to race. Christ, it suddenly dawned on me I could be detained while they call the police. My father would probably kill me if I ever came home in a cop car. Then there are all those nosy neighbors. I could hear my mother telling me how I shamed the entire family. And how dumb is this? I'd forgotten Gabe's birthdate in case this *stunad* tries to trip me up with such a simple question. I heard they do that sometimes. I obviously hadn't thought this thing through very well. I felt a knot in my stomach and stopped breathing. So now what? Maybe I should make the first move, but what the hell would I do? I could try to stare him down, but he's a goddamn bouncer in a bar for God's sake, so it might be smarter just to snatch the card out of his hand and make a beeline toward the exit.

I watched his mouth open to draw a breath and speak. Here it comes, I thought, fight, or flight. "Thanks, Gabriel." He handed the card back to me and looked at the next person in line.

"Thank you very much," I replied, overextending

myself, then fumbled the ID back into my wallet with a sigh of relief. I stepped over the threshold and found it exhilarating, as if I just entered a members-only secret society. Still, this was as close as I needed to get to the college scene.

The four of us stood at the entrance scanning the layout. The room was dark, smoky, loud, and lively. Clusters of small tables cluttered with beer glasses and smoldering ashtrays surrounded a packed dance floor. Lights flickered down on a footloose mob gyrating shoulder to shoulder to a driving beat, reverberating to my core. The music drew my eyes toward the back of the room, where a live band with brass instruments was rocking the crowd from a small stage. A guy-girl duet was belting out the song, *I Want to Take You Higher* by Sly & the Family Stone. I caught myself bobbing to the beat. To the far right, an extended saloon countertop stretched along the front wall, crammed with people three deep as bartenders rushed back and forth behind it. It was SRO at Socrates Cave on a hopping Friday night.

I noticed the rough textured walls constructed to resemble bedrock. It created an underground effect. I didn't realize it at the time, but the theme of this bar was a clever take on Plato's parable, *The Allegory of the Cave.*

In it, Plato has his mentor Socrates compare different perceptions of reality. The story begins with a group of prisoners inside a dark cave. Chained since birth, they face nothing but a wall and are unable to turn their heads. Behind them, a massive fire burns brightly with puppeteers casting shadowy shapes of people, animals, and objects on the wall in front of them. The prisoners give names to these ghostly figures and often have lengthy, detailed discussions about them. After all, Socrates explains, the wall is their entire world. The shadows are their reality. Then one of the prisoners is set free to the sunlight above ground. He finds the climb out to the daylight physically and mentally painful. Once outside, everything seems confusing until he is enlightened by the real world. Socrates then examines the challenges the prisoner faces with this knowledge back inside the cave after his illuminating revelation.

Great reading for inquiring minds perhaps, but not so much for impetuous, young racks – not yet, anyway. Still, it's a creative name for a gathering place of bright people.

The four of us began drifting toward the dance floor and commandeered a table as a couple stood to leave. Leo grabbed two more chairs, and we all sat down. An attractive waitress soon approached. She seemed a bit frazzled and spoke without making eye contact as she collected the empty beer glasses and wiped down the table.

"You boys want to start off with a pitcher?"

"Yeah, that sounds good, doll," Leo said. "Why don't you take a break and sit down with us for a drink?"

Her response was an abrupt look and a fake smile. "I'll be right back."

"Ouch!" I said, ribbing him as she walked away. "I guess that's why they call you the *Rapper*."

He twitched his eyebrows at me and we both laughed.

Of course, the only alcohol served at a student bar was a cheap brew called three-two, as in 3.2 percent alcohol. Twenty-one was the legal drinking age in Ohio for anything harder.

We waited patiently for our drinks. Four brash, dapper fellows from across town, dressed in our traditional Banlon shirts under black leather jackets, sharkskin pants, and spit-shined *Regal* dress shoes. Regal was the affordable brand in our neighborhood and a proper rack had several pairs in different styles and colors. I was wearing blue wingtips.

I studied the appearance of the collegians while sipping my beer. *Madonne*, these girls were pretty, garbed in stylish halter-tops, bell-bottoms, and miniskirts then accented in earrings, headbands, wide belts, and beaded necklaces. The vast majority had long, straight hair and some parted it down the middle. Others had bushy Afros.

The majority of guys wore striped or tie-dyed T-shirts with bell-bottom jeans. A few were dressed *preppy*, that is, with button-down polo shirts, khaki slacks, and penny loafers. One was even smoking a pipe. Seriously? My grandfather Pasquale owed the same one. Their hairstyles were also very different than our slicked back look. Most wore it long, shaggy, dry, and natural.

I began to understand some of the annoyed and uneasy looks we were generating, then thought about the three girls in the foyer.

We continued drinking our beers and smoking cigarettes, quietly watching everyone having fun while engaged in conversation. I couldn't make out what they were discussing but imagined it was the likes of politics, economics, and the arts and sciences. I also sensed their confidence, which was intriguing and truthfully, a bit intimidating. We began sharing our thoughts by the third pitcher.

"Those potheads over there look like wimps."

"This swill tastes like piss water. Let's go get some real beer."

"I think I'm in love with that girl over there. She keeps looking at me."

"Yeah, she's got one eye on you and one hand on the mace in her purse."

"You're so full of crap your eyes are brown."

"Didn't you get the memo about girls finding him adorable?"

"Yeah, but his mother don't count."

"Hey, shut up about my mother."

"This band is damn good. I want to get out there and boogie."

"They should play more Motown."

"Is it me, or is everybody staring at us? Do we stick out?"

"Like buck teeth, brother."

Once our riveting analysis subsided, we unanimously decided to return the following night. Then Paul made an observation I was already contemplating.

"We gotta go *mod*," he suggested, "if we're gonna blend in here."

Each of us nodded and raised our glasses. "Here's to going mod." It was really that simple. We began discussing plans for the following day.

The next afternoon we headed to Parmatown Mall in a western suburb to find a new wardrobe. I bought two cotton pullovers and a pair of bell-bottom jeans. Later that night, the Cabretta leathers and Regal shoes stayed home. We even officially announced *the wet head is dead!* I liked our new look.

Weeks passed as we melded into this new world, and soon more of the boys back home began crossing the river with us. We were showing up two, three, and sometimes four nights a week. At that rate, it didn't take long to become one of the regulars. Regulars just called it *the Cave* and didn't wait in line or need to show any identification. The bouncers greeted me with a quick nod and a *"hiya Gabe"* as I walked straight through the doors. Sometimes the off-duty cop working security picked up the tab for the regulars.

"Hey, barkeeper," he yelled, over the music, "get Gabe here a pitcher on me."

"Do what, now? No, no, wait!" I hollered as the bartender pulled the beer tap handle.

"What, I can't buy you beer when I feel like it?"

"No, that's not it."

"So, what is it?"

"It's just, well, I don't know." I wasn't about to tell him the truth.

"Then don't worry about it, Gabe," he said, leaning in, "they never charge me for it anyway."

"Ah, well, okay, I guess. Thanks, man."

A couple of girls stopped me on the way back to my table. Don't ask me how I ever managed to keep my two identities straight.

"Hi Jerry, love your hair! Did you tie-dye that shirt yourself?"

"Nah, a girl from CSU made it for me."

"Boy, you sure look a lot different than the first time we saw you here."

One put her lips up to my ear. "We should dance later, okay?"

"Count on it," I said. I was having the summer of my life!

Our evenings always started at the Cave, but we eventually began to venture out to similar college spots across the bridge. Places like the Agora, the Plato, and Fat Glenn's were now options as long as Gabe let me borrow his draft card. I was meeting all sorts of people and making new friends on the other side of town. It was a milestone summer-fling, full of changes, and I didn't want it to end.

When I returned to West Tech High School in the fall of my senior year, just walking down the hall that first day back caused quite a stir among the faculty and students. Tech was a school steeped in conservative traditions, and the long, shaggy mop on my head clearly violated the strict dress code. Mr. Fabian, my hip, young homeroom teacher gave my new look two thumbs up, but bet me I wouldn't make it through the day without being sent to the office.

Miraculously, I won the bet. The worst I endured from the faculty were a couple of references to a dirty bum and a good-for-nothing hippie. My fellow classmates, on the other hand, overwhelmingly approved of the new me.

A few notable events followed my summer of summers. I finally turned eighteen in the fall, registered with the Selective Service System, and received my very own and very legitimate draft card. I finished the school year respectably by hitting the books harder than ever, surprising some people, including myself. To top it all off, my peers voted me *Mr. Hair* in the senior class yearbook.

Yet, the biggest surprise came soon after graduation when I registered for college. I helped my parents pay tuition fees by working part-time at a small factory down the street from our house. Then later by tutoring students at nearby Walton Elementary School, once I enrolled in the College of Education at CSU. Eventually, with the support of old friends and the aid of new ones, I became a schoolteacher.

~~~

Now, my dear children, as Papa reflects on my summer of '70, it was undeniably unconventional, to put it mildly, with life lessons acquired in the most unorthodox manner. Nevertheless, if you look very carefully and use just a bit of imagination, I swear there's a twisted version of Plato's cave allegory in there somewhere. Then again, I'm no Greek philosopher.

THE HOME FAMILY CLUB

MY FATHER WAS MY HERO growing up in the 1950s, and I felt privileged to share his given name, well, sort of his given name. When Gennaro arrived here in America from Italy in 1930, our melting pot country tagged him with the name Jerry. And after three daughters, it's the name he gave me. I was the only boy and the baby in our home, which is undoubtedly hitting the perfecta in any Italian family. Most of our extended clan referred to us as *Big Jerry* and *Jerry Junior.* At least, my maternal grandparents, Pasquale and Santa called me *Gennarino*, which translates to little Gennaro. We lived on West 33rd Street in an ethnic pocket of Cleveland named for the two main intersecting streets in the community – Clark-Fulton. There were many more Italian families in our working-class neighborhood near the Cuyahoga River. And it seemed to me the men were always busy somewhere out there earning a living – working hard to provide for their families just like my pop.

By day my hero labored as a skilled concrete finisher

and brick mason. Tools of his trade included a strong back, big arms, and broad shoulders. He looked intimidating as hell but had a gentle, quiet soul. His business card read; *No Job Too Big or Small – sidewalks, driveways, patios, basements, and more. Call Shadyside 1-1149 & ask for Jerry.* Of course, his best advertising came from word of mouth by satisfied customers.

Pop worked long hours, including weekends, until the winter frost forced him into hibernation for a couple of months. He did all he could to support my mother, three sisters, and me. My parents even sponsored a teenage cousin from Italy that lived with us for five years before she married. Accepting the responsibilities of immigrating relatives was a common practice for Europeans already rooted in America, especially during the first half of the twentieth century.

Nevertheless, if Big Jerry had any time and strength left in the evenings after dinner, you just might find him over at the *Home Family Club*. It was a private Italian lodge located right on Clark Avenue near the busy corner of Fulton Road. There were similar clubs in the neighborhood, and a patron's hometown back in the old country influenced the one he or she supported the most. This particular club had many members from the southern regions of Italy. Pop came from Casamassima and Ma's family from Capurso, two communes in the province of Bari of the Puglia region. That's the heel of the boot-shaped peninsula.

These home-grown clubs operated as fraternities for immigrating countrymen or *paesans*, with the specific purpose of sponsoring social activities, and to promote community for its members and their families. However, they also did something else equally important. They served to keep these Italian immigrants from entirely assimilating into the American mainstream. Members found refuge within the confines of these havens if only for a few hours.

The Home Family Club owned and operated a banquet hall above a print shop in a small two-story brick building. The club rented it out for wedding receptions and dinner banquets. My family attended many such events up there. My personal favorite as a child was always the club's annual Christmas party. It included an after-dinner special guest appearance by Saint Nicholas himself, who passed out presents to all the children. He donned a wrinkled Santa suit, cotton-ball beard, and spoke with an accent. Dancing to live music followed for all the adults. There was something fun for everyone.

Still, if the banquet hall was the heart of this close-knit society, then the soul had to be the attached clubhouse tavern in the rear of the structure and its adjacent bocce court. This hideaway is what really drew Gennaro and his paesans like a magnet in the evenings. My pop didn't drink alcohol or gamble very much, but he sure loved to play the game.

My mother, Anna, was also on the go day and night. She was a classic, old-world daughter, visiting her parents nearly every single day. They lived just two doors down from the club in one of a half-dozen homes interspersed among the businesses at the intersection of those two main streets. I never really minded going with her on that five-minute drive, though I rarely had any choice in the matter being so young. My grandmother always had plenty of good food, and I loved playing at their house. My grandfather was also in the construction business. He kept all of the heavy equipment in his big backyard – a front-end loader, a cement mixer, scaffolding, an old dump truck, plus many other construction contraptions and whatchamacallits. But hey, it was all just one gigantic playground to an unattended child.

When I got tired of the Italian jungle gym, I'd dash to the back door into grandma's kitchen to feast on her homemade pizza. So thick you could slice it horizontally and layer salami, mortadella, and prosciutto inside for a delicious sandwich. With a little luck, I'd also find Italian pretzels called *taralli*. I am addicted to the damn things to this day. After that, it was off to the front porch to sit with family, friends, and neighbors who gathered to discuss whatever it was grown-ups talked about back then. I preferred sitting on the front porch steps just watching Clark Avenue itself. The loud heavy traffic of cars, trucks, buses, and busy sidewalks was a commercial-free reality show. It was like watching live television with black exhaust fumes.

This was all well and good for most kids, but being Big Jerry's son gave me one more option other kids didn't have back in the residential part of the neighborhood. After dusk, I would head over to the club to watch my father in action.

"Ma, I'm going now," I'd yell from the sidewalk over all the street noise.

"Don't stay too long," she'd shout back, "and don't' eat too much junk either or you're gonna get sick! You hear me?"

"I'm not gonna!"

The club had something memorable for every one of my senses starting the minute I arrived at the end of the long, dark, narrow driveway.

The bocce court was lit up like a professional arena by bright lamps attached to the tavern. Courts vary in shape and size. This one was hard crushed limestone around thirty-some feet long by eight-to-ten feet wide. A two-foot wall of wooden planks framed it with extended six-foot wire fencing at both ends designed to protect patrons from misguided balls hurled as a strategy rather than rolled.

Bocce is a competitive sport played the world over in one form or another and dates back to before ancient Rome. The primary objective is to roll balls toward a smaller target ball called the *pallino* with points awarded to those stopping closest to it. There are strategies and techniques in the game if you're skilled enough to block the pallino or knock the opponent's balls away from it.

To resolve discrepancies, sticks were used to measure the distance between balls and the pallino. There was no need for fancy measuring tapes when you had sticks of various lengths set aside. And hold on to your hat whenever there were challenges because some competitors were dead serious about winning. Heated discussions were routine.

The patrons were exclusively men, or so it seemed, and usually gathered in small groups around three sides of the court. The fourth side had a long, rough-cut wooden bench anchored to the tavern allowing onlookers to rest their feet up on the courtside planks. Some men held glasses of beer or whiskey, and most used tobacco in one form or another as they analyzed the game in progress. I seldom understood the conversations at the club because the men spoke in their native language. And while I knew a few vulgar words picked up on the city streets, my parents only spoke English to their children. By design, they wanted us to be Americans first and foremost. Nonetheless, the language barrier never stopped me from going there.

It never seemed odd being the only child at the tavern in the evenings. No one ever appeared to mind my presence, so I always felt welcomed. Honestly, if I didn't get to my father first to ask for snack money, chances were one of his paesans would take care of me. Either way, it ended in a payday.

"Here, *Jeddy*, take the money, go get some-ting. You daddy's playing now."

"Thank you!"

"Aw, you a good boy, Jeddy." It usually ended with a hardy pat on the head or a rough pinch on the cheek.

A white-haired bartender with yellow teeth watched the game by leaning out one of the tavern windows just above the extended bench. He fiddled with a crooked stogie between waiting on the grown-ups both inside and outside.

I'd stand tiptoed on the bench under his windowsill to place my order. Yet no matter what I said to him, he'd return with a six-ounce bottle of Coke and a bag of potato chips, peanuts, or a chocolate bar – *always his choice*. He'd smile and waft his hand at my coins so I would reach up to pay him and then take a seat to enjoy my bounty.

Watching Pop play was always a special treat. He had the funny habit of making a *toot-toot* sound after releasing the ball as it rolled down the court. It made me giggle every time. He always appeared to be having fun even when the other men weren't. Except for one time when I overheard him tell my mother he felt terrible after punching someone in the nose for being disrespectful.

25

A trip to the club was never complete without stopping inside. So when I got antsy enough, I would clutch my little Coke bottle and head toward the tavern door by looping back around the court through the standing spectators. One time a man chewing tobacco was so engrossed in the game, he spun around without looking and spit on my arm. He quickly pulled a handkerchief out of his vest pocket to wipe me off, apologized the best he could, and then gave me a quarter. I wondered if he was the guy Pop punched in the nose.

The tavern had the unforgettable musty smell of beer and cigars. I started at the bar. There, men sat on stools along the counter, quietly nursing their drinks and watching the fights on the portable black and white television perched on the top liquor shelf. Not much ever happened along the boring counter, so I never stayed very long. I'd meander toward the tables where men played cards under the dangling light fixtures that exposed the thick fog of tobacco smoke in the air. I didn't know what games they were gambling on, but they seemed to be having more fun than the men were back at the bar. Sometimes, if I stood there long enough, one of them would flip me a nickel.

However, I always saved the best for last by heading to the rowdy corner of the tavern. That's where men engaged in a game so unique, it could only be described as bizarre, exhilarating, and terrifying all at the same time.

Morra is another ancient competition. A hand contest similar to the kid's game rock-paper-scissors. Two players stand face-to-face, both with a number from zero to ten in their heads. Each shouts out his number simultaneously while exposing a subset of fingers. The player to correctly match the combined total of fingers scores a point. They simply tally points until a winner emerges.

Now here's the thing. Played in the proper spirit and tradition, Morra is no kid's game. It was rock-paper-scissors on anabolic steroids, a mesmerizing contest that could really get your heart pumping. In fact, the face-off could get so intense it resembled more of a western gunfight in the street at high noon. Some men placed bets before the shoot-out.

The showdown commenced quietly enough with a menacing stare-off. It was a chance perhaps to calculate the other's first move until one of them flinched. Then hands extended out at blinding speeds. In a blaze of glory, fingers flew toward the opponent while firing out a number point-blank in Italian, of course, so loudly it made me cringe. Most participants engaged in this type of showmanship, but some players went even farther with their theatrics, thrilling the crowd like a real wild west show. They usually played standing over the corner card table.

One evening I watched as two *finger-slingers* took their places across from each other. They started in the usual fashion, but this showdown quickly amplified into one I'll remember the rest of my life. Their screams swelled the veins in their necks and foreheads as they slammed the backs of their hands down on the tabletop with such force, one of the men's knuckles began to drip blood. While it didn't seem to faze him one bit, I was certainly dumbfounded as the crowd went ballistic with every slam, bang, and boom. The fierceness ended in hooting, hollering, and backslapping after the final draw. Everyone had a fun time, including me, standing not much taller than the tabletop itself, sipping my Coke, and taking it all in stride. It was really a spectacle to behold at any age.

Then it was back outside to the bocce court to let my dad know I was leaving, that is, if I could catch him between games. He played a lot because he won a lot. He'd shoot me a wink, a nod, and a smile from afar and then watch me leave the bright lights and chatter behind to disappear back down the dark, quiet driveway.

I seldom spoke at the club, sometimes not a single word the entire visit. Still, it never mattered because all my senses had been sufficiently tantalized. My mother was usually ready to leave when I returned to her. And to top off the night, Pop would return home and scatter more potato chips, peanuts, and chocolate bar treats on the kitchen table for everyone to enjoy.

This extraordinary tradition lasted most of my childhood, but just as childhood activities wane with age, so did my visits to the club. Eventually, with paesans and a club of my own, they stopped altogether.

Regardless, Big Jerry continued playing his favorite pastime well into the next decade. There was great excitement in our home one night in 1965 when he returned as the interclub bocce tournament champion and had the spoils to prove it. A thick, golden trophy almost three-feet tall with his name boldly inscribed on the front declaring him champ of the neighborhood. It was the most massive damn trophy I ever held in my hands. Our home buzzed all week with friends, family, and neighbors stopping by to congratulate him and to see his prized possession. We were all so very proud of him and his accomplishment.

The club displayed the trophy on a shelf for nine years until members presented it to my mother in 1974 after our strongman lost his battle with cancer. I was only twenty-two years old.

Now, it's been well over a half-century. The landscape in my old neighborhood has drastically changed, especially around the intersection of its namesake. Yet, I'm happy to report the club survived and thrives in a western suburb of Cleveland thanks to its dedicated members.

~~~

The original Home Family Club served my father, his paesans, and their families well. I shall always be grateful for its existence. Just imagine the collective comfort and joy generated in and around that strong cultural fortress. Papa's trips to the club as a child remain fixed in my memory. I can still see the wining, dining, and dancing upstairs in the banquet hall. I hear all the camaraderie inside that smelly old tavern. And I can almost taste those sweet treats I enjoyed sitting on that rough-cut bench. It's my honor and a unique privilege having been part of a place so many called their home away from home. And to think it was all captured by the five senses of your papa when I was just one happy, quiet, little Italian boy from Clark-Fulton.

RELATIVE IN ITALY

SONO IL FIGLIO di Anna e Gennaro Il'Giovine. Loosely translated it means, I am the son of *Annie and Jerry Young* – at least in the United States. My Italian parents were both born in Ohio, but each has a unique twist to their childhood story.

Anna's parents raised her in a neighborhood close to downtown Cleveland, yet she couldn't speak a word of English the day she first entered kindergarten at Walton Elementary School. Still, by the time she was an adult, most people could not detect an accent in either language, even when she visited family in Italy.

Gennaro's parents settled in Lancaster, a glass factory town just south of Columbus. They stayed only two years before returning to their native country. And that's where he grew up the next sixteen years until his solo trip back where he lived with relatives in the same neighborhood as my mother. He spoke no English upon his return arrival.

After an old-world courtship shrouded in secret

rendezvous, parental threats, and an eventual elopement, they were happily married for the rest of their lives. Three daughters followed before I was born and given my father's new-world name.

The name Jerry was so American, so simple, and so prevalent during the middle of the twentieth-century. There was one issue with it involving a nun in Catechism class, when Catholic parents were expected to name their children from the list of our saints.

"So, what is your real first name? It doesn't say here on your record."

"Its Jerry."

"No, child, that's a nickname. I mean your Christian name. Is it Gerald?"

"No."

"Has anyone ever called you Gerard or Jeremy?"

"Somebody called me Gary once."

"You're making this difficult. I'll bet its Jerome. Yes, Jerome sounds Italian."

"Oh, I know. They call me Jerry Junior."

"Don't be ignorant. There's no Saint Jerry, but you're a junior, you say? What's your father's name?"

"Big Jerry."

"For the love of God, child, how do you not even know your own name?"

I questioned my mother when I got home. Ma showed me my birth certificate from Lutheran Hospital. I was technically correct. My official given name was Jerry, but my Baptism certificate had the added middle name, Raymond. Ma added it to satisfy the church. She told me she prayed to Saint Raymond during her pregnancy with me.

That simple name worked just fine in public school, especially when learning to read using the basic primers. One featured *Dick and Jane*. The other, however, was my favorite for obvious reasons. It starred *Alice and Jerry*. I loved listening to my classmates reading my name aloud. It made me feel special.

But then something began going ironically askew. I eventually figured it out. My last name was an incredibly challenging tongue twister for everyone around me. In fact, my American first name and Italian surname diametrically opposed each other in complexity.

This irony followed me throughout school. Teachers, principals, students, friends, neighbors, and yes, even some extended family members remained baffled and bewildered by it.

I get it. It's a name comprised of five vowels sprinkled between four consonants, plus I have punctuation. The apostrophe is the last nail in the coffin. So, allow me to help with the enunciation.

It's pronounced ill-JEO-vin-neh. Say it slowly and aloud, ill-JEO-vin-neh.

Again, slurring the accented second syllable nice and easy, ill-JEO-vin-neh.

Now, one last time for good measure letting it roll off your tongue, ill-JEO-vin-neh. It may even be easier if you use your hands a little as you say it.

Oh sure, people everywhere bravely made their attempts: ii-GLO-veen, LI-go-vin, ol-JEE-zeen, IG-loo-vine, GOL-zone, I-joe-bean, and most common and palatable, El-joe-vanni. To make life easier, my elders conceded to all the tongue twisting and yielded to the bastardized three-syllable pronunciation, ill-JOE-veen. Please don't assume it made my life easier.

The gym teachers in high school often addressed the boys using their surnames as if we were in the military. I was the exception and learned to accept it.

"I need four men to come down to the equipment room with me. How about you four – Mastro, Kazel, Jerry, and Romano."

Some teachers used the title, *mister*, to formally address their male students. I became Mr. Jerry at that point. Giggles, accompanied by an apology often followed.

However, one teacher, in particular, deserves individual recognition. Hats off to Mr. Rall, my machine shop teacher, who set himself apart on the very first day of class. He stands alone as a good man with a no-nonsense style of instruction. Mr. Rall had a zero-tolerance policy for any irregularities in his shop – misconduct, or otherwise. Known for his southern drawl and quickness with a paddle, he had our full attention.

"Roll call. Mr. Polo."

"I'm Here!"

"Mr. Bossa."

"Here!"

"Mr. Conforto."

"Right here!"

"Hmm. What's this?" Then after a short pause, "Where is this I-L-G-I-O?"

"That's me. I'm here!" It stuck. He called me the first five letters of my name for the entire semester. Give it up for Mr. Rall.

I tried using *Jerry Young* for a few years after college, but I eventually abandoned it. While it made life easier in some respects, I learned common names come with a price. For example, you often get mistaken for other people. I picked up the wrong Chinese take-out order because of it. What a twist for me. The biggest reason for going back, though, is that I missed all the *Italian* that went with my name. I guess you don't know what you'll miss until it's gone.

It never got better as an adult. So I used it to entertain myself as people tried to tackle the pronunciation. I let them go for a while before putting them out of their misery. *Ah salute* for at least trying!

~~~

It was only after retirement that I had what Buddhists call an *awakening* to the true nature of reality. My wife Judi and I had to travel 5,000 miles across the ocean to Italy to learn this teaching. It began the moment we went through customs at the Leonardo da Vinci airport in Rome.

"Next. Passport, please." A woman officer waved me forward and then held out her hand without looking at me. She opened my passport and briefly scanned it before looking up. "What is your purpose in this country?"

"My wife and I are here as tourists. We're going to visit many of your cities."

She stamped a page in my passport and handed it back to me.

"Thank you, Mr. ill-JEO-vin-neh."

I think my mouth was open when I reached for my passport. The agent looked a bit confused at my expression.

"Is there anything else, Mr. ill-JEO-vin-neh?"

"No... no, thank you," I responded.

We picked up a connecting flight to Naples, where a limo driver was waiting to take us to our hotel in Sorrento. After gathering our suitcases at the baggage claim area, we walked into a large lobby where a group of chauffeurs stood holding signs with written names on them. A young man in a blue suit stood out. His read, *Grry il Giovine*. I swear it's true.

"Hello, I believe that's me," I said.

"Are you Mr. ill-JEO-vin-neh?" There it was again.

"Yes," I replied, "and what is your name?"

"I am Vincenzo," he said. "You go to 'otel, Antiche Mura, si?"

"*Si, grazie.* That's where we're going. Antiche Mura in Sorrento," I responded proudly. I just spoke Italian in Italy!

We arrived at a beautiful hotel where all the employees were dressed in uniform black suits. One of them behind the desk greeted us.

"Buonasera, buonasera." He looked down at our passports. "Ah, welcome Mr. and Mrs. ill-JEO-vin-neh." Judi and I looked at each other and smiled. It was becoming a habit. A second employee approached, and both began working on the computer. They spoke softly to each other in their native language, until the second man turned to us and nodded.

"Buonasera," he said to me. "Good evening, signora," he said to Judi.

"Buonasera," I responded.

"You are Italiano from America, no?"

"Yes. Si," I said. "Born in Ohio, so I speak very little Italian, I'm afraid."

"Si, Ohio, but here, your family is from the south," he replied with certainty.

"Yes, in Bari, but how did you know?" I asked, happily puzzled.

"Ah, *Barese*," he said, "I am from the south as well. I am Napolitano – from Naples. The spelling of yours tells me. It means *the young man*, you know? JEO-vin-neh all by itself is more common." In other places, you will see it *il giovane*.

I knew what it meant, but had no idea the spelling was relative in Italy.

"Well, thank you for saying it beautifully. We are not used to hearing it that way in America. Tante, grazie!" I said, shaking his hand. We all looked at each other and laughed.

"Prego," he replied, "you are most welcome, sir."

And from that point on, a warm, hearty, and verbal welcome greeted us every time we entered the lobby – always by our last name.

"Buongiorno, signora ill-JEO-vin-neh!"

"Ciao, Mr. and Mrs. ill-JEO-vin-neh!"

And that's not the only place we were impressed. The locals addressed us as matter-of-factly as the desk clerks in Sorrento throughout our tour of over twenty cities. Then there was that bellhop in Rome who wrote my name without asking how to spell it. He even did it while talking on the phone. What a difference 5,000 miles can make!

~~~

It took a trip to Italy for Papa to realize what was going on here. All this time I thought we were the ones with an Einstein equation for a surname. Now, we know I was looking at the whole thing backward. In reality, it's just as easy to say we have a simple name that others find difficult to handle. As Albert might have pointed out, it's all relative.

STICK-MATA

IT WAS NO SURPRISE I saw my first emergency room at age ten. By 1962, I was meddling with the tools in my dad's shed, climbing trees, and hopping garage rooftops. Even playing *fire escape tag* after school on the three-story iron staircase at Sackett Elementary. Finding things to do in our ethnic neighborhood on the near west side of Cleveland was never a problem for this imaginative little Italian boy.

It happened at Billy Weidmann's house. He was one of my best friends from school and lived only one block away from our home on West 33rd Street. We were in his attic playing with a chemistry set like two mad scientists, mixing a concoction I named *Presto* when we heard his mother yell up from the bottom of the stairs.

"Hey boys, why don't you go outside and play now? You've been up there in that musty attic for over an hour. Go get some fresh air."

"We have the window open, mom."

"Go!"

"All right," Billy shouted back. "Hey, let's go in the backyard and pour the Presto on a bug to see what happens." So, we went outside and poured it on a bug, and nothing happened.

"What do you wanna do now?" Billy asked.

"I don't know. Let's see."

We stood up to survey our options. Billy's backyard was similar to most in the neighborhood. Weeds and dirt patches speckled the sparse lawn with clusters of grown-up *stuff* scattered around, apparently deemed too valuable to throw away. There was an old truck rim, a rusty lawnmower minus a wheel, roof shingles, a wooden door, an abandoned doghouse, and a stack of used aluminum siding piled alongside the wood and wire fence.

Yes, there was certainly enough here to make do when suddenly two girls from our classroom appeared in the adjacent yard. One of them launched a stone at us that landed at Billy's feet as the other twirled the one in her hand, making sure we saw it. They stood there, giggling, waiting for a response. At first, we ignored them. After all, they were simply two pukey girls to us until a second stone whizzed right past my head. Clearly, this was the best option for a little excitement, so we each found a projectile and returned fire.

It only took a minute for the exchange to escalate, an empty can, a soda pop bottle, and then a doorknob. Just when I thought it couldn't get any better, a long, wooden board came whirling over the fence, which got the biggest laugh. It looked as though it came off an old picket fence. I decided it would be funny to hurl it back. So I picked it up with my right hand and held it high above my head like a sword. But when I tried to whip it back over the fence, the strangest thing happened – it never left my hand. I tried again without a second thought, but with the exact result. Then I let go of it, but it never hit the ground. I even shook my hand with no success. I was puzzled and zoomed in for a closer look.

Releasing my grip revealed the head of a nail, flush against the wood. I gently pried the board away from my palm to see in between. A nail had penetrated the skin, but I couldn't determine its size. It couldn't' be too long, I assumed since it wasn't poking out through the back of my hand. I tugged on it firmly, but it didn't budge, as if the damn thing was super glued on.

Again, with a little more care, I pulled it away from my skin, this time toward the sunlight. That's when I realized the extent of my problem. It wasn't small at all. In fact, it was quite the opposite. Carpenters use these nails to frame houses, only this one was bent and rusty. It had pierced the center of my palm, then twisted up into my index finger to the top knuckle. It bulged out below the skin like an internal splint, locking my finger's position straight out. How the hell did I manage to do this without feeling any pain? I needed a second opinion.

"Billy, come here quick and look at this!"

"Holy crap," he gasped, staring with his jaw dropped. "I'll go get my mom."

"Hurry up," I yelled as he ran back into the house.

The girls sensed trouble and ran off like scared rabbits. Now I was alone with only my thoughts. The first was, *didn't Jesus die from this?* Luckily, I was distracted by the sound of a screen door slamming. I turned to see Mrs. Weidmann rushing toward me as she wiped her hands on her apron. She examined my injury with care, after which I detected a sense of urgency.

"Let me get you up to the front porch," she said, stabilizing my arm as we walked. "I want you to sit down on these steps and don't move! I'll be right back, don't move," she repeated.

I sat at attention, clutching the wooden weapon across my chest like a soldier holding a rifle *port arms*. Billy stood dutifully by my side. Once Mrs. Weidmann returned, she sat down beside me, seemingly much calmer.

"Your mom's on the way," she said, gently cradling me. "Does it hurt?"

"No," I replied. "Why doesn't it hurt, Mrs. Weidmann?"

"Let's be thankful it doesn't," she said, with a painted smile. Then we all sat in silence, waiting for my mother's arrival.

Now, if the world's largest *splinter* wasn't already the most oddball thing I had ever witnessed in my young life, what happened next may just have topped it. The sound of a loud, whining engine simultaneously raised our heads. A small, red, convertible sports car came screaming up the street toward us. The woman's hair in the passenger seat caught my eye. It was blowing wildly in every direction as the car drew nearer. I thought it was my mother for a split second, but how ridiculous would that be, right? Ma speeding around the streets of Cleveland in a little red convertible, until the woman signaled the driver to pull over to the curb. It *was* Ma.

"I'll be damned," slipped out of my mouth. Mrs. Weidmann glanced down at me, then fixed her eyes back toward the vehicle as it screeched to a halt in front of us. It barely stopped rolling before Ma leaped out and was standing in front of me with her crazy, windblown hair.

I sat speechless, trying to make sense of what was happening as she examined my injury. I looked back at the car and recognized the driver. It was my twenty-three-year-old neighborhood idol and relative, Junior D'Ambrosio.

He occasionally stopped by our home to visit the family. They were having coffee and bakery when Mrs. Weidmann called the house. Junior offered to help. I watched him jump out over his car door, and was with us in three giant leaps.

"*E Madonne*, why do you do these *stupit, stupit* things?" It was the first thing out of my mother's mouth. "Why,

why, why? Christ almighty, you're gonna be the death of me yet! And forget about ever leaving the house again! You hear me?"

Italians have this extraordinary reaction to drama and tragedy. They get angry before they can show compassion. I'm sure it has everything to do with the initial adrenaline rush, but I learned to wait it out since it never lasted long. I knew doting would soon follow. It always did, and it's no wonder I now exhibit this same trait as an adult.

And just for the record, it wasn't until junior high school that I discovered I was saying the word *stupid* incorrectly. It also explains my solitary visits to the speech teacher twice a week in fourth grade. *"I hated dem stupit speech lessons!"* Of course, it's not surprising once you realize English was a second language for half of the neighborhood.

Junior scooped me off the steps and followed Ma to the car. He sat me down on her lap with the board sticking up over our heads, then ran around to the driver's side and jumped in over the door. Ma held me tight and kissed the back of my head.

"Good thing I had the top down today," Junior said calmly, "or you'd have to sit on the roof!" He put the car in gear, revved the engine, and winked at me. "Okay, buddy, this car's a rocket. Are you ready?" I nodded and smiled as we sped away from the curb. If Junior was trying to distract me, he did a great job.

Zipping down Sackett Avenue to West 25th Street, we arrived minutes later at City Hospital, recently renamed Metro General. I felt the eyes of everyone in the waiting room on me as we approached the front desk. Even the nurses stopped to stare.

We waited behind a closed curtain after my X-rays, stick included. I was lying on a gurney with my mother seated at my side. An ER nurse was present, busily preparing equipment. I could see Junior standing outside the slightly open curtain, watching all the ER action until he politely drew it back for the incoming doctor.

"Okay, champ," the smiling physician began, "I understand you won't let go of your baseball bat. I hope you at least hit a home run. Now, let's have a little peek at that Louisville Slugger."

He abruptly dropped the smile and nodded earnestly at the nurse, making me nervous all over again. I looked for Junior. He was still standing out there like my personal bodyguard.

The nurse pulled a second gurney beside me, stretched my arm across it, and draped a white sheet across my shoulder, shielding my view.

"Keep him steady," the doctor ordered. The nurse gently but firmly held my arm. I felt the pinch of a needle and yelped as Ma squeezed my other hand. Soon all the feeling beyond my covered limb went numb. Another doctor stepped in, and the two quietly conferred. Shortly after, my arm began to twist and turn. It didn't hurt but made me queasy. Ma stroked my hair.

I became a little self-conscious as staff members filed in and out to have a peek. They were like gawkers in a circus freak show tent. Unfortunately, I was the main attraction. I imagined Junior out there selling tickets – *"Step right up folks and have a peek at the human pin cushion, only twenty-five cents!"*

This spectacle went on for about twenty minutes until I watched a nurse leave the room with my wooden appendage. The tent cleared out except for the doctor, who approached my mother with his prognosis.

"He's going to be fine. The X-ray showed no bones were injured, and I see no serious damage to the tissue. I'll get the nurse back in here, and she can finish up."

"Thank you, doctor, thank you so much," she replied, grabbing his hand and shaking it briskly.

"I'm back," the nurse said, returning with a hypodermic needle in her hand. "I have to give you a shot in your arm because the nail was rusty, but then I'll bandage your entire hand up so it looks like you had a bad injury. That way, you can pretend this was all a terrible ordeal and show off to all your friends."

Did I hear her say *pretend* it was terrible? Are you kidding me? Didn't this lady just see me nailed to a piece of wood a few minutes ago? That's kind of a big deal to most Roman Catholics. Still, I guess it's just another

Saturday afternoon at the city hospital. By the time she finished dressing my injury, you would have thought a surgeon had sewed my severed hand back onto my wrist. She even tied my arm up in a sling.

"There we go. This will keep your hand nice and elevated to minimize the swelling. Now, about that stick you walked in with, would you like me to get it for you? You know, as a souvenir."

I shook my head while mumbling, "No." I just wanted to get the hell out of there.

Later that evening, the Tetanus shot made my arm hot, red, and swollen. It hurt worse than my hand. My mother considered taking me back to the emergency room. She called the hospital, but a nurse advised her to wait until morning. The swelling did go down, but my arm remained sore for a couple of days.

I spent that time relaxing on our sofa with a pillow and blanket while everyone sufficiently pampered me. My mother smothered me in hugs and kisses and showered me with my favorite treats. The following day she made Italian wedding soup, usually reserved for holidays and special occasions. We called it *Jerry soup* in our house because it was my favorite.

My father and I watched more television together than I can ever remember, including plenty of cartoons and cowboys shows. Even my three older sisters made a big fuss over me, fluffing pillows, playing games, and serving my favorite lunch on a TV tray – fried baloney on white bread, a side of potato chips, and chocolate milk. My old school pal Billy even dropped over with three new comic books for me to read during my convalescence.

Yessiree, the nail hole in my hand was a hot topic all week, drawing more visitors, coddlers, and treat bearers. I guess there is nothing like a good old-fashioned crucifixion to bring people together.

~~~

Nevertheless, my darlings, it healed without incident, leaving behind a noticeable round scar right in the center of Papa's palm. I used to tell people it was divine stigmata, like the wounds of Saint Francis. But over the years, the scar faded away along with my tall tale. Nobody ever believed dat stupit story anyway.

THE ANNUNCIATION

LIFE WAS ABOUT TO RADICALLY CHANGE once Beto LoBianco, a schoolmate of mine since kindergarten, introduced me to fifteen-year-old Gabriel Del Mare back in the mid-1960s. The three of us lived within a short walking distance of each other in our Italian neighborhood near downtown Cleveland, and soon became the best of friends.

I hadn't met Gabe any sooner for a couple of reasons. For starters, he went to parochial grade school at our local parish, St. Rocco, while Beto and I attended public school at Sackett Elementary. By the time Gabe moved closer to my house, he was getting ready for high school at West Technical since he was a year older. Beto and I had one more year at Thomas Jefferson Junior High. My newest acquaintance also ran with a completely different crowd of boys and had different interests than most of my other friends.

Gabe didn't want to play catch, ride bikes, or climb trees. Instead, we shot BB guns and blew off firecrackers.

He was also the first friend I had that smoked cigarettes. However, fishing for jumbo perch in Lake Erie is what he loved best. Beto and I were very excited when he asked us to join him. We didn't waste any time heading to Zayre Department Store to buy fishing equipment. Angling became my new favorite pastime.

We decided it would be fun and economical to make our own sinkers, so we gleaned some scrap lead from a local print shop and bought a sinker mold at Ted's Tackle. Beto's *nonna* let us use her basement to set up shop. She had an antique gas stove down there, the kind with tall legs from the 1930s you see in old photos. She also supplied the cast iron pot used to melt the lead. We took turns pouring the liquid metal into the one-ounce molds, then divvied up the finished product after filing the rough edges smooth. It seemed we made enough of them to last us a lifetime.

Gabe, Beto, and I spent a lot of time angling off the government pier at Edgewater Park during the summer mornings, trying our best to get there by sunrise. There were times when we took a small commercial ferry across the two hundred foot harbor opening for fifty cents round-trip, allowing us to fish off the breakwall. The breakwalls are made of large blocks of cut stone and concrete. This particular one juts out into the lake, runs parallel to the coastline, and then stretches back out again. It is approximately a mile in length, but we

rarely trekked all the way out to the West Pierhead
Lighthouse at its tip.

Most anglers never bothered crossing over, which
meant the long barrier strip was ours, and ours alone.
Maybe the other anglers thought fifty-cents wasn't
worth the price, but it was probably more of the isolation
once you made it to the other side. It left you at the
mercy of the ferry skipper. He was our only way back,
and timeliness was not his strength. Mother Nature
was another consideration. There were no facilities or
shelters on the breakwall, so our weather forecasting
abilities played a large part in the decision to make the
crossing. Erie is the shallowest of the Great Lakes and
can quickly kick up without warning. Ominous skies and
choppy seas were quite unsettling stranded all alone on
the other side. Rainstorms soaked us more than once
by misjudging the early morning skies. Still, there was
always something very magical about being out there in
the middle of nowhere.

After baiting our hooks with live minnows and casting
out our lines, it was all about patience and rhythm. There
is more than one way to detect nibbles on your lure. You
can watch for movement, or you can feel for it. Either
way, a shift in the tempo will grab your attention, and a
tug on the line gets you up on your feet and reeling. And
watch out for the excitement that followed when a school
of perch passed through. We could catch two fish at the

same time with two baited hooks on each of our lines. It was double the pleasure, double the fun. The feeling never got old.

Nevertheless, those slow mornings were just as satisfying – all alone with nothing but the sights and sounds of seagulls, ships, and water washing over the rocks below us. It was such a sharp contrast to the bustling city streets.

We could be as serious or silly, lazy, or crazy as we wanted to be out there, secluded from the rest of the world. On most occasions, we'd each find a slab of stone to lie on, put our hats over our faces, and reflect. That is if you can call it a reflection.

"Hey, Gabe... Gabe. Gabriel!"

"Huh?"

"What are you doing? You awake?"

"I am now. What do you want?"

"I'm just laying here thinking."

"Well, that's different."

"How do you say, *I want fish?*"

"What?"

"I said, how do you say, I want fish – in Italian?"

"Voglio pesci. You woke me up for that?"

"Yeah, you wanna know why?"

"Why?"

"Vohlyoh pehshee, Gabe." I heard Beto snort under his cap.

"Oh, that's real funny," Gabe responded. "Now, say *voglio tranquillo*."

"Vohlyoh trrrankwihloh. What's that mean?"

"It means you're a dumbass *baccala*." We all laughed.

~~~

Traveling to and from the lake was no problem once Gabe was old enough to drive, but in the beginning, we had to find someone willing and able to give us a lift. If no one was available, we took the city's Cleveland Transit System. CTS bus drivers never appreciated a trio of amateur *pescatori* climbing aboard their bus with all that tackle. Especially the return trips home when we were hauling our catch of the day. One bus driver gave us a particularly hard time in the Edgewater parking lot when he saw the buckets of perch we were carrying.

"Uh-uh fellas, you're not getting on this bus," he said, looking down through the open doors. "Not with dead fish."

"But you can't leave us stranded here."

"No, sir, no way."

"Are you kidding? We gotta get home."

"Then leave the fish."

"We're not leaving the fish. It took us all day to catch these."

"I see a payphone over there. Call a cab."

"We don't have that kind of money."

We took turns pleading our case. The stubborn bus driver wouldn't budge an inch.

"C'mon. They don't smell."

"It's not happening, boys."

"They're fresh fish."

"What part of *no*, don't you get?"

"There's nobody on the bus."

"I'm on the bus for Christ's sake, and I mean *all day*. It's hot in here too, and I don't want you stinkin' it up. Now, step back."

"Listen, you..." I grabbed Gabe's arm before he could finish.

"Okay, guys, let's just tell him the truth," I said, staring at my friends. "He seems like a reasonable man." Both gave me a curious look. I turned toward the driver and delivered an acting performance worthy of Hollywood. "Please don't make us beg anymore," I groveled. "We're desperate if you wanna know the truth. We got a guy back home willing to pay a buck a fish, a buck and a half if we clean 'em first. You know how hard it is to make ends meet these days. I'll bet you have kids. All we're trying to do is help put food on the table, that's all. And the faster we get these fish home, the sooner Mama will have money for groceries. I can tell you're a decent man. You even remind me a little of my papa. Now, what do you say?"

The determined driver paused for a moment and then buckled. "Oh, just get in for Christ's sake." He waved his hand to come forward but then raised his palm toward us. "But I'm warning you, so help me Christ, you sit in the back row, and I mean the goddamn back row, or I swear to the almighty above we're not moving."

Gabe smiled and shook his head at me, so I twitched my eyebrows back as the three of us gathered up our tackle and buckets of fish to board the bus. We each thanked him as we boarded. "Yeah, yeah, yeah," was his response. As I passed, he added, "And just for the record, I don't have any kids." My smile did nothing to change his apathetic glare. He watched us through the large rearview mirror above his head and waited until we sat down on the bench seat in the very last row. The doors finally closed as the bus lurched forward.

In truth, I always split my fish between Gabe and Beto. My mother wasn't about to behead and descale fish, not when the local Pick-N-Pay on Clark Avenue sold frozen filet packets. On the other hand, their mothers were willing and able to gut and clean anything put in front of them.

~~~

After spending so much time with Gabriel, he decided it was time for Beto and me to meet his former classmates from Saint Rocco. It was a large group of mostly Italian boys. Most were a year older since they also attended West Tech with Gabe. Nevertheless, the church grounds were still the gathering place both day and night, seven days a week. It was the official home turf of the *Rocco Boys*.

"Are you guys interested in joining the Hi-Club at Rocco's?" Gabe asked.

"What is it?"

"A club organized by the church. There's a meeting tonight."

"But what's a Hi-Club?"

"Hell if I know, a high school club, I suppose. They say it's a social club, but I think the priests just want to keep an eye on us."

Gabe may have been right. It was a club, sponsored through the Catholic Youth Organization and formed when his class began attending West Tech. Still, with the churchyard as a full-time hangout, it was also an excellent opportunity for adults to influence the young minds of these impressionable parishioners.

"That depends. Does it cost anything?"

"There's dues, but they're cheap. We throw dances and car washes to raise money to do stuff."

"What kind of stuff?"

"Oh, I don't know, field trips, I guess. We have plans to go to New York City next year, and they're talking about a rec room in the basement of the school. We'll be able to shoot pool, play Ping-Pong, and cards. This guy Myron is even gonna donate a pinball machine. He repairs the ones at Kovar's."

"What's Kovar's?"

"Kovar's Korner, the little coffee shop across the street from Rocco's. Mary and Stan own it. Well, he just died, so she's running it by herself now."

"I thought that was a soda shop. My older sisters used to go there."

"It was once, now she mostly sells coffee and donuts. She'll still grill you a hamburger or a toasted cheese sandwich if you ask. She's cool. We're there all the time."

"So, what do you do when you're not at Hi-Club or Kovar's?"

"You mean most of the time. Mainly hang out around in the churchyard. There's crazy stuff too."

"What kind of crazy stuff?"

"Once in a while, other gangs come down trying to prove something, like the boys did across Twenty-fifth Street last week. Big mistake once the older guys got a hold of 'em. They don't mess around."

"Who are the older guys?"

"They're like eighteen and hang around the church too. Nobody messes with 'em cause they can get a little *pazzo* in the head. They're almost like older brothers. The cops came down a couple days ago cause they were shootin' off fireworks and Roman Candles at us. One hit Bonesy in the ass and burned a hole in his pants. I laughed my ass off."

"The cops showed up? Does that happen a lot?"

"Sometimes."

"When was the last time?"

"Um, yesterday. One of the guys broke into the traffic control box on the telephone pole and was controlling the light manually. It was so funny."

"What did you do when they came?"

"What we always do, hop some fences, and run. Just disappear for a little, then come back after they leave. They're just trying to scare us. Father Dominic wouldn't let them do anything to us. Not really. He went and got Rizzo released after they picked him up for drinking beer in the parking lot last Sunday."

"And they just let him go?"

"Yeah, the padre's got connections. So you joinin' or not?"

Beto and I looked at each other. This all sounded way too intriguing. St. Rocco was my family's parish and less than a ten-minute walk from my house. And while I was never really much of a Sunday churchgoer, at least I would be able to tell people I went to church regularly, and technically wouldn't be lying.

"Let's go," Beto said.

"I'm in."

"Good. Meet me in front of the church hall before seven," Gabe added, "and I'll take you around and introduce you to the boys."

~~~

A little uneasiness crept in walking down Fulton Road that evening. A good first impression is essential. And not just for me, but for Gabe too. He was sticking his neck out for us. This was no church club of boys I was joining. It was a gang of boys who just happened to be in a church club. And I wanted in!

I arrived at the parking lot entrance twenty minutes early. A couple dozen teenagers were already standing in front of the church hall. A half-dozen or so were girls. I began drifting between the small groups looking for any familiar faces. There were none, of course, which did nothing to calm my concerns. So I slowly recirculated through the crowd.

I stopped to watch an assembly of boys playing a kind of pain tolerance game. One of them braced his right hand under his left armpit, palm out, and then shielded his eyes with his left hand. Another kid stepped up, reared back, and cracked his palm so hard it made me flinch. I knew it hurt by the look on his face. The culprit immediately slipped back into the hooting crowd. The one that was slapped had to guess who inflicted the pain. His incorrect guess drew more laughter and meant he had to take another turn. I wasn't quite ready for that just yet, so I moved on.

I wasn't sure what to do with myself after completing

another lap. It became harder to stay inconspicuous. That's when I heard a voice.

"Are you here for the meeting or are you just lost?" I turned around to a pretty girl smiling at me. Her girlfriends giggled.

"Oh, uh, the meeting," I said. "Have you seen Gabe anywhere?"

"No," she answered, "but I just got here myself. Try inside." She pointed to the open hall doors.

"Thanks," I replied, trying to remain calm, cool, and collected.

My mind began racing to formulate an escape plan as I walked up the hall steps. If my fishing partners aren't here by the time the meeting starts, I'm going to leave. No, wait. How is it going to look if I take off and then show up for the next meeting? That would be so awkward. You only have one chance at a good first impression. I took a deep breath and exhaled, though I couldn't stop overthinking the situation.

Three people were setting up folding chairs as Father Mario shuffled papers near the stage inside and no sign of Gabe or Beto. "Damn it!" I walked back out and stopped at the top of the stairs for an aerial view of the yard. That's when I saw them across the street walking from Kovar's. *Bless you, Saint Rocco!*

"Hey, there you are," Gabe said, as I met them halfway. "I just went to grab some smokes." He opened the fresh pack of cigarettes and offered one to us. Surprisingly, we both obliged. Neither of us smoked.

"Come on in!" someone yelled from the hall doors. Everyone filed in, and the meeting commenced. Gabriel was asked to announce us to the group, and we were officially welcomed into the fold. When the meeting was over, Beto and I walked around with Gabe so he could introduce us individually. Most of his friends were very sociable, a few seemed indifferent, and one or two were quite unimpressed by our presence.

Overall, the evening went very well, and from that point on, the churchyard became my new home away from home. I was now one of the gang. There's a pecking order in every social structure, and over time, I found my sweet spot.

~~~

"Good-bye! I'm going to church!" The sound of that sat very well with my mother as I walked out the door each night after dinner. What mother wouldn't want to hear those words?

"Okay, but it's cold out, no?"

"I'll be fine, Ma."

"Don't come home too late, you have school tomorrow."

"I'll be home before dawn."

"Hah, hah. Say hello to the priests for me if you see them!"

"Oh, I'll see 'em all right, and I'll ask them to say a special prayer just for my Mama. Bye."

"Don't be *stupit*. Give me a kiss."

I loved my mother with all my heart, yet she was so blindly unaware of the adventures and misadventures that awaited me. In reality, this was true for me as well. I never knew exactly what I was walking into. Whatever it was, you can be sure I was an enabler, a participant, or an innocent bystander depending on the circumstances.

In any case, our high-spirited lifestyle continued in the churchyard over the following months. Going to hang out with the gang was my top priority. It also gave me many opportunities to hone my street smarts.

Meanwhile, our monthly club meetings continued as scheduled. So did our fundraisers. The dances were a huge moneymaker for the Hi-Club. The church hall was packed with teenagers every month. Our success was due, in part, to the local band we employed that featured two of the older guys.

The good news is the Hi-Club saved enough money to plan several field trips over the next couple of years. The bad news is once New York City met the Rocco Boys, it was the end of field trips – forever. It was also the end of Hi-Club – forever. We caused quite a ruckus at the Hotel Edison, enough to get us banned for life. Looking back, it was all justified. And finding willing chaperones after that would have been near impossible. *Forgive us our sins, Saint Rocco!*

~~~

Beto and I eventually graduated from junior high. We finally hit the big time by joining many of the other Rocco Boys at West Tech High School, which was over three miles away. And I didn't own a car in tenth grade. To get there in the mornings meant walking a couple of blocks to the Fulton Road bus stop in front of Tony's Auto Parts, transferring buses at Lorain Avenue, exiting at West 89th Street, and then walking one more block to the school. It was a real pain in the ass, so once Gabe bought a car, I accepted his offer for a lift without hesitation. All I had to do was make the short trek to his house, giving me an extra fifteen-minutes of sleep every morning. What a relief!

My new morning routine was a simple one. I would knock on Gabe's back door and enter the kitchen to find his mother already busy. Pots simmering on the stove, the sound of a churning washing machine, and an ironing board flanked by wrinkled and folded clothes suggesting she'd been up for quite some time. My presence never seemed to slow her down.

"Good morning, Mrs. Del Mare." She would nod and motion toward a kitchen chair, usually with a cutting knife or a wooden spoon in her hand. I'd nod back. Gabe's mom spoke no English, and my Italian was limited to swear words, so there was little use trying to disrupt the silence. Our quick game of charades sufficed. Besides, she had a good rhythm going, and I didn't want to break her tempo.

I watched from the kitchen table as she prepared his lunch. It was almost similar to mine. Two lunchmeat sandwiches shrouded in wax paper, then packed into a used paper lunch bag. But then she would add two cigarettes. I wondered which of the food groups tobacco was in. It made me smile every morning. He'd buy a carton of milk and a cookie in the cafeteria like the rest of us. Then Gabe would whoosh into the room and grab a piece of toast for the ride. A brief but intense conversation in Italian would ensue. It sounded like all hell broke loose.

"Ready?" he'd ask when it was over.

"Yes. Is everything okay?"

"Yeah, why?"

"Oh, nothing. Goodbye, Mrs. Del Mare. Have a nice day." She'd give me the international one-shake nod of approval with a straight face as he grabbed his keys. We'd shoot out the door and into his latest automobile.

Gabe had an unusual arrangement with his parents. Neither drove. He was put in charge of family transportation while they paid the bills. A match made in heaven for any sixteen-year-old. This agreement explained the rapid turnover in vehicles – about every six months. We rode to school in luxury cars, muscle cars, and even foreign sports cars.

I hitched a ride with him until my sixteenth year. That's when I became the proud owner of my very own set of wheels – a big old family sedan. It fell miserably short of my good friend's standards, but I can still remember that awesome feeling of owning my first car.

~~~

Papa remained close friends with Gabe and Beto throughout our teen years. But just as you might expect with adolescent relationships, the three of us began branching out in different directions as our lives took root. Still, I can't even conceive what my early adult life would have looked like had I not met Gabe. In an act befitting of his namesake, Gabriel announced me into an extraordinary fraternity that allowed me to forge friendships with some of the wildest and craziest characters you could ever imagine. Now, they are all Papa's old friends meaning – friends forever. Hey Gabe, wherever you are, I want to say, "Voglio ringraziarti."

THE HARD WAY, KID

DEAR OLD WEST TECH, WE'LL ALWAYS LOVE YOU. It's the opening line of my high school alma mater. I probably sang the damn thing a thousand times, but the first was in 1968. West Technical was not only the largest school on the west side of Cleveland; it was once the largest high school in Ohio. A massive state of the art public school with programs providing employable skills to those bound for the workforce after graduation and this included an impressive selection of vocational trades. In addition, the school offered a college prep program for those seeking higher learning. There was something for everyone and each student chose a program to fit his or her needs.

Yet somehow during my first year, I found myself assigned to the Industrial Arts Department, and for the life of me, I don't know how the hell I got there. Nevertheless, the trades are noble and valuable occupations, and while I wasn't really interested in machine shop, welding, printing and all the rest, that's where I settled, indifferent to my circumstances, spending a good portion of each day in the basement of the school where most of the technical training rooms were located.

I obviously hadn't given any thought to my future. Maybe growing up in a working-class Italian neighborhood made my post-high school strategy seem rather uncomplicated. There was no shortage of skilled laborers in our community or my family for that matter, and there appeared to be a fair amount of construction work in the foreseeable future. So, who needs a school guidance counselor? The writing was on the proverbial brick and mortar wall.

My father, Gennaro, was a young barber when he came to America from the old country, but he jumped at the chance in construction work when a friend told him he could easily double his income. He became highly skilled at cement and brick masonry, eventually branching out on his own. Everyone called him *Jerry* by the time I was born, so it's the name he gave me, and by the time I entered high school, customers and colleagues were routinely calling the house asking for Jerry, now a well-established and reputable tradesman in the business. So you see, finding employment with him or one of his paesans would be too easy, and then I'd simply train on the job. Hell, prospective employers were calling my house literally before I even graduated. I'd let nature take its course.

"Jeddy?"

"Oh, hello, Mr. Leone. Pop is out back in his garden. I'll go get him."

"No, Jeddy, I call for you. You need da job? You pour concrete, no?"

"No, well I mean, I've been on a couple small jobs, but those were on weekends with my dad. I'm still in school."

"Ah, you gotta stay?"

"Yes, I'm going to stay and graduate."

"Okay, okay. You stay Jeddy, but you call me first. You *capisce*?"

"Yes, I understand, Mr. Leone. Thank you." These calls only reinforced my belief in fate.

Yet, surprisingly, Pop had different ideas for me. He wanted an easier life for his only son. Despite having the strength of a diesel bulldozer, he'd come home exhausted every night and stretch out on the floor in front of a fan until dinner was ready. One evening, I sat down beside him to ask about his day. Instead, he gave me a short but powerful piece of advice I'd remember the rest of my life. It was a warning from the heart, *padre a figlio*, father to son, to use my brains instead of my back.

He spoke them with his eyes closed. "Make the people pay for your mind," he said, "or you will be sorry. Not right away, but it will come." Then he looked at me and said, "Maybe then it's too late, eh figlio mio? Go to college."

These simple words resonated in my mind, sending

me into a deep dive of what the hell I've been doing at school in those subterranean workshops. Besides not being interested in the work, I wasn't very good at it either. So far, I only knew what I *didn't* want to do with my life, and yet these were rapidly becoming the most likely prospects. It also became quite clear where college fit into the equation. Without any prerequisite classes, I simply wouldn't be eligible.

As for my friends, many had colonized in the classrooms upstairs, spending the better portion of their days shuffling between business and college prep courses. I wondered about the options they'd have after graduation, ones *not* available to me.

It was a sinking revelation as regret settled in and I worried it might be too late to do anything about it. In order to give myself even half of a chance, I had to position my studies toward something more in line with business and at least the possibility of college. Now, the question was how to go about it.

Of course, the only idea I had involved my guidance counselor. I've heard him speak to groups before, but we never actually spoke face-to-face. Not only would we have to meet, but I also had to admit my current course of study was an oversight, no, a huge mistake on my part that I let go far too long. This wasn't going to be easy for me. I enjoyed my anonymity at school and was perfectly content flying below their radar.

I gathered the courage to trek up to the office of Mr. Hubbard. He was sitting behind his desk in the middle of a good laugh with one of the student athletes. The varsity jock was tilted back on the hind legs of his chair with one foot propped up on the desk. I quietly stood in the doorway waiting to be acknowledged. When I wasn't, I softly interrupted.

"Excuse me." They both quickly turned to look up at me.

"Can I help you?" Mr. Hubbard asked. I'm sure he thought I was lost.

"Uh, well, I was wondering if I could talk to you about changing my major."

"Changing your major?" he repeated, in a rather ambiguous tone. The jock snickered through his nose. Their responses put me on the defensive.

"Maybe I should come back some other time."

Mr. Hubbard held his index finger up at me and then looked at the jock. "I'll catch up with you later." The big man on campus slowly set his chair down on all fours, stood up and waited for me to step aside. We bumped shoulders when I didn't move fast enough. "Well, come in and sit down," the counselor said, waving me forward and gesturing toward the chair. "Now, who are you again?" He rested his elbows on his desk, cupped his hands under his chin, and waited for an answer. That's when my mind went completely blank.

Of course, he had no idea who I was and why would he? It was an enormous school and I was one unassuming student, partly by design, partly by nature. Counselors usually know the standout students; the ones involved in sports and extra-curricular activities or the super bright, and even the troublemakers. I was none of the above.

I don't even remember how I started explaining my dilemma, but I do remember the face he made causing my monologue to fizzle out like a dud firecracker. I call it the *stupid look*. He raised his eyebrows, tilted his head and smirked. I felt my face flush and it stopped me dead in my tracks.

"And you waited until now to decide this because?" He held the last syllable.

"I don't know," was my poor but honest reply. I sensed his lack of empathy and he looked quite dismissive. I had to think fast and say something compelling or this was going to be a very short consultation.

"I come from a large family of builders," I blurted out. "My father is in construction. All my uncles and cousins are in construction. My grandfathers were too. So were their fathers. They don't need another builder. They want a businessman in the family."

It was mostly true, and the best I had to offer. It was also enough to change the expression on his face. I had to keep my momentum going.

"My father wants me to use my brains," I added, "not

my back." It drew a slight smile from him. "If I don't do this, I'm going to be sorry for it the rest of my life."

Now he looked much more considerate and after a short pause, pursed his lips and lightly nodded.

"Okay, tell you what," he said. "Let me at least pull your file and take a quick look. How do you spell your last name?" He grabbed a pen and a small piece of paper. I spelled it for him twice, and he still wrote it incorrectly. "French?"

"Italian," I answered.

"Of course, Italians and architecture." He smiled and stood up. "I'll be right back."

I sat quietly reminding myself why I was doing this and trying not to care if he thinks I'm a big *cafone*. He was gone for quite a while.

"Sorry it took so long," he said on his return. "It was filed incorrectly."

He sat down, opened a folder and began leafing through the papers.

"What's that?" I asked.

"Hmm? Oh, it's your permanent record," he muttered, never looking up. I heard of permanent records but thought they were just myths, used primarily as a threat to keep students in line.

I watched his face, wondering if another stupid look was coming. He stopped once and peered at me above his reading glasses.

"Do you plan on going to college?"

"I, I think so. I'd like to have the option."

"You may fall short on credit hours. This could be a problem."

He stared at me, lightly rapping his fingers on the desk, then browsed a few more pages. He removed his reading glasses and rubbed his eyes.

"Look, I'll be honest with you," he said, leaning forward again. "You want to leave the trades for business. They're two very different curriculums, different animals, you see. We're talking apples and oranges here. Do you think you can handle a drastic change like this?"

"I don't know."

He squinted at me as if the answer was written on my face.

"You're doing this the hard way, kid." He waited for my reaction, so I improvised once again.

"Sometimes it's the only way, Mr. Hubbard." I'm not sure he liked my response, so I gave him a slender grin. There was another moment of silence and more finger rapping.

"You do understand there's no turning back if we do this, right?"

"I understand, thank you."

"I'll see what I can do," he said, standing up, "and I have to call your parents."

I left his office relieved it was over, and nervous for

what I had just set into motion. This was by far the most pivotal thing I had ever done for myself, not to mention a real boost for my confidence.

That evening my mother mentioned the phone call. "Oh, school called today and said you want to change your classes, so I said it was okay with me if that's what my son wants, but then he said something I didn't understand about you running the family business someday."

"He said that?"

"Yeah, do you know what it means?"

I smiled. "I have a good idea."

It wasn't long before typewriters, adding machines and accounting ledgers replaced welding rods, lathes, and grinding wheels. Now, classes related to bookkeeping and business filled my days *above ground*. I'll admit there were times when I struggled a bit with the transition. It seemed I was always scrambling to keep up with my new classmates.

Nevertheless, the caption under my high school yearbook picture lists my course of study as Business. No interests, hobbies or sports, no quotes, no honors or awards, not so much as a nickname, and they didn't even get my last name quite right, but none of it really mattered to me because I graduated, went on to college, and willfully enrolled myself into the Education Department.

Dear old West Tech survived eighty-three years before closing its doors to students in 1995. Today, this historical building contains private lofts, a school museum and is home to the West Tech Alumni Association. The *crimson and gray* spirit is still very much alive with scheduled tours and events, a newspaper, scholarship program, Hall of Fame, and even more. *Go Mighty Warriors!*

~~~

Upon college graduation, Papa accepted a teaching position in a quaint little school in the suburbs. After six enjoyable years, I attended night school to explore a relatively new industry known as Data Processing, later renamed Information Technology. I was enticed into this more lucrative and booming profession much the same way construction lured my father away from his barbershop, only I became the architect and builder of mainframe computer software. The tools of my trade were a keyboard and my imagination. An office served as Papa's construction site until I eventually retired after two rewarding careers.

WATCH AND LEARN

I WAS JUST MONTHS AWAY from my sixteenth birthday, and by now a Rocco Boy for almost two years. It was the summer of 1968; the season I received one of my many memorable life lessons. It was subtle yet, powerful and a result of being in the right place at the right time, but not necessarily for the right reasons.

The church of St. Rocco on Fulton Road in Cleveland was my family's neighborhood parish. It not only served the spiritual needs of a large, inner city community of Italians but also hosted a significant number of its youthful parishioners. Now let me rephrase that second part again in plain English. A sizeable, rowdy band of good-natured teenagers overran the church's four-acre complex. We roamed freely between the half-dozen buildings and spacious parking lot like wild buffaloes on the western plains, easily observable in our natural habitat all four seasons of the year. Every evening brought new adventures. How many young teens can boast they walked to church everyday.

Fortunately for us, there was a mutual understanding between the priests and the gang. After all, we were part of their everyday surroundings, which meant we were an inescapable presence in their daily lives. The arrangement of our coexistence was simple. They did their best to tolerate us while we tried our damnedest not to get caught at whatever the hell we were doing. It was a pretty sweet deal, at least from our perspective, when you consider all the time we spent growing up literally in their backyard.

One priest, in particular, Father Mario, attempted to harness the unbridled energy by organizing a youth club. He was a likable character, shorter than most of us, smoked cigarettes like some of us, and spoke with an Italian accent more than all of us. He was also the youngest, the most sociable, and the most popular of the clergymen. The idea was to fund field trips and a recreation center in the school basement by raising money through monthly teen dances in the church hall and Sunday car washes in the parking lot. It was one tough assignment given our collective adolescent behavior, not to mention a noble mission. I can't imagine the number of times Father questioned this undertaking. He had the determination and principles of Saint Rocco himself, an advocate for fighting pestilence.

Father used some of his extended vacation time off to visit his family back home in Italy. Whenever we knew he was planning a trip, we'd ask him to buy jewelry for us like gold crosses and chains, knowing he would get good deals. He was kind enough to oblige, often returning with a surplus he gave away or sold at-cost to any interested parishioners. Just one more thing we loved about him.

When I heard he had some nice looking wristwatches, I decided it was time to have a look and maybe even do a little haggling. I asked to see what he had in stock.

"Okay, you come inside, and you pick one out," he said. I followed him upstairs to his wood-paneled office. He sat down behind his desk and opened the side drawer. "Go ahead, pick," he said, pointing to a half-dozen styles and colors.

I held up my favorite after browsing his inventory. "How much for this?"

"How much you have?"

"Four bucks."

"Four dollars, that's it?

"That's all I got, Father."

"It's okay, that's how much it costs."

"Can you do three?"

"Eh, sure, why not. Three then."

I put it on my wrist for a closer look. It was much larger than the youth watch I received as a gift for my Confirmation a few years earlier. The deal sounded too good. Still, I knew Father was a man of integrity and would never steer anyone in the gang wrong, so I handed him three dollars and pocketed the fourth. I showed it to all the boys. Yes, I was pretty pleased with the way I negotiated that afternoon.

You can imagine how I felt five days later when my new watch stopped working. All of a sudden, three dollars seemed like a whole lot of money. I decided to take it back to see if he'd honor any sort of warranty on it.

I didn't think he'd give me any spiel about all sales being final or purchased *as is*, but just in case he tried, I prepared myself for a little quibbling. I'd take a page from my dad's book on haggling. I watched Pop barter with car salespeople before and marveled at his negotiation skills. He could sure make them sweat, finagling his way to good deals, even bargaining for a used car at a local dealership by throwing in some brick and cement work. How ingenious. Now it was my turn to step up and deal.

When I got there, Father Mario was sitting outside the rectory having a smoke. I handed the watch to him.

"Hey, Father, that thing is junk."

"Junk? No, not junk. Why junk?"

"Cause it stopped working already. Good wristwatches don't do that. I want another one."

He fiddled with it for a few seconds. "Eh, it's no problem. You come and take another one – come and choose." We returned to his office desk, and again, he sat down and pulled the drawer open. "Go ahead, have a look," he said. So far, so good, I thought to myself. I wondered if any more of them were defective though I couldn't imagine someone actually cheating a priest.

Then, from the corner of my eye, I zeroed in on one in particular. In fact, it was the most dazzling watch I'd ever seen in my life. The damn thing had me hypnotized to the point where I started speaking without thinking. "Okay, Father, you want me to pick out a watch? I'll pick out a watch. I want that one – that one right there," I said, pointing to his wrist.

He was wearing a *Vintage Ernest Borel Cocktail* watch. It's no ordinary analog timepiece. The square outer case was sleek and gold, and the matching band was a Twist-O-Flex, a trendy brand at the time. However, the main attraction of this model was the animated face. In place of a second hand, a disc of spokes created a mesmerizing kaleidoscopic effect as it rotated, one, second, at, a, time. Borel watches are noted for this unique feature. It wasn't the first time that fine jewelry piece on his wrist bedazzled me. It caught my eye whenever he wore it.

If that weren't already enough, the flipside was equally captivating. It had a clear crystal back, exposing the gears as they rotated. Also visible were several of its seventeen ruby jewels. It was distinctive, front and back, and as beautiful as it was classy.

Father Mario looked up at me, somewhat puzzled by my proposal. "You want this one?" he asked, pointing to it. Now I could see *his* gears rotating.

"Yeah, that's right," I replied. "That's the one I pick." I waited for him to burst out laughing except what happened next is something I never expected.

He shrugged his shoulders and tilted his head. "Eh, sure, why not? You can take this one if you want it." He slid the gorgeous timepiece off his wrist, placing it into my hand. I just stood there like a cafone, grinning and waiting for a punchline that never followed. He was serious. The awkward silence deflated my grin. In fact, I suddenly felt lousy.

"Wait. What? You're giving this to me?" I mumbled. "Are you kidding?"

"No, I am not kidding. It's yours." If he was using some sort of reverse negotiating technique on me, it was working.

"No, no, no. I'm not taking this," I said, pushing it back at him.

"Sure, you can. Why not?" he replied, brushing my hand away.

"Why not? Well, for starters, it's worth way more than three bucks and more than I could ever afford."

"It's okay. I want you to have it. Try it on."

"People like me don't have watches like these, Father."

"What the hell does that mean, *people like you?* Put it on. Go on!"

"I don't know about this," I said, sliding it over my hand. "What can I say?"

"How 'bout thank you," he said with a sincere smile.

"I'm... I'm... Thanks, Father." I was tongue-tied. It was the most beautiful thing I ever owned. "Thanks a million." That evening I showed my parents my newest acquisition and told them the whole story.

My father examined it, front and back. "It's a damn good watch for three dollars," he said. "You did good." That made me proud.

"The truth is you received a generous gift," my mother countered, "not a good deal. You thanked him, no?"

"God, I sure hope I did. To tell you the truth, I don't remember."

"Well, you should thank him again tomorrow just in case!"

Of course, my mother was right. It was one helluva lesson in generosity from one of my early role models. His concern for the boys was genuine, and this selfless act of kindness is just one of many testaments to his character. I wonder if he realizes the lasting impression he made on me.

~~~

Now, here we are over fifty years after that lopsided negotiation. Father retired and moved back to his native home after a long and successful mission at our beloved St. Rocco. Papa is not happy with the prospect of never seeing him again. Though honestly, he crosses my mind every time I wind that precious keepsake. The damn thing still keeps perfect time, and I always enjoy wearing it on special occasions. It fascinates me how this attractive timepiece never fails as an effective icebreaker at social gatherings. Inevitably, it will catch the eye of someone interested in taking a closer look. Then like clockwork, they ask for the story behind it, and your papa can tell them the most wonderful tale of a most generous man and the timeless gift he has given me. Grazie, Padre.

INCIDENT AT SOCRATES CAVE

I DISCOVERED THIS COLLEGE BAR on the east side of Cleveland with a few older friends, back when I was still in high school and not quite eighteen. I managed to get past the bouncers by borrowing a draft card, repeatedly, until I became old enough to carry my very own college ID. By that time, ironically, I didn't need any identification. I became a familiar face and was considered a regular. I just moseyed right into Socrates Cave as if I owned the damn place.

I was also one of the Rocco Boys, a large gang of teens that grew up on the streets near our local parish, Saint Rocco, on the near west side of town. There was a large population of Italian families like mine in the neighborhood at that time. Most of my young paesans were good-natured but high-spirited. I'll even admit sometimes too high-spirited. A few bordered the fringe of society, and one or two of them were just downright incorrigible. Still, they were brothers to me, thick as thieves, and quite a few of them were there this particular Saturday night in 1972.

It all started typically enough. The place was filled with plenty of people, music, and cold beer. A live band had an energetic crowd up on their feet, rocking and rolling to the greatest tunes of our generation. Everyone seemed to be having an enjoyable time. And to top off the night, the bar was passing out free T-shirts with the Socrates Cave logo printed on the front.

I was sitting with a few old friends from high school when Hector, another one of the regulars, rushed the table out of breath and visibly concerned. He cut me off in mid-sentence.

"Man, you'd best come quick!" he shouted over all the noise.

"What do you mean? What's wrong?" I asked, now half standing up.

"It's your cousin, Frank, man. He's gonna fight. There's these dudes."

"Frank's here? Who's gonna fight?"

"They're looking for trouble, and he's gonna give it to 'em. Better hurry!"

"Sorry, I have to go," I said, abruptly leaving the table to follow him. "Tell me what happened, Hector." He didn't respond as we bobbed and weaved our way through the dense crowd, stretching our necks to find any sign of unusual activity. I saw nothing out of the ordinary and no cousin.

Frank was four years older than me and recently

married. He and his new wife, Pam, made an appearance that evening. She was pretty and kind and a great addition to our close family. I enjoyed spending time with them, and by now, most of the boys knew they were my relatives.

Hector threw his arm out to stop me and pointed toward the sidewall. "They were right over there a minute ago, but now they're gone."

"Can you please just stop and tell me what the hell's going on?"

He explained that Pam was dancing with her girlfriend when four drunken rowdies taunted her with whistles and catcalls from a nearby table. She was able to ignore the rude behavior at first until two jumped up to cut in. When Pam refused their advances, one of these *stugots* physically pushed her on his way back to his seat. His drunken-ass antics only drew more taunting from the table of troublemakers.

I don't know how Frank found out about this incident. What I did know is he had tracked them down somewhere close by, but I couldn't find him. Keep in mind Frank wasn't a big man, but was lean and in excellent shape. My cousin was also as loyal and honest a man as you'll ever find, and I can tell you is he never flinched when it came to *famiglia*. This situation was a ticking time bomb.

"Okay, let's split up," I suggested. "Check the men's room. I'll go around to the other side of the dance floor."

I waggled my way through the standing crowd, making inquiries along the way. I had no luck until I looked across the room and noticed my friend Nick gesturing toward the entrance as if he knew my mission. I fought through the crowded foyer, threw the front door open, and stepped out onto the sidewalk. The heavy door slammed behind me, muffling the loud music and chatter inside. Now all I heard was the sound of men arguing.

There was Frank, not far down the dimly lit sidewalk, standing toe-to-toe in a shouting match *with all four of them!* He had his back to me, looking up at one of them, poking the man's chest. The others began forming a semicircle around him.

Time suddenly stopped, and I remember thinking this was not going to end well, yet I was compelled to get involved. I took a deep breath, clenched both of my fists, and walked toward the confrontation to make my presence known. I stopped behind my cousin with my heart pounding in my chest, and rightfully so. Getting my ass kicked was not on this evening's agenda. I remained silent as the situation deteriorated in front of me. Then suddenly it got quiet. I'm talking eerily quiet. Christ, here we go, I thought, trying to anticipate who to swing at first.

Instead, the four tough guys froze at attention. Their faces paled, and expressions sobered. They slowly began gravitating to the parking lot behind them. Frank advanced, demanding satisfaction. I reluctantly followed.

The one having his chest poked carefully raised his hands in submission and began apologizing profusely for his misconduct. One by one, the others expressed their deepest regrets and begged his pardon as they turned in unison. I was baffled but relieved enough to relax my fists.

Their final departure was a fast break into a two-door sedan. The driver had the engine started before the doors were closed. Frank directed his barrage of insults at the car as it sped away, then stood like an alert watchdog until the taillights vanished into the darkness. The night air became still except for the muffled sound of music. Time began ticking again.

Frank spun around so quickly he bumped into me. We stared at each other for a moment, and then he glanced over my shoulder. "I'll be damned," he uttered. We made eye contact again as a smile eased across his face.

That's when I erupted. "What's so goddamn funny? You could have gotten us both killed out here." He just continued smiling. "Frank, have you gone completely *gagootz*?"

Again, he glanced over my shoulder, prompting me to turn my head. Gathered behind us in deadpan silence and poised for trouble stood a dozen Rocco Boys. It made me smile too.

"So, what took you so long?" Frank teased.

"You're an idiot, you know that, right?" I threw my

arm around his neck, and everyone laughed as we headed back inside. That night ended the way most of them did back at the Cave – with lots of fun and lots of friends.

~~~

Papa recently came across that old Socrates Cave T-shirt. It was tucked away in a box of old clothes in the attic for decades. How in the world did it manage to survive all these years? It brought back a rush of faded memories from Papa's glory days at my beloved college bar, including this heart-pounding incident with Frank and the boys. I lifted the vintage souvenir out of the box and stretched it across my chest. After that, I became consumed with only one thought. How in God's name did I ever fit into this thing?

THE MONSTER BARBER

MY FATHER LEFT HIS BARBERSHOP to work in construction years before I was born, yet he never stopped cutting hair. If you knew Gennaro well enough to visit his Italian home in Cleveland's inner city, it entitled you to free kitchen haircuts for life. Try finding that in any book on proper hosting etiquette. In any case, it was one helluva perk for his family, friends, and one improbable guest in our ethnic neighborhood.

I returned home from playing outside one Saturday afternoon in 1963, just eleven years old, to an all-too-familiar sight. Someone plunked down in the middle of our kitchen draped in a pinstriped barbershop cape receiving the royal treatment. Two empty coffee mugs and an open pastry box from Hough Bakeries were sitting on the table. Pop stood behind the swaddled figure, positioning the man's head downward about to groom the back of his neck. I naturally glanced to see who it was as I made my way toward the living room.

At first, my young mind grappled with identifying

the daunting face. It caused me to slow down for a closer look, until a cold shiver shot down my spine, with the worst of my fears confirmed. This was no friend and most definitely not family. It was *Marteen*, our neighborhood's equivalent to Frankenstein's monster – minus the neck bolts.

Only this village monster roamed freely throughout our streets dressed in a tweed coat, drooping pants, and worn-out boots muttering to himself uncontrollably with intermittent outbursts to scold nothing more than pure air. He also practiced a bizarre ritual of tossing litter from the sidewalk to the curb. Adults passing Marteen on the street sheltered their eyes and quickened their pace. Children like me just shamelessly ran the other way.

When he wasn't patrolling for litter, chances were you'd find Marteen in front of our local parish, St. Rocco. There, he made a real spectacle of himself by kneeling on the concrete steps, while passionately crossing himself in a rapid, repeated succession. He spewed fire and brimstone at no one in particular or worse, to unsuspecting passersby caught in his crosshairs. He was always first to the altar for communion at Sunday masses, then would wave the congregation forward with both hands. Grown-ups used words like demented and deranged to describe him. No one knew for sure if he was homeless. Rumor had it he took refuge in the cellar of one of the church buildings.

So you see, there was never any real justification for engaging our monster. Yet, for some ungodly reason, he was in my kitchen in the middle of a shave and haircut no less. Pop was a kind, quiet man and my hero. He had a way of teaching me things without ever saying much. Strong too, but really, what the hell was he thinking inviting Marteen into our home? Now he's snipping away as if it were cousins Freddy or Joe, Uncle Rico, or my godfather Chucky sitting there. Even our old watchdog Rusty slept on the floor with one eye open. I stopped to gawk. Hell, I'd never been this close to him before, close enough to touch – and smell.

I lapsed into a spellbound gaze standing there as Marteen kept his chin glued to his chest. I noticed the wiry hair on his head was peppered gray, but his eyes and brow were jet-black. So were the wild hairs budding from his nostrils and ears. And that look of contempt chiseled on his haggard facade remained fixed even as he sat still.

Suddenly, there was movement from our monster, startling me out of my hypnotic trance. Marteen began contorting his forehead, shifting his face my way while straining to keep his head down. I felt another shiver as our eyes made contact through his bushy eyebrows, and would have fled, but was unable to move my arms or legs. I was literally scared stiff.

But what happened next in that frozen moment was the damnedest thing I could never have imagined as a child. A half-crooked grin rose tenderly up the side of his cheek. Marteen was smiling at me! Then his face dropped back to the floor before I could wipe the repulsion off of mine. I regained the feeling in my limbs enough to dash to the living room, now more confused than afraid.

Turning on the television, I tried watching my favorite cowboy show starring *Roy Rogers*, yet my bewilderment lingered. Later that hour, I crept to the kitchen archway for a little covert surveillance. My father was alone in the room sweeping the floor. Then from the bathroom off of the kitchen, I heard the toilet flush and the door opening. My kneejerk reaction was a beeline back to the television, but eventually, curiosity got the best of me. I tiptoed back, carefully peering into the kitchen only to find them sipping wine at the table, sharing a relaxed conversation like two old paesans. If that wasn't already odd enough, Marteen's appearance gave me another surprise. He never looked better. I ducked around the corner as he glanced my way, only this time, I wasn't as frightened. How peculiar.

Finally, I returned for one last peek when I heard them leaving the table. Pop helped Marteen with his coat and even offered him a couple of dollars, which the improbable guest agonizingly refused to accept.

"Go on, take it. It's okay," Pop said, and Marteen reluctantly obliged him.

"Grazie," Marteen said, nodding awkwardly.

"Tante grazie."

"Prego," Pop replied, "you're welcome."

Marteen silently left our home. As always, Pop methodically cleaned his barber tools and carefully put them back into the black case he kept stored in the closet.

~~~

Papa's quiet hero delivered yet another one of his subtle life lessons in that simple act of kindness. Then I understood my earlier confusion. My father didn't see a monster. All he saw was a needy man and offered a helping hand. Now, I don't see monsters anymore.

TOSRV '79

FRIDRICH BICYCLE, INC. ON LORAIN ROAD has been around since the turn of the twentieth century, making it one of the oldest bike shops in the country. My first visit to this historic institution was with my parents in the late 1950s when we went shopping for my first two-wheeler. Once inside the rustic building with creaky, wooden floors, there was row after row after row of bicycles in every shape, size, and color imaginable. This place, I thought, must be bicycle heaven.

The three of us picked out a twenty-four inch, red and white *Cadillac*, a Fridrich's name brand at the time. We added a wire basket, a handlebar bell, and handle-grip streamers, giving it that authentic 50s look. It was a bicycle any child would have been proud to ride that summer, except, in my case, there were a couple of minor glitches. First, I didn't know how to balance on two wheels, and second, my legs weren't long enough to reach the pedals. I think the rationale here was to buy one bicycle I would eventually grow into and have for the rest of my childhood. Practical? Maybe, but in the meantime, all I could do was admire it and use my imagination.

To address this dilemma, my father picked up a smaller framed, twenty-inch bicycle for fifty cents at the junkyard. It was rusted solid, and missing a seat, chain, and pedal. Also, both tires were worn flat, and the sprocket was bent. It resembled more of a Pablo Picasso sculpture than a bipedal mode of transportation. Ma insisted he throw it in the trash. Instead, our artist wired my tricycle seat to the frame, then found a secondhand chain and pedal from God only knows where, probably that dilapidated shanty of his next to the garage. He kept one of everything there. Once he *somewhat* straightened the sprocket, patched the tires, and greased all the fittings, I ultimately learned to ride the damn thing. Pablo would have been impressed with Pop's masterpiece, though I rode it with extra caution. The chain, seat, and pedal habitually fell off while I was in motion, which usually sent me crashing to the ground. After that season of trial by fire, I could balance on anything with a wheel.

I rode my Cadillac everywhere, sometimes on faraway adventures to deliberately get lost. I must have had a good sense of direction since I always found my way back. I once made it clear out to Cleveland Hopkins Airport over ten miles away, traveling on busy city streets like Pearl, Brookpark, and Snow. Always home by suppertime, I was smart enough never to tell Ma where I'd been all day.

My next purchase from Fridrich's came during the mid-1960s when I was a young teenager. This one was a handsome, three-speed racer with chrome fenders that I paid for with my savings from delivering newspapers. It was much lighter and faster than the Cadillac and the first bike I owned with handbrakes.

I learned a valuable lesson in aviation from independent front and rear brakes. Did you know you could oppose gravity with enough ground speed, torque, and a front handbrake? It happened while riding down the steep, twisted brick road to Brookside Park at Fulton and Dennison. I straddled the handlebars spread-eagle and landed on my hands and knees after applying just the front. My shiny new bike landed right on top of me. Ouch! That extreme stretch of road was the scene of many car accidents and permanently closed once renovations under the Fulton Bridge completed. I had some fun times on that bike too.

Then, as they say, the third time's a charm. I returned to Fridrich's in 1978 to purchase a ten-speed black racer, the bicycle of my childhood dreams. The tall, *Ross Professional Tour Model II* was suitably fit for my lanky, six-foot body. I customized the add-ons with black handlebar wrap, a leather saddle, leather-trimmed stirrup pedals, a water bottle holder, and accenting yellow saddlebag. The finishing touch was an aluminum bike rack attached above the rear wheel to hold my gear. My dream came true.

Now, almost twenty-six years old, I rode religiously. These weren't short rides around the neighborhood. They were long outings lasting hours, mostly on weekday evenings and the weekends. Many of these excursions were with my cousin Frank riding next to me on his *Falcon*, a European touring bicycle. We enjoyed riding throughout a series of nature reservations encircling Greater Cleveland, known as the *Emerald Necklace*. And yes, I still tried to get lost.

Frank and I were peddling along a stretch of Big Creek Parkway in Parma Heights one autumn afternoon of that year when I broached the subject of entering an honest-to-goodness bicycle tour. The one I had in mind was Ohio's Tour of the Scioto River Valley, *TOSRV* for short, pronounced toss'rawv.

It was a 210-mile, round-trip journey through some of the most beautiful scenery in the southern half of the state that paralleled the nearby Scioto River, Ohio's longest interior waterway. The course stretched 105 miles from the state capitol building in Columbus to the small town of Portsmouth on the banks of the Ohio River, with the return trip the following day. Frank had already completed the journey a few years earlier. I'd never ridden over 100 miles in a day, let alone doing it two days in a row. Still, it sounded like a worthy challenge.

"I won't kid you. It's not easy," Frank admitted, "but I did it, and so can you."

"You think Dennis would be interested in coming with us?" My cousin Dennis is Frank's brother and lived in Columbus at the time. I knew he enjoyed bicycling.

"I'll ask him," Frank replied. "Either way, we could stay at his house the night before so we won't have to drive there in the morning." Cleveland is a two-hour drive to Columbus.

"TOSRV '79, here we come!" I said. It fell on Mother's Day weekend in May. We felt pumped after that conversation and rode an extra ten miles. Later that week, I learned Dennis agreed to join us.

To build my endurance, I continued riding as often as possible while staying active during the winter months by playing indoor volleyball. I also joined a floor hockey team as the goalkeeper until the winter thaw.

Now, twenty-mile jaunts weren't enough to prepare for this two-day event. The bar was set much higher at fifty-to-sixty-mile excursions. I wasn't even sure if this new conditioning routine would be enough, but it had to suffice with my schedule.

Frank and I drove my Dodge van to Columbus one evening in early spring to discuss our tour plans with Dennis. We filled out the registration forms, and Dennis offered to send them in together. He also mentioned that one of his friends asked to join us, which was fine with me. My cousins and I literally talked until dawn before heading back to Cleveland the next morning. You can do without sleep when you're that young!

On Friday, May 11, Frank and I loaded our bikes and gear into my van and drove to Columbus to stay with Dennis. The three of us went to bed early that night, but honestly, I was too restless to get a good night's sleep.

We arrived in front of the Ohio Statehouse just before sunrise on Saturday morning, May 12. Over three thousand enthusiastic participants were buzzing the streets as we pinned our race numbers onto our shirts. Mine was *3272*. I felt pretty good about this test of will and endurance despite my lack of sleep.

During the prestart preparations, I learned volunteers would be patrolling up and down the course in vehicles called *sag wagons*. It brought me some comfort though I hoped we wouldn't need their assistance. The weather seemed to be cooperating too. This weekend was surely going to be one helluva experiment.

Dennis introduced us to Matthew, our fourth riding partner. Matt had another person standing with him. "Davie, what are you doing here?" Dennis asked. "I didn't know you signed up for the tour too."

"I didn't," Davie replied. "I'm going to drive down to Portsmouth just to hang around with you guys tonight." Then he pointed to a Volkswagen bus parked at the curb. "I'll double-back once in a while to check on you guys," he added, "so if any of you need a rest, you can just throw your bike in the back and ride with me for as long as you'd like."

Well, I'll be damned. We had our very own sag wagon. But to be perfectly honest, I felt apprehensive about it. I wondered if this was going to make it too damn easy for us to quit out there, especially during those mental and physical lapses of weakness and exhaustion. I promised myself right then and there not to climb into that bus during the tour. Still, it was a heartfelt offer to test my mettle further.

With my adrenaline pumping, we departed the statehouse amongst a large pack of cyclists, but it didn't take very long before the crowd thinned out. Since this was not a race, we were determined to maintain our own pace, despite the urge to peddle faster every time a uniformed cycle team sped passed us. *"On your left,"* was the audible signal they gave whizzing by like a train of boxcars.

Our first stop of the tour was in Circleville, almost thirty miles south of the capital. Time flew by quickly with all the excitement stirring around me. Davie was waiting for us in the assigned area. Hundreds of cyclists were spread out all across the park, resting on the grass and having fun. Juices, fruits, peanuts, and candy snacks were bountiful and complimentary. And as a sign of the times, it was also the right place for us to take a cigarette break. I said it was 1979!

Next, it was on to Chillicothe, less than twenty-five miles away as we cycled deeper into beautiful southern

Ohio. Ancient glaciers carved these gently rolling hills, leaving behind countless acres of fertile soil for the picture-postcard farms to till. Soybeans, corn, and wheat fields were plentiful. Grazing livestock also dotted the landscape – what a stark contrast to big city life.

The first signs of fatigue began to set in during the end stretch of this leg, despite the remnants of excitement still with me. I sensed I wasn't alone as my team quieted down. We arrived at the designated rest area to replenish ourselves just as the skies began to cloud over. Soon moisture filled the air. We capped off our break with another cigarette.

The first raindrops fell right after leaving for our third stop, Waverly, less than twenty miles away. The thick skies darkened to black storm clouds mixed with strong headwinds. Next came the thunder and lightning, followed by pelting rain, making it difficult to keep my head up. The downpour soaked us to the bone within minutes. It came down in buckets on that desolate country road with seemingly no shelter in sight. Then right around the bend and barely visible through the dark and deluge, a farmhouse appeared just forty feet off the road. The *bike gods* had taken pity, providing a dilapidated barn leaning next to the house, and an old man rocking in a chair on the front porch. The farmer watched us drudge across the face of his property, then stop in front of his picket fence. He continued swaying back and forth.

"Excuse me, sir," Frank yelled. "Would you mind if we stood in your barn for a little while until this rain lets up?"

"Nope, go ahead, door's open," he replied, without breaking his rhythm.

"Thank you!" Sopping wet, the four of us walked our bicycles inside the leaky structure. We found a dry place to rest and ate the snacks in our saddlebags. It was almost thirty minutes before the hard rain let up into a constant drizzle. It was time to get back on the road again. Our elderly savior was still in his rocker.

"Good luck to you, boys." I think most of the folks down there looked forward to this annual event. Everyone treated us kindly.

The short-shorts I was wearing, another sign of the times, exposed my inner thighs to the wet leather saddle, therefore chafing my skin. This developing rash, the humidity, my stiffening joints and muscles, along with a thorough drenching, were about as much fun as it sounds. The next twenty-some miles of road was more of a struggle – nothing close to fun or excitement.

"Is anyone else's bike squeaking?" I asked the group. The downpour had washed most of the grease off my bike.

"Yes, look for a sag wagon," Frank suggested. "They'll have grease." Neither bike gods nor sag wagons were with us that part of the journey. We squealed our way into Waverly an hour off our pace.

I found a piece of dry pavement between the puddles

to eat my trail mix. I struck up a conversation with a fellow rider dressed in a traditional cycling outfit, right down to the cotton cycling cap. Safety helmets were scarce back in 1979. He let me borrow a tube of grease.

"Thanks," I said, returning it to him. "How long have you been here?"

"Oh, about ten minutes. I'm getting ready to head back out soon."

I was pleased to think we weren't too far behind someone that looked like he came out of a cycling magazine. "Well," I said with self-confidence, "I guess I'll see you in Portsmouth then."

"Oh, no," he responded, "I was there already. I'm headed back to Chillicothe."

"Wait. What? Where did you start?"

"Columbus."

"When?"

"Not long after dawn." It took a few seconds for that to register. Damn, this guy started around the same time as us, completed the first 105 miles, and was already a quarter of the way back. Mea culpa! I just met one of those bike gods. Now my ego felt as bruised as my body. I wondered how many cigarette breaks he stopped for along the way. I was too tired to give it any more thought.

When the smoke break was over, we mounted our bikes to head south on the last thirty-miles for that day. We rode into an overcast Portsmouth, where volunteers directed us to our accommodations. The sleeping bags and clothing changes we loaded onto a truck back in Columbus were waiting for us at the town's community college. The gymnasium floor was our assigned sleeping quarters for the night, along with hundreds of other cyclists. It might not sound very cozy in any normal situation, but a warm, dry sleeping bag on any surface seemed perfectly acceptable to me. So did a hot shower, a hot meal, and a hot cup of coffee.

After that hot shower and some dry clothes, I felt surprisingly good. Now, it was time to eat. The tour had food available, but my team collectively opted to explore what the small town had to offer us. We locked our bikes up and piled into Davie's bus.

After a very short drive around town, we found a local restaurant and had a quiet, sit-down meal. We were all genuinely fatigued except for our energetic chauffeur, who did most of the talking.

"It's supposed to rain again tomorrow," Davie said, making small talk. It wasn't exactly what anyone wanted to hear at that moment. We were wearing the only dry clothes we had left. When dinner ended, it was back to the bus.

There were festivities in town sponsored by the tour, so we stopped to check it out. It was mostly music with a few vendors peddling bicycle parts, equipment, and souvenirs. We each bought a cheap plastic poncho for the return trip home just in case the forecast was correct, then headed back to the college campus.

Davie chose to sleep in his bus somewhere nearby. "See you boys tomorrow morning," he said. "I'll check with you before I head home to Columbus in case anyone wants a lift back."

Matt's ears perked up. "I might take you up on that offer."

I remembered the promise I made before the tour began not to quit if things got tough. I repeated that vow to myself several times before passing out into a deep, deep sleep on that hard, hard floor.

Morning came much too soon as I awoke to the sound of people stirring all around me. My first conscience thought was a strategy on how to peel myself off the floor. Every fiber in my body ached, including my eyelids. I felt deep-seated soreness in the palms of my hands from leaning forward on the handlebars all those hours. Just trying to uncurl my fingers was painful. It took a minute to stand and the next to gain my balance. Grabbing food and coffee and a second hot shower to loosen up seemed to help. I stood most of the morning in fear of not being able to get up again. Yet nothing could have prepared me for the experience of sitting on my bicycle seat for the first time. Maybe a burning hot saddle of broken glass might come close to describing it. How the hell was I going to endure this level of discomfort for the rest of the day?

To make matters worse, if that was possible, the sky was a thick, dark gray. Threatening weather aside, we collectively refused Davie's final offer for a ride, bidding him farewell as the four of us began the first leg of our return trip. It took every ounce of my mental strength to ignore the stiffness in my body, not to mention the hot broken glass beneath me.

The rainfall came just two miles down the road prompting us to don the plastic ponchos we bought the night before. The precipitation leveled off to a steady drizzle as we ever so strenuously propelled ourselves forward.

Once again, the swarm of riders rapidly thinned as it had at the beginning of the tour. At one point, we found ourselves alone on a quiet stretch of road, until the unmistakable whining sound of a Volkswagen engine approached us. It was Davie backtracking.

"G-zus, what now?" slipped quietly from my lips as we pulled over and stopped.

"Hey, you guys, there's another big storm just ahead. It's raining cats and dogs with thunder and lightening too. I figured I'd check to see if you're ready to quit."

Matt was the first to speak up. "What are you guys going to do?" Again, Davie's gesture was kind and thoughtful, but I felt I had to get started soon before I buckled.

"I'm good, really. Thanks, but no thanks." It pained me to lie out loud.

"You sure?" Davie asked. "Cause I'm headed back for good this time."

"We're more than halfway through this," was my response. "When I'm old and telling this story to my grandkids someday, I want to be able to tell them *Papa made it*." It got quiet for a few seconds.

"For the grandkids, then," Frank replied.

"I'm in too," Dennis added.

"Help me with my bike," was Matt's response to Davie. They loaded his bike into the bus, and both climbed aboard.

Davie rolled his window back down. "Last chance!" The three of us waved goodbye in the rain.

All we had to do now was finish busting our humps back to my van parked in a downtown lot ninety miles away. I wondered how much of our decision to continue was perseverance versus stupidity. Oh well, so much for semantics.

We pedaled diligently through dreary weather for the next few hours until the sun broke through the clouds somewhere between Chillicothe and Circleville. The air was muggy, but the sunshine gave us the mental boost needed for that final leg of the trip.

We rolled up to the administration table in Columbus, where all three of us received a colorful Certificate of Recognition. More importantly to me was the stamped *GOLD SEAL OF COMPLETION*. I stopped at a souvenir stand

and bought a commemorative coffee mug and T-shirt.

Frank and I parted ways with Dennis in the parking lot before loading everything into my van. "Now, all we have to do is stay awake for the drive home," I joked.

"Not even funny," was his response. "Wake me up halfway there, and I'll drive the rest of the way." Then he closed his eyes and fell fast asleep. I took him up on the offer somewhere near Mansfield.

I opened my eyes as we pulled into Frank's driveway. He unloaded his gear, and then I drove home still weary but proud of our ambitious weekend accomplishment.

I was a schoolteacher and had prearranged to take Monday off work. Thankfully, the school administrators supported this little venture of mine and allowed me time to recuperate.

I slept late the next morning, then made the stupid mistake of cutting the grass in the afternoon heat. I quit in the middle of my chore and retired to the living room couch despite using a gas-powered, self-propelled, walk-behind mower. All of my self-determination was left behind in the Scioto Valley the day before. This bicycle tour was my first organized ride, but not my last.

~~~

Time has a way of eroding details from our recollections. What remains are the underlying feelings. For this momentous weekend in May of 1979, the most outstanding sentiment I recall is the utter joy in creating all those miserable aches and pains. And best of all, with the help of famiglia, I have the perfect ending to this story for you, my dear bambini. Papa made it!

THE LICORICE STICK

I RAN HOME FROM MY ELEMENTARY SCHOOL with the application in my hand. It was only one block. I didn't bother to pack it into my school bag so I could show it to my mother the second I got home. I knew she would be in the kitchen when I got there, and that is precisely where she was, washing a pasta bowl in the sink. I startled our dog, Rusty, from his afternoon nap by slamming the door behind me.

"Ma, look what I have!" I said, trying to shove the paper into her wet hands.

"What's this all about? Let me at least dry my hands," she said, wringing them on the dishtowel flung over her shoulder.

It was the fall of 1961, and the day I've been waiting for had finally arrived – patiently waiting since last year for the fourth grade so that I could play a musical instrument. This was the grade students at Sackett Elementary were offered beginning orchestra lessons. There was a wide range of string, brass, and woodwind instruments to choose from, and I had a pretty good idea which one I wanted to pick.

Music permeated our Italian home for as long as I can remember. The mandolin was my father's favorite instrument, yet he was skilled enough to win a music contest playing his guitar. He brought dozens of beautiful songs from the old country. My mother had a lovely voice and sang with him in both English and Italian. Sometimes they would record their music sessions on a portable cassette recorder. My three older sisters, Anita, Sandra, and Linda, harmonized to modern songs as they washed and dried the dinner dishes in the evenings while I swept the floor.

Our large kitchen was the epicenter for much more than just eating great food. Friends and family often gathered around our table to sing and play beautiful music together. You might call them *kitchen concerts*, and I had every intention to be a part of it all.

"Oh, this," she said, scanning the paper, "I knew this was coming from the last school meeting I went to. Me and Dad already talked about it."

"You did? So I can be in the orchestra?"

"Of course, I think it's a great idea. I want you to learn an instrument."

"Oh good, cause I want to choose the trumpet," I said, grinning in relief.

She looked down at me, smiled, and then pinched my

chin with her damp fingers, "Well, I was thinking the clarinet would be better for you."

"But I want the trumpet. Why can't I play the trumpet?"

"Because it's hard to blow into a trumpet and you'll get headaches and maybe even rupture a vein in your head. Is that what you want, to rupture a vein in your head? And besides, they're very loud."

I didn't know anything about ruptured veins, but it sounded painful, like something I wouldn't want to happen in my head.

"Is that what Dad thinks too?" I asked.

"Yeah, he doesn't want you getting hurt either. He thought the clarinet was safer. You heard of Benny Goodman, no?"

I heard grown-ups talk about him before, but I never actually saw him. He was a famous big band leader in the old days that also played the clarinet when he wasn't conducting. I shrugged my shoulders.

"But what's a clarinet, Ma? I never seen one before."

"You're gonna love it, you'll see. It's long and thin and makes a beautiful sound," she assured me, looking happy enough for the both of us. Moreover, she was very convincing.

"Okay, please sign me up," I said, and that was it. I was so excited to be in the orchestra. I didn't really care what instrument I played. However, looking back now, I'm not as sure this conversation was as much about my health as it was about trumpets being very loud. That evening, I watched Ma fill out the application and check the box next to the clarinet. I turned it into my teacher first thing the following day.

"Oh, you're going to play the *licorice stick* just like Benny Goodman," she said, reading my application. "How wonderful." I didn't know what the hell she was talking about, so I kept quiet and smiled.

A week later, just before the final bell, the music teacher summoned students enrolled in Beginning Orchestra to the auditorium. Our instruments had finally arrived. Eight of us rushed down the hall jumping with excitement. I was one of three pupils receiving a clarinet. The music teacher handed me a long, black case with scuff marks all over it, a telltale sign of its age and use. There was no time to open it at school, so I quickly ran home to fidget with it.

The house was empty when I arrived, and the kitchen door was locked, which occasionally happened when my mother ran her errands. I sat cross-legged on the floor in the small foyer and began to examine the case from top to bottom. There was something stenciled on the side. It was badly faded, but I was able to make out the words. It said *Property of the Cleveland Public Schools: 1950.* I took a deep breath, slowly unlatched its two hinges, and carefully raised the lid with the expectations of an archeologist about to open an ancient crypt.

Inside, a crushed blue velvet lining worn with age carried the familiar musty smell of my grandmother's jewelry box. It cradled a long, silvery metal gadget with holes and levers attached from one end to the other. I couldn't seem to count them all, so quite frankly, my first impression of a clarinet was one of intimidating disappointment. What a stark difference from the three valves of that godforsaken trumpet I wanted so badly, and it certainly didn't resemble any licorice stick I'd ever seen before. Of course, I had no idea my teacher referred to the slang term given to black, wooden clarinets, which many professionals use.

I carefully lifted the instrument out of its case to inspect the barrel from end to end, and then held it up like a telescope to peer inside. I examined what I correctly guessed was a mouthpiece, but a clamp secured to its circumference had me baffled. If that wasn't confusing enough, the case held a small container labeled *Cork Grease*. Cork Grease? What the hell did I just get myself into by letting Ma pick my instrument?

I managed to attach the two pieces and decided to give it a go. I blew into the mouthpiece producing nothing more than the sound of rushing air, trying a little harder the second time but with the same result. I pressed some of the levers down and blew with all my might the third time – still nothing. I yanked the two pieces apart, shoved them back into the case, and slammed the lid. Maybe this wasn't such a great idea, after all, I thought. I sat and waited for Ma to come home so she could explain how the dumb thing worked.

After fumbling with it for a few minutes, it became apparent my mother never saw a clarinet up close either. She sensed my frustration and offered a consoling suggestion.

"You know, Uncle George will be at Grandma's house tonight. What if we take it to him? I bet he can tell you everything you want to know. How about it?" Again, she sounded convincing. All three of her brothers were musically inclined – three of the coolest uncles a boy can ever have.

"Okay, Ma!" Happily, my mother was right.

"You're missing a reed," Uncle George said, examining the mouthpiece in his hand. "It's like a sliver of bamboo. The clamp holds it on, then you rest the reed on your lips and blow into the hole. The air vibrates the reed, which makes the sound. To play different notes, press the keys, and cover the holes. It didn't come with a reed? Let's take another look."

He fished around inside the velvet case and, sure enough, found one tucked inside a paper sleeve. It was under the cork grease, which he also explained allowed the mouthpiece to slide on easier. There was a chip in the corner tip, but he clamped it on anyway. *Voilà!* At least now I was able to squeak and squawk some exciting sounds that evening. My uncle sure came through for me. Once again, I was excited to be in the orchestra.

Our music teacher, appropriately named Miss Notestine, initially grouped our lessons by instrument. First, we learned to read notes and play the scales up and down, and then progressed into simple songs like *Hot Cross Buns* and *Baa, Baa, Black Sheep*. Before long, all eight fourth-graders became part of a larger orchestra, and were allowed to leave the classroom together whenever the teacher announced, "Musicians may now go to rehearsal." It made us feel very special.

By fifth grade, I played a secondhand, black wooden clarinet that my parents purchased for fifty dollars from Whitney's Music on Fulton Road. The shop even threw in a complimentary new case. I studied there for a year to supplement the school program and then switched to Master Music on West 25th Street in sixth grade.

There were plenty of school concerts at Sackett Elementary, where I featured in several solos. I played from seventh to ninth grade at my junior high school, Thomas Jefferson, but the last year was strictly to please my mother. It took me that long to convince her I was no Benny Goodman.

That was right about the same time I learned a few chords on one of my father's guitars. In an instant, I had a new favorite instrument and turned to folk, pop, and rock & roll music, the genres of my generation. The guitar also allowed me to sing along in the kitchen concerts, something I wasn't able to do with my clarinet. It's been stringed instruments ever since.

~~~

For some strange reason, Papa was never able to part with that old woodwind. It sat around collecting dust on one shelf or another my entire adult life. I can go years without seeing the damn thing. Then, every now and again, I'll take it down from the shelf, and we'll visit like old friends. We reminisce of the good old days together, playing on school stages, and around the table at those earliest kitchen concerts. Today, it's out of commission, with most of the working parts brittle and stiff. I smile because Papa is kind of the same way too. Then, I'll carefully close it up and put it back on the shelf after remembering why I keep it. It's my old licorice stick.

BUICK RIVIERA

I WAS VERY HAPPY with myself at West Technical High School after taking the initiative to change my major study from Industrial Arts to Business during the 1969 school year. I had abandoned the trades to focus on a white-collar profession. It might not sound like much to most people, but the switch was a giant leap for me and proved to be quite a turning point for someone who began high school with no plans for the future. That's not to say it was smooth sailing afterward because it wasn't at all. I took my lumps leaving machine shop and welding equipment for the chance to sit behind a desk.

Take bookkeeping, for example. I'd be the first one to raise my hand in an opinion poll on the subject. Half the time, I found the accounting difficult. The other half was just mind-numbingly dull. Is there some wet paint I could be watching dry? At times, I didn't know my assets from a hole in the ground and grappled to keep up with other students who seemed to take it all in stride.

Now before you go laughing at me, keep in mind

I've traveled through life favoring the right side of my brain. I would have much preferred doing something that involved creativity and the arts. That's what I was most interested in, and yet, I yielded to the critics that warned me this was the fast track to the depths of poverty, and my best and safest path to succeed in life was in business.

"The world doesn't need another starving artist."

"Better find yourself a sugar momma."

"Your imagination and the change in your pocket won't buy you a cup of coffee."

But before you go feeling too sorry for me, I'm happy to report, bookkeeping aside, I enjoyed most of my other classes except for one general business course that sticks in my craw to this very day. The class started easy enough, and I seemed to excel in the course work. I even stood out a little among my fellow students, which was good for my confidence. Things were humming along smoothly halfway through the semester. Then one day, Mr. Letting announced he had a substantial business project for us that would account for a good-sized chunk of our grade. Each student received the task of designing a product.

"The boys in this class are to design an automobile – the girls will design a fashion outfit," said Mr. Letting. Remember, these were the days before the awareness of political correctness. "Use your imaginations and give me something the public finds interesting. You have two weeks to produce your illustrations and a detailed report."

Wow! I remember feeling very excited about this assignment. It was the ideal opportunity to exercise that creative itch of mine, and a good grade could seal the deal on the perfect score I had going in class, especially with the brilliant idea I had concocted. Are you ready for this? I was going to redesign next year's model of a beautiful and popular luxury automobile – the *Buick Riviera*. Who knows, if I do an excellent job on this project, it could lead to a career at General Motors.

I rolled up my sleeves and plunged headfirst into the mindset of an honest-to-goodness automobile designer. I studied the lines and curves of the current model by picking up a pamphlet from a dealership. Then, I began sketching out some fresh concepts of my own, remembering to preserve the famous brand's identity. You should always protect the integrity of a good product.

Once I decided on a preliminary design, I used my Mechanical Drawing training to blueprint the details – top, front, side, and rear, ensuring the form remained to scale. I also designed new wheels and gave the dashboard a facelift.

Lastly, my written report covered all the specifications of the new look. The finished product was neat, clean, and precise, and surely worthy of praise. "Wait 'til they get a load of this beauty," I thought. "I bet Letting never saw anything like this before in his class." I couldn't wait to see my results.

Three weeks went by before he had our projects graded and recorded. He smiled at me several times as he made his way up and down the aisles passing back our projects. I peeked at the proposals around me, and at the risk of sounding fatheaded, the work appeared shabby and elementary compared to mine. I was a quiet student in high school, always shying away from any kind of limelight, but I was sure this was going to get me some positive attention.

Finally, he stopped at my desk, deliberately saving me for last, I presumed. I smiled and reminded myself to thank him. He returned the smile and then hovered my project high over my desktop before allowing it to free-fall. It landed on my desk with a thud and gush of air.

That's when I felt my heartbeat in my throat. I stared down at three bold, blood-colored strokes. Slashed across the top of the first page was the letter "F." Below it, the fraction, zero over one hundred. I was frozen for a moment, the way you feel after hammering your thumb. There is no initial pain, but you know it's going to hurt like hell in a few seconds. And the sharp sting soon followed.

I gasped while looking up at Mr. Letting. His smile was gone, replaced by an ice-covered, demonic sneer. He appeared to be savoring my response. I swiveled my head around to see if anyone was watching. Oh, yes, the room was quiet, and the entire class was gawking at us. I felt the flush of humiliation wash over me and wanted to crawl under my desk.

Once Mr. Letting seemed sufficiently gratified, he strutted back to the front of the classroom and began his lesson of the day, as if nothing happened. I missed every word he said the rest of that period by trying to make sense of what the hell just happened. I was sure I did everything right. How did the lunkhead next to me score higher with his crayon doodle? That didn't seem right. What was to become of my cumulative grade? And while I wanted nothing more than to escape, I knew I had to confront him after class. My final grade depended upon it. It was probably the worst day of school and only got worse after class.

"You thought you were so smart, didn't you," he started, with another sneer. "Do I look stupid to you? Do I? You thought you could get away with it, huh, well not in my class, mister."

"Get away with what, sir?" I asked. "I'm sorry, I just don't understand."

"As if I couldn't recognize a Buick when I saw one. You didn't know I own a Buick, did you? Maybe not a Riviera, but a Buick nonetheless!"

Okay, now I was beginning to understand. "Let me explain." I started humbly defending my brilliant idea, but he would have none of it. My reasoning went in one ear and out the other.

"I even went down to the automotive shop to show your drawings to the auto teacher down there. And do you want to guess what Mr. Clay had to say about it?"

"I don't know. What'd he say?"

"He said, and I quote, 'This *could be* a Buick Riviera, unquote.'"

"But that's good. Don't you see it? I safeguarded the brand." Again, I tried to explain the cleverness behind that exact intention, but it was all in vain. "Don't I at least deserve *some* points for all the work I put into this? It's worth more than a zero."

"I don't give points for plagiarism," was his response as he stuffed papers into his briefcase.

"Can I have some time, then, to do it over?"

"Not for cheating, you can't!" he replied, without eye contact. "There's nothing else to discuss here. Now, if you'll excuse me, I have another class to teach upstairs." He left me standing alone in the room.

I'm not sure how a better student would have responded, but this incident broke something in me. I never had a school experience like this – ever. Accused of lying and cheating by a teacher, and then brushed off trying to defend my principles.

The shock wore into doom, which festered into deep-seated anger. If he was trying to adjust my attitude, he did one helluva job. Unfortunately, it was in the wrong direction. In protest of my perceived injustice, I became deliberately silent for the remainder of the semester. At times, I swear I bit my tongue until it bled just to piss him off.

Mr. Letting countered my insolence by purposely calling on me for answers to his questions as I sat with my arms folded. In return, I'd volley with an immediate response of *"I don't know!"* before he could finish. It really pushed his buttons until one day he finally exploded, slamming his textbook down on his desk with such force, the entire class collectively jumped.

"That's it! I've had it with you!" he shouted, then opened his grade book and scribbled something inside it. God only knows what he wrote, but apparently, my silence was never enough to involve the administration. All I received were his sneers and jeers. As unsettling as it was, my resolve surprised no one more than me.

I still passed the course with a decent grade, and luckily, never had him for any other classes. It was my first and last role as the class bad boy.

~~~

The teachers that Papa encountered in the Cleveland Public Schools were excellent representatives of their profession and offered students a top-notch education. Perhaps the irony here is that Papa used this isolated incident to become a better educator in my teaching career. It made me keener on understanding my students' intentions over the face value of their actions and outcomes. A valuable lesson learned.

WILD KINGDOM

THE CLARK-FULTON NEIGHBORHOOD on the near west side of Cleveland had plenty of churches from which to choose. But for an ethnic area packed with working-class Italian families like mine, there was really only one choice, and that was Saint Rocco. Its origin is what makes it so unique. A group of local Italian immigrants conceived the idea for a church to call their own back in the early beginnings of the twentieth century. Paesans in the community were more than capable of handcrafting a small, brick chapel on Trent Avenue by themselves. They conducted celebrations of their highly revered patron saint in and around this facility. Eventually, the Roman Catholic Church recognized the unofficial chapel in 1922. It became Cleveland's first west side Italian parish.

Membership in the small church soared by the mid-1920s, inspiring the clergy to purchase property around the corner on Fulton Road, where workers built a new, larger church with an attached school.

After WWII, the Italian community pulled together

again to self-build an even larger, more elaborate church on the same property. They completed the structure in 1952. The existing church was converted to a banquet hall and school gymnasium. Members of the congregation also erected several other buildings on the property. Our people seem to have a passion for architecture and construction.

Now let's fast-forward to the next decade, albeit not nearly as illustrious, and another chapter of this one-of-a-kind parish. It was during the mid-1960s when my generation, the baby boomers, exploded onto the scene. A young and tumultuous band of teenage parishioners seemed to overrun the church's landscape. In fact, our ever-presence was so commonplace we became known as the Rocco Boys. And back then, our numbers reached well into the thirties and even forties, averaging half of that on any given day.

We saw the churchyard as an open-air clubhouse. And thanks to our talented forefathers, there was plenty of space to roam freely between the well-constructed buildings.

Generally speaking, these structures were arranged two-by-two on the property. From left to right, the church and rectory sat nearest to the street. Next, came the connected grade school and hall, with the convent and kindergarten school in the rear. The entire right side of the property was a long, asphalt, parking lot extending from the main road back to the kindergarten. This open, spacious area bordered the rear property lines of a string of houses on Roehl Avenue. Fences helped to keep us out or in, depending on your point of view. The left perimeter of the property bordered a narrow lane named St. Rocco Court, connecting Fulton Road to West 33rd. And there you have it. This hallowed ground was our natural habitat.

The majority of us came from good homes. Still, with so many adolescents flooding this urban community, things occasionally got reckless, even volatile at times – at least enough to keep us on our toes. We were streetwise.

All right, so we were squatters, forcing the priests into a relationship they mercifully accepted, enduring our ever-presence from sunup to sundown and beyond. Looking back at this most unusual arrangement, it was nothing short of a miracle. The clergy's tolerance was indeed a labor of love, perhaps more precisely an exercise in the biblical patience of Job. *Bless you, Saint Rocco!*

I'm not saying we didn't wear on their nerves because we surely did. When it happened, most were willing to express themselves in a clear, concise, and straightforward way. A way our impulsive young minds could quickly grasp without any room for misinterpretation. Anything else would not have registered.

"What's wrong with you morons? You're a pack of wild jackasses. I feel like I'm watching television right outside my window. *Mutual of Omaha's Wild Kingdom*, and it's not even Sunday night."

"Sorry, Father, we'll keep it down."

"Go home, you idiots."

"Aw c'mon Padre."

"Can't I get just one evening of peace and quiet around here?"

"Sure, we're going over to the *Red Barn* now for hamburgers." It was a fast-food joint on Clark Avenue. One of the boys worked there and gave us his *five-finger discount.*

"Neighbors are calling here asking me what the hell is going on!"

"Aw, it's probably just Uncle Augie. He'll pass out soon enough." Augie wasn't really anyone's uncle. He was a tenant living on the second floor of a rental property on Roehl. His back porch, like others above the parking lot, served as an upper box seat to our asphalt jungle. We grated on Augie's nerves, especially when he boozed it up, which was often. Then he'd lose his inhibitions sparking disruptive outbursts of his own. Augie looked like Mussolini on his balcony once he got going, pounding the rail and shouting down at the crowd below. He even appeared with his shotgun a few times and held it up in the air once pulling the trigger. You should have seen the stampede it created. Then depending on his mood, he'd show up in the churchyard with a cold case of beer to discuss plans on buying uniforms for the boys so he could coach us in baseball. Augie liked us calling him *uncle*, and we loved him bringing cold beer.

"It's not just him," Father fired back. "Half that street

is up in arms. You know you're lucky the neighbors call here instead of the cops."

Father was right. They did call the priests first *most* of the time, but when the cops did show up, we'd simply scramble like roaches, only to return after the coast was clear, unless it was Officer Angelo. He was a parishioner of the church. In his case, we'd stick around for a lecture through the open window of his cruiser while his partner quietly observed.

"Christ guys, we had a half-dozen calls this evening. I don't know exactly what the hell you're doing here, but if we get one more call tonight, it won't be me coming back, and trust me, the next guy won't be so nice. Somebody's ass is going down to the station, capisce? And another thing, don't think I can't smell the beer, and I know you little stunads aren't old enough to drink. Just know Father Dominic isn't always gonna bail your sorry little asses out of trouble. Last warning, got it?"

"Okay, Ange, we're sorry. Thanks." We liked Angelo. He spoke our language too, just like the priests, but his lectures seldom reached us.

~~~

Father Dominic was a prominent figure around town, including down at the Second District Police Station, where he exercised his clout more than once on behalf of the boys in our wild kingdom.

His poker-faced humor and sarcastic wit were legendary among the gang. Still, we saw through it all to his underlying benevolence. Father Dominic's creativity was exemplary once he had enough of our antics, especially when it came to the rectory porch. It was a perfect place for us to sit and watch passing traffic and maybe raise a little too much hell. He'd throw a pale of cold water down on the gathering from a second-story window or worse yet, lit firecrackers. Sometimes he'd deliver a verbal scolding by stepping onto the porch in his slippers, open collar, and evening cigar. It was wise never to stand too close to him if you valued your arm hair the way he wielded that cigar around as he spoke. His animation made us laugh while making his point.

Father also seemed to have nicknames for some of us. Mine was *Zeke*. Don't ask why because I haven't a clue, but compared to some of the other tags he dished out like Pork Chop, Pineapple, and Choochy, mine wasn't so bad.

"What's your story, Zeke? Don't you have anything better to do? Why do you waste your time coming here every night?"

"I don't know, Father, I guess because it's fun."

"Fun, huh? So, which one of you dummies pulled the fire alarm again last night? That's the third time this year. You know the fire chief called me today. If it happens again, I swear he's getting a list of names and addresses, and you can all answer directly to him. I wash my hands of it all. So who's going to fess up?"

The answer to his question was always the same. "I don't know." Of course, it was always Mick Shubert. He was a loose cannon friend of ours from another gang, but I swear he spent more time hanging around in the churchyard. He also had the most experience inside the police station. Mad Mick had an infatuation with the fire alarm box on the telephone pole in front of the church. He'd pull the damn lever when no one was looking, then watch and wait to see who'd be the first to notice the approaching sirens heading our way. It created chaos.

"Uh-oh, do you hear that?" Looking at Mick whenever you heard sirens became a habit.

"Christ Mick, did you pull the goddamn alarm again?"

"Maybe I did, maybe I didn't. Why don't you stick around and find out."

"Damn it, man!"

"Here we go again!"

"I swear, Mick, one of these days."

"See you boys later," Mick yelled, giving us a half salute as we scattered out of sight. "Time to burn some of that *gabagool* off your fat asses!"

False alarms are considerable trouble, so sticking around wasn't an option. Some of the boys hopped fences to backyards along Roehl. Others hid behind the convent in the back of the property. I preferred the open road by ducking out behind the church toward the court and heading to West 33rd toward my house. I never appreciated these emergency evacuations, but clearly, they were often the best option in certain situations. Despite the hassle, no one ever snitched on Mick. A day in the life of a Rocco Boy.

~~~

Our social network was large enough and diverse enough to safely say that someone was probably engaged in something, somewhere, crossing the boundaries between smart and dumb, right and wrong. Most of the boys were good-natured individuals who were willing and able to appreciate the rowdiness and keen enough to sense nearby danger. *Trouble radar* was a must in our wild kingdom, and so were quick reactions. The former without the latter could put you in a dangerous position.

Things swiftly got out of hand one summer night when Milo showed up with a starter pistol. It looked and sounded like a real gun. The gang of boys under the streetlight near the rectory got a hold of it first and began improvising. I was standing in the middle of the churchyard with another group of guys watching this all unfold.

"G-zus, will you look at what they're doing over there."

"Uncle Augie will be out with his shotgun in no time."

"Nah, he's out already – out cold."

"They're too close to the street with that pistol. They shouldn't be that close."

Yet, they were, and within minutes, their shenanigans turned into a street performance of mock hold-ups. Car passengers at the red traffic light made great witnesses as they took turns robbing each other.

"Look at that. Now they have cars crashing the red light."

"I'll lay odds Mick's in the middle of it all."

"I won't take that bet."

"This isn't going to end well, fellas."

"You're right. Time to get out of here."

"I'm surprised we haven't heard any sirens."

"Let's go before we do. Who's up for the Red Barn?"

Unfortunately, we never had the chance to leave. From nowhere, a squad of Cleveland police officers stormed the parking lot. They had us surrounded within seconds, no sirens, and no place to run. Someone managed to ditch the starter pistol behind the Virgin Mary statue in front of the rectory as the officers, armed with rifles and revolvers, ordered, "Everyone freeze!"

We were gathered together and lined up shoulder to shoulder for a little interrogation. The officer in charge was not very cordial. One by one, we stared into his flashlight to state our name, address, and what our business was at church. No one had a good reason. He made each of us swear out loud to leave the premises and never return. I hope he didn't really expect that to happen though you can't blame him for trying.

In hindsight, we should have stuck to something less conspicuous, like a friendly game of Gray Ghost, a variation of Hide-n-Seek, inside the locked school building. We had a very clever method of getting inside without technically breaking in. Marco would climb the two-story downspout, enter through the unlocked roof hatch, and open one of the side doors to let us in. It was admittedly a lot of fun chasing each other through the dark halls and classrooms. I'm happy to report we were always careful not to disturb anything in the building. Damaging church property was strictly taboo in our wild kingdom.

This game went on for quite some time until a priest we nicknamed Ozzie put a stop to it. I don't know how he knew we were inside the school, but he nabbed us. A skinny kid we called Bonesy was hiding in the boy's restroom, standing on a toilet in one of the stalls as footsteps approached him. Some of us saw the lights turn on and then heard the stall door creak open. I heard Bonesy yell, "Gray ghost on Oz!" The last thing I remember was sprinting to the exit amongst the snickering and footsteps in the darkness. Father Oz escorted Bonesy out the door by the scruff of his neck after a thorough grilling. The roof hatch remained locked from that day forward.

With mischief like this so easy to find, more severe trouble sometimes found us. There was no telling who might show up in our wild kingdom. At the time, there were other neighborhood gangs on the west side of town, which brought about lots of trash talk, occasional saber-rattling, and even physical confrontations.

Fortunately, we had a built-in deterrent to help keep the peace. It was a group of churchyard inhabitants we simply referred to as *the older guys*. They were precisely just that, boys roughly three years older than we were, which is a sizeable gap between teenagers. Their no-nonsense reputation was widespread amongst the other gangs enough to keep relations civil, *most of the time*. They were like our big brothers. We were like their kid brothers. Over time, our big brothers became scarce once cars, girlfriends, and high school graduation entered their lives.

~~~

A few of us were sprawled out on the hall steps one hot summer afternoon when Donny's car pulled up in front of us. He was an older friend of Marco, who wasn't there with us that day. Donny wasn't a Rocco Boy, but a likable enough person, so we invited him to sit down and join us. We rested on the steps while admiring his pristine muscle car, a Pontiac GTO. It was a beauty to behold.

Our admiration for Donny's *Goat* was soon interrupted when a Ford Bronco entered the churchyard and slowly coasted our way. Its tinted windows prevented anyone from seeing inside the vehicle. We didn't think much of it since there were no gang alerts in effect, so we remained calmly seated on the steps as it came to a stop behind Donny's car. But I sat straight up the moment the passenger door swung open. Hell, I would have preferred a rival gang to who was stepping out of that car. *Saint Rocco, pray for us!*

It was *Toro*, a raging bull psychopath with a five o'clock shadow. I didn't know if Toro was even his real name or where he lived, but I knew enough not to make any sudden movements. No weapons were visible, though he had a reputation for carrying them. He comfortably positioned himself in front of us as if he were about to deliver a speech. We watched as Toro silently scanned his captive audience. Suddenly, he exploded into a tirade that ended before I began listening. The first and only thing I understood was a command issued to Donny.

"You, stand up," he ordered, and Donny reluctantly rose. I think Donny was chosen for looking older. There was a communal gulp. The ratcheting sound from an emergency brake made me look toward the Bronco. A shifty-looking character stepped out of the driver's door as if Toro needed reinforcement. He didn't. I turned my head back toward Toro just as he squeezed his fist into a tight ball and socked poor Donny right in the kisser. It sent Donny straight down to the ground. Still, no one moved.

"Anybody else wanna piece of that?" Toro asked, pointing to his victim sitting on the concrete. No one responded. "No? I didn't think so," he said, outwardly pleased by his action.

"You guys don't seem so tough," the driver added.

Then Toro said something I prayed would come back to bite him in the ass, something to make him regret this whole incident.

"And that goes for dem older guys too!" He looked down at Donny, now rubbing his jaw. "You tell 'em I said so." They got back into the Bronco and drove away. It all happened so fast though it felt like an eternity.

We lifted Donny up and dusted him off. He appeared a bit woozy, but okay, except for a bright red strawberry blossoming on his cheek. Once we collectively began breathing again, the decision to wait for the older guys was unanimous. And boy did they get an earful. We even reenacted the scene for them on the hall steps and emphasized Toro's menacing threat.

"And he said to tell you, *'that goes for you older wussies too!'*"

Yet despite our best efforts, the only reaction we surprisingly evoked was petty disinterest. "Don't worry about it," was the overall consensus. They were more preoccupied with their evening plans than hearing about this madman coming here on our turf and clocking some unfortunate innocent bystander in the face. I never thought I'd see the day! What the hell is happening to the order of our universe?

However, the order in our universe was restored the following day after receiving confirmation of Toro's emergency room visit the night before. Witnesses say three unidentified young men confronted him in front of a convenience store. Toro was *excessively subdued* after he brandished a handgun.

We knew better than to ask questions back then. Sometimes it's better to leave things unsaid in our wild kingdom. Besides, the universe doesn't owe anyone an explanation, though we eventually learned all the details. In any case, that was the last time I ever saw Toro.

~~~

Much like the older guys, the churchyard slowly became a meeting place to decide the evening's agenda as we too turned our attention to cars, girlfriends, and high school graduation. Most of us were now in either full-time employment or college. The Selective Service even drafted a few of the boys due to the unpopular Vietnam War. I ultimately chose college.

My days seemed dedicated to school and a part-time job, and my evenings to a girlfriend, leaving very little time for the churchyard. And I wasn't the only one. The same was also true for most of the boys. Perhaps the time to put away our childish things had, at last, come to pass.

Since I hadn't seen my friends in quite some time, I drove down to the old stomping grounds late one weeknight after a long study session. Sure enough, I spotted a lone figure sitting on the rectory steps. It was Artie, one of the newer faces around the churchyard. I pulled into the parking lot and took a seat next to him on the steps, remembering to use *proper rectory porch etiquette*. We quietly talked for twenty minutes before I checked my watch.

"Well, Artie," I said, "It's been one helluva long day."

"Yeah, I hear you. I'm headed home too."

We walked back to our cars.

"Okay, Artie, I'm glad I stopped. I guess I'll see you around."

"Not if I see you first!"

And that was the last time I ever sat on the rectory steps. There were plenty of other *last-times* in our wild kingdom too. Playing handball against the gym hall, football in the parking lot, shooting off fireworks, hall dances, car washes, Gray Ghost, shooting pool in the rec room, giving chase, and being chased were all behind me.

Somehow we all managed to survive our wild kingdom. Somehow the priests managed to survive it too. I suppose we have a lot to thank them for – but how?

~~~

Let's fast-forward again, only this time a half-century. The west side's landscape looks very different now, with all the new construction taking place and the continued revitalization. I'm happy to see the money, time, and effort invested into the community I've felt so sentimental about for all these years.

And while some things change, others remain the same. It's not surprising that many of those high-spirited boys still roam our open-air clubhouse. Only now, my good-hearted paesans give back to the parish with the same hard-working dedication as our forefathers. They dutifully and repeatedly repay with their loyalty, unselfishly offering their services to keep old traditions alive – maintaining the buildings and landscape, organizing fundraisers, and managing the ever-popular annual Feast of St. Rocco. They also bring with them new generations to help support their beloved parish. And together, along with the existing community, the good work will continue for decades to come.

~~~

Papa's life may have taken me away from my beginnings, yet, I continue to wear a keepsake of all those special memories. It's a medallion of Saint Rocco and his trusted dog. An extra inscription on the backside, Rocco Boys, reminds me of all the crazy characters who share my days of auld lang syne. Your papa makes it a point to return to Clark-Fulton for the feast whenever possible, and I can't wait to reunite with the boys down there at Christmastime. We come together over a delicious spread of homemade food and drinks. We catch up on the latest news, and swap photos of our grandkids – even reminisce of crazier stories better left untold here. When the celebration is over, I return home with all those freshly stirred memories still swirling around in my head. Then, I anticipate my next journey back to our wild kingdom. Thank you, Saint Rocco!

THE CLEVELAND PRESS

I REMEMBER FEELING A LITTLE SAD after learning the Cleveland Press halted its publication for good back in 1982. It was Greater Cleveland's afternoon newspaper, delivered to the doorstep of thousands of subscribers returning home after a busy day at work. It gave them a chance to digest the contents before, during, and after dinner. Back in the day, it was a major institution and considered one of the most influential newspapers in the nation, published six days a week, Monday through Saturday. Nevertheless, my connection to the Cleveland Press was more sentimental than admirable. Carrying the news to my neighbors on three inner city streets was my first job. I was nine years old.

When our paperboy, Monty Dennison, began high school in 1961, he found the paper route cutting into his after school sports programs. Monty lived across the street from my family's home on West 33rd, so he wasn't just our paperboy, he was a neighbor. Fortunately for me, Monty had a solution to his new problem.

"I'm looking for a *helper*. Are you interested in making some money?"

I knew a classmate at Sackett Elementary making $1.50 a week helping on a paper route. That was a lot of money to a nine-year-old. I jumped headfirst at his offer.

"Yes! I'll be your helper," I exclaimed, waiving all details.

"Good. How does three bucks a week sound? Is that okay with you?"

"Holy crap!" I couldn't believe my ears. Not only was I joining the workforce, but I was also going to be rolling in some serious dough. "When can I start?"

"Meet me at Olee's at four o'clock tomorrow. That's where the truck drops off the papers." Olee and his wife were the owners of a tiny grocery shop everyone called *the corner store*, located at the intersection of Sackett and 33rd. "And bring that wagon of yours," he added. Every nine-year-old kid in the neighborhood had a little red wagon.

I couldn't wait to tell my parents what I had done all by myself. Everyone in our ethnic neighborhood seemed hardworking to me. I felt a real sense of pride in this accomplishment.

I showed up early for my first day of work. Monty found me sitting on Olee's steps, eager to get started. Shortly after, a blue truck with the familiar Scripps Howard lighthouse logo on its side rolled up to the corner and squealed to a halt. The sliding side door was already open. The driver applied the emergency brake and quickly grabbed two stacks of wire-bundled newspapers and tossed them down to the curb. Then he counted out a few more and handed them to Monty.

"Howdy boys, here you go!"

"Hi," Monty replied. "Ed, this is my new helper, Jerry."

"Nice to meet you, kid. Listen," he said, jumping back into his seat. "I'm telling all carriers to throw their wires away after unbundling the papers, especially if you're not going to snip them. Some dumbass is threatening to sue us for getting tangled up in one on the sidewalk. He fell and broke his arm."

"On my route?" Monty asked.

"Nah, I'm just supposed to tell everyone, that's all. So, throw 'em away," Ed repeated. "See ya tomorrow." Then he stepped on the gas pedal and zoomed off to stay on schedule.

"What did he mean, Monty?" I asked.

Monty explained how most carriers start a delivery by pulling papers from the center to avoid snipping the metal band. Left on the sidewalk, these circular wires make perfect snares. "Just make sure you take yours home and throw 'em in the trash."

"Got it!" I just had my first lesson in the newspaper business.

Our route spanned West 33rd on both sides of Sackett

Avenue, with some customers on Trowbridge and Meyer too. Some of the houses were two-family dwellings. In total, we had fifty-eight cash-paying customers, not a shabby sized route compared to some of the others in the area. Since it was my first day, Monty showed me the ropes by walking beside me as I pulled my paper-filled wagon.

"People are fussy about where you leave their newspaper," he said. "Trust me. If you don't get it right, you're gonna hear about it." He went on to explain how some people wanted it folded and placed between the rungs of the porch rail or the back porch or laid under a doormat. Others requested the top of the stairs, the bottom of the stairs, or between the screen and front door. A couple of people even asked us to put it inside the milk shoot. Several homes in the neighborhood had them, but almost no one had dairy products delivered anymore. Then there was Mr. Armaro, who rocked on his porch every afternoon waiting for the newspaper. I placed the papers exactly where my boss told me to while he watched from the sidewalk.

Friday deliveries took longer because it was collection day. Some people left the fifty-cent fee where we placed the paper, but for most, we had to knock and yell, "Paperboy!" Monty carried a big metal ring of index cards on payday. Handwritten on every tag were the customer's name, address, and delivery location preference. The week numbers of the year were also printed on the cards to keep track of customer payments. He used a hole-puncher to clip out the current week for those that paid. The newspaper's share and my salary came from Monty's cashbox. The remainder was his profit.

Most of our customers were generous enough to add a few extra coins for a tip, some did intermittently, and of course, a few never left a penny more. One lady on Meyer Avenue would go weeks without paying and then short change us when she did pay. I eventually gave her the secret nickname, *Hell Bat*.

"Excuse me, you owe for four weeks, and there's only $1.50 here."

"No, I only owe you for three weeks."

"But, the holes aren't punched out for the last four Fridays."

"Well, then I guess you missed a week, didn't you. That's your mistake."

"Hell Bat."

"What did you say?"

"I said, *'my bad.'*"

Splitting the route meant Monty could stay at school longer while I started the delivery, and we'd still finish at a reasonable time. His plan worked beautifully – and so did mine. The money I had pouring in seemed exorbitant. Three dollars a week was more than enough to supply me with all the garbage treats I could consume from

Olee's glass candy counter. Then there were times when he asked me to do the route alone and paid me extra on those weeks. With all this additional cash flow and with the help of my mother, I started my very own savings account at Cleveland Trust on West 25th Street. That meant my very own passbook that I watched grow with every deposit. When they added the quarterly interest, *Madonne*, I felt like a newspaper mogul.

At one point during this early undertaking, I saved $109 in my bank account. It was also around the time I went to my mother with my very first business proposal. It had to do with an ad in the newspaper from Sears and Roebuck. It was for a portable black-and-white television *now on sale from $129 to $119*. I knew my idea was a bit far-fetched based on my family's general lifestyle. Our household was one of the last in the neighborhood still without a color television in the living room, so being a two-television family seemed improbable. Sure, the odds were stacked against me, but I was determined to try. Hell, with no electrical outlets in my bedroom, I pitched my proposition to Ma as a *kitchen television*. I approached her with the advertisement in my hand after rehearsing a few times in the mirror and gave it my best shot.

You cannot imagine my shock when she agreed to my terms and drove me to the bank to withdraw the cash. We headed straight to Sears and Roebuck for my first major purchase. Ma even made up the difference in price and paid the taxes. Now that I think about it, I probably could have negotiated a better deal.

Regardless, everyone in my family was delighted with our newest appliance, everyone except my father. Pop wasn't crazy about another electronic device in the house. He wanted us to return it, saying, *"It will burn more electricity and cost more money."* Ma came to the rescue again and talked him into giving it a chance. He agreed but insisted that both televisions could not be on at the same time, which only lasted a few weeks. Eventually, he bought a rolling stand to set it on.

My business arrangement with Monty went on for months until he took it to a whole new level. "My basketball games are about to start in a couple of days. Are you ready to go solo permanently?"

His question caught me by surprise, but I answered without hesitation.

"Yes, I'm ready!" My first promotion in my first job – it was a real chance to take on more responsibility. It also sounded like a very lucrative step up, except Monty never mentioned money. I felt awkward broaching the subject with him, so I kept quiet through the entire route. Thankfully, he brought it up on the way home from our last delivery.

"Oh, wait," he said, stopping in his tracks. "I almost forgot to mention that all the money is yours since you'll be doing all the work." That sealed the deal for me. The route was mine going forward, though we never officially transferred it to my name, keeping the transition seamless and straightforward.

Seasons passed, and like our mail courier counterparts, neither snow nor rain nor heat nor gloom of night kept me from my appointed rounds. Of course, delivering newspapers solo in the sometimes-harsh Cleveland winters was never enjoyable. Luckily, my house sat smack-dab in the middle of my route, allowing me a halftime break to thaw out before completing the other side. I'd stand on the furnace register in our kitchen, sipping a cup of Ma's hot chocolate until I was ready to complete my daily duties. It worked out well.

I kept my paper route for two more years. Long enough to rebuild my depleted savings for the next major purchase on my wish list. I had my sights set on a three-speed racer with handbrakes. After that, I gave the route to a kid on the next block.

~~~

Papa's paper carrying days were over. Nevertheless, the Cleveland Press was much more than just a means to an end for me. It was an overall positive experience, with lessons in people skills, money management, and just one more happy memory from my childhood growing up in Cleveland.

THE GOOD OL' FACTORY

IT WAS GOING TO BE CONVENIENT having the factory down the street from our house up and running again. The small, brick structure sat vacant for a while, but someone recently moved into the building. They even painted the entire exterior white to give it a fresh, new look and hung a shingle above the door that read, *Kooper Products.* Yes, with so many manufacturing jobs hemorrhaging out of Cleveland's near west side in 1971, this little factory was a welcomed sight.

It was quite a beehive of activity too, with trucks coming and going all day, loading and unloading boxes of different shapes and sizes. I had no clue what went on inside that clean, white building, but whatever they were up to created the most exotic aromas you could ever imagine. A worthy trade-off for an old neighborhood once subjected to the downwind stench of the Cleveland Union Stockyards just thirty blocks west. That was the one place no one missed after closing their doors for good in 1968.

I said the factory was going to be convenient because

I saw it was the ideal place to apply for a part-time job. I had recently graduated from West Technical High School and started classes at Cuyahoga Community College. Think of the time and money I could save by walking to and from my job, and if they let me work on Saturdays, I could go home for lunch. It was a perfect plan. Now, all I had to do was go there, fill out an application, and convince them to hire me.

I took a quick detour to visit my old friend Beto as I headed down the sidewalk toward my future employer. He lived right around the corner from the little shop of smells.

"Big Jer, what's up?"

"Not much Beto old boy. I'm headed over to that white factory around the corner to apply for a job."

"What's with that place, anyway? It always smells so good over there."

"Hell if I know. I just need a little scratch while I go to school," I answered, rubbing my thumb against my fingertips. "It seems like the perfect place to make some spending cash."

"What kind of job are you applying for?"

"I don't really care as long as it's part-time. Hey, do you want to come with me? What's it gonna hurt?"

Beto shrugged his shoulders. "Yeah, what the hell, all right."

When we got there, the tall garage door usually open

and bustling with business was down, so we entered the front door. A narrow hallway led us to a small but nicely decorated reception area. A young woman was sitting at a desk with her head down diligently pecking away on a typewriter. I noticed the long ash on her cigarette burning in the ashtray.

We stood quietly at her desk, politely waiting for her to greet us. I glanced at the transistor radio perched on the windowsill. It was dialed into the top rock-n-roll station in Cleveland at the time, *WMMS*. She remained focused on her typing, so we focused on her. In her late twenties, well dressed, and from where I was standing had an attractive figure. Beto looked at me and flicked his eyebrows. I nodded and smiled just as she looked up to greet us. She was pretty too.

"I'm sorry about that. Thanks for your patience. I have to get this letter finished before lunch. Can I help you?" She reached for the last of her cigarette.

"Yes, we're here to apply for a job," I said, confidently.

"Both of you?" she asked, taking the final drag.

"Yes, please," I said, again speaking for both of us.

"Okay, sure." She opened her desk drawer, pulled out an application pad, and tore off two sheets. "Fill these out first, and then I'll have Jack come out to talk to you." She held up a coffee mug of pens, and we each took one and then sat down.

Once we both finished, she collected them and excused

herself to find the shop manager. We stood up to examine the artwork on the paneled walls as the number one hit song *Brown Sugar* played in the background. My perfect plan was finally set into motion. It was almost too easy.

The metal door leading to the shop swung open about ten minutes later, and a husky man in his mid-thirties entered the room. He was dressed in jeans and a plaid shirt and was holding our applications. A brown powder lightly dusted his hair and shoulders, and he reeked of sweet perfume. The pretty receptionist followed him back in and returned to her typing. Our informal interview began standing in front of her desk.

"I'm Jack Walcott, the plant manager. So you guys are looking for part-time work?" He was all business and sounded like a no-nonsense kind of guy.

"Yes, sir," I said. Beto answered the same.

"Do you know anything about our company?"

"No," we confessed.

"Well, for starters, we make products sold primarily in head shops and novelty stores," he said. "Flowers made of resin with magnets on the back so they stick to the refrigerator. We also make them with green wire stems and sell them in bunches for vases. They come in all sorts of colors too. But by far, our main product is incense."

"An incense factory? You've *got* to be kidding!" I said.

"Nope. People love incense these days, especially *Tokers*. They love burning this crap while they're smoking joints. I guess it masks the smell of the marijuana or maybe they just like the aroma. Who knows? We carry a wide variety of different fragrances too. There's sandalwood, frankincense, lilac, coconut, pine, vanilla, peppermint, um," he stared up at the ceiling trying to recall more, "cinnamon." He glanced down at the receptionist for help.

"Okay, well, let me think. There's also lavender, rosewood, and jasmine," she answered, then added, "oh, and patchouli."

"That's right! That's what this is," Jack replied, brushing off his shoulders. "I was back in the shop where the sticks are cut and dipped. They're making a batch of patchouli right now."

He explained how the concentrated liquid solutions came from a company here in the states, but the unscented sticks were imported from Asia. These sticks consisted of a dried, slow-burning paste bonded to a sliver of bamboo. The brown powder floating around the back of the factory was residue from handling the raw, dry sticks. The air was dusted further by the band saws, used to shorten the bottom by an inch to fit into the plastic packets. The shortened sticks got soaked in whatever fragrances they were making that day then laid out to dry. Workers assembled the wire display racks after stuffing and sealing the packets with the assorted scents. Shipping and Receiving filled orders that came from all across the country.

"Maybe you've seen our display racks on counters in some of the local stores around town. They're labeled as *Old Ben's Franklin Scents.*"

"I don't think I have," Beto admitted.

"Me either, but then again, I'm not much of a toker," I added, fishing for a smile. I got nothing.

"It doesn't matter," Jack said, looking down at our applications. "You both graduated and that's good. Actually, it's great. We don't get many graduates gracing our presence back in the shop. I want to add a little brainpower around here, at least over in shipping and receiving, so I don't have to do *all* the thinking. We're introducing more products soon, and I suspect business is gonna be picking up. I see you boys live in the neighborhood. How long?"

"Born and raised in this neighborhood," I said, assuming it was a plus.

Beto followed with, "I've lived around the corner most of my life."

"That's good, too," Jack replied. "Most of these *grunts* have to ride the bus here. They don't or can't drive for one reason or another. Oh, I'm assuming you both drive, right?"

"Yes, we both do," Beto assured him.

"That's important cause you'll be taking the company van to the airport once in a while and making local pickups and deliveries too. Are you okay with that?"

"Yes," we replied in harmony.

"And we're getting a forklift pretty soon. Think you can handle a forklift?"

We both agreed again. I glanced down at the secretary as she lit up another cigarette. We smiled at each other. My perfect plan was hatching perfectly.

"Well then," he said, "I like you boys, but I can only hire one of you today."

That wiped the smile right off my face. Beto and I looked at each other and had no comeback. There was an awkward moment of silence.

"Tell you what then, I'll flip a coin," Jack said. "Heads it's you, tails it's you."

He reached into his pocket for a quarter and flipped it, and a second later, Jack congratulated Beto as the new hire. It felt like a punch in the gut the instant I realized my mistake, now so painfully obvious. Never take competition with you on a job interview. And it must have been one helluva look on my face the way Jack reassured me how they would need more help soon, and he would keep me in mind. Still, it was no consolation at the time. I went straight home to sulk.

Time passed, and production at the little white shop expanded just as Jack had anticipated. So much so, he asked Beto to work full-time, and he accepted. It took a few more months before Jack gave me a call. My mother took a message one morning while I was away at school.

"Some guy named Jack called here asking for you. He said you should come down to the factory if you're still interested in a job. You're not quitting school, are you?"

"No, Ma, it's part-time work. It's that little white building down the street."

"The one that smells so pretty when I go by? What do they do over there?"

"It's an incense factory."

"An incense factory? You've *got* to be kidding!"

To Jack's credit, I started working the day after we talked. My perfect plan to go to school and work just down the street had finally come to fruition. He came through for me, too, making sure my work hours never interfered with my college schedule. Some quarters I went to school in the mornings and worked in the afternoons. Other quarters, my schedule flipped.

Beto and I did a lot of good work together. However, with all the expansion going on, Jack still needed to hire another full-timer. We recommended a friend from our neighborhood gang. His name was Danny, but everyone called him *Doc* because he was the smartest person we knew that never went to college. He was a year older than Beto and me, a hard worker, and would be an excellent addition to our company. His interview was just like ours minus the coin flip.

Having Beto and now Doc at the busy shop made working there even more fun. Jack seemed pleased to have three employees around that he didn't see as grunts. He finally had people to converse with that brought a sense of normalcy to his workday inside the shop. We all found what we were looking for in the end.

~~~

Jack was a decent man, but he developed a very short fuse working longer and longer hours as the shop continued to expand. His mood swings were as erratic as the shallow waters of Lake Erie. One minute calm as glass, the next a gale force. And when it happened, we would issue ourselves a *small craft advisory* and stayed the hell out of his wake. I noticed Jack always kept a bottle of antacids in his desk and gobbled them up like gumdrops.

Much of Jack's pressure came down from the owner, Mr. Kooper. A man in his mid-forties considered by many as a twentieth-century Scrooge. He was tough on all his employees, but most of all, Jack. Mr. K kept mostly to the front offices, so it usually spelled trouble when you saw him in the shop. He had no qualms about belittling our boss in the middle of the shop floor in front of everyone. It was degrading, and I wish just once, Jack would have punched him in the nose. Jack took it in stride.

Doc, Beto, and I gauged Kooper's mood by the car he drove to work that day. The dark Mercedes meant he was strictly business, while that yellow Porsche of his transported a mellower Ebenezer. And on those rare

165

occasions when his parking spot remained empty, well, we all breathed just a little easier.

Then came the pressures from below by Jack's so-called grunts. Their work ethics were low, and their thought capacities even lower. Kooper Products measured employee retention in months, weeks, and even days. I once asked Jack why he didn't hire better people, and his response had merit. "Who else will do those crap jobs back there for low pay and no benefits?" Maybe he had a good point, but there were times when his management style wasn't much better than Mr. Kooper's.

One of Jack's motivational tools was the tall stack of applications deliberately kept on his desk in plain view. He used it on anyone giving him heartburn. "Do you see this pile of applications? I can replace you in one hour!" I heard him say it many times, but Jack's most famous threat was his go-to, signature zip line. He used it with ease and could zip in any warning to fit the situation. "The next person to [*place transgression here*] is fired on the spot!" Sometimes it even came in the form of a sign. "Notice! The next person to *leave this door open* is fired on the spot!" Doc, Beto, nor I ever gave him cause to reach for his stomach pills, which I'm sure he appreciated.

Jack was also a private man and seldom shared his personal life. So we knew it was serious when he began opening up about the problems in his home life. The long hours and stress of his job were taking their toll on him and his family. He neglected them so often he almost missed the birth of his last child. I was genuinely concerned for his well-being. He was looking weathered and gray, but as Beto and I were about to find out, a double-bout of agita was heading *our* way.

~~~

The Vietnam War was raging, and the fighting remained on-going with seemingly no end in sight. Graphic movie footage of the fighting overseas led the television news every evening. Anti-war marches and demonstrations in the streets and universities intent on bringing our soldiers home were given equal time. Many protests were nonviolent, while others involved terrible clashes. Young men burned their draft cards while thousands moved to Canada to dodge the draft. Peace concerts sprang up all across the country. I even composed a protest song myself when I was just sixteen that began...

Here I am, Uncle Sam, you can't get me where I am,
Uncle Sam.
It's cold up here, but you see, I must have my liberty,
Uncle Sam.
Well, I don't want to sail across the sea,
Shoot a gun or have one shoot at me,
Charge a hill and take the enemy, you see, Uncle Sam...

Meanwhile, close to home, four college students were shot and killed at Kent State University when the governor of Ohio called out the National Guard to stop the protesting students. This unpopular war was extraordinarily volatile, and our government was having difficulty finding a fitting way out of it. The times were troubled and uncertain for families throughout the nation. Nevertheless, the government needed soldiers and was sure to get them one way or another.

The date was Thursday, August 5, 1971, and as usual, I went to work that afternoon after my morning classes finished. This workday was going to be anything but usual. That day, Beto and I were about to find out our fate for the next two years. The Selective Service was holding its annual draft lottery for all young men born in 1952, and we were both card-carrying members. The radio was already on in the shipping area but dialed to a live broadcast, not WMMS.

The process was simple. The draft board randomly drew birthdays along with numbers. The smaller your birthday number, the bigger your chances were of going to the armed forces. Simple yet complex at the same time.

Beto and I listened attentively to the announcer as we taped and labeled out-going boxes. I froze when they pulled my birthdate.

The deep voice proclaimed it was number fourteen.

Beto let me process the information for a few seconds before he spoke. "You can't get much lower than that," he said delicately.

"No," was all I could muster.

Then it was Beto's turn. He didn't fare much better at sixty-eight.

"Looks like I'll be joining you," he muttered, wide-eyed.

"Well, misery loves company," I said with a forced grin. I finished my work that evening and went straight home to tell my family the results.

"Won't college keep you out?" my sister asked.

"Right now, I'm a class away from a full-time schedule, so I don't think so."

"You're not going anywhere," my mother vowed. "Not for *this* war."

In a calm voice, my veteran father added, "I'll take you to Canada myself." I swear he meant it too.

For the next six months, I could hardly stand watching or reading the news and tried not to focus on the giant monkey-wrench thrown into my once perfect plan. Then in the quirkiest twist of fate, the draft board rejected me for a medical condition. Ironically, a chronic stomach issue was enough for a reclassification. "As it turns out," I later told Jack, "agita has its rewards." My plans to go to college and work just down the street remained solidly intact. Eventually, I became a full-time student.

There was more good news. Even though my good friend Beto was drafted, he never left the states. Shortly afterward, the war geared down, and the military drafts ended.

~~~

Kooper Products continued to flourish with expansions into new markets that included perfumes, shampoos, herbal teas, and temporary tattoos. With this growth came the need for more workers and floor space. The company leased a warehouse on the other side of town and added a new crew. I made pick-ups and deliveries there with the company van a few times a week.

It was around the same time Jack hired a full-time replacement for Beto, who was now somewhere in the south receiving basic training. Norman was in his early twenties and a high school graduate. His work application listed *formal forklift training* as one of his skillsets, so Jack gave him exclusive rights to the forklift. It bothered me some because I had fun stacking and arranging pallets as part of my job. It was second only to driving the company van. In any case, that was Jack's decision, and I needed to focus on the bigger picture – completing my last couple of quarters at Tri-C then transferring to Cleveland State University. Besides, Norman and I got along well enough to take our breaks together occasionally.

One sunny day a tractor-trailer loaded with a shipment of fifty-five-gallon drums of scented shampoos pulled up to the curb of the open garage door. I was labeling boxes for the afternoon pick-up as I watched Norman hop onto the forklift and head down the pitched driveway toward the back of the semi-trailer. He drove quickly and confidently, stacking the pallets of shampoo right outside the door. He'd restack them inside once the truck was gone. I noticed something odd out there and went to have a closer look.

"Norm!"

"What's up, Jerry," he said, stopping the forklift next to me.

"Hey, should you be stacking these pallets three-high on this slope? It doesn't look very stable."

"Nah, it's fine," he assured me.

"Hmm. That end stack looks like the leaning tower of Pisa," I joked.

"They won't be here long. I want to get this trucker back on the road."

"Okay then," I said, "let's take a break after you're finished."

"Sounds good," he replied and drove off to finish his task. I went back inside to continue mine. Ten minutes later, Norman approached me with a push broom in his hands.

"Jerry, come with me," he said, desperately. "Now!"

I followed him outside, and sure enough, one of the top barrels had fallen to the ground, jolting the lid off. Fifty-five gallons of creamy, yellow, lemon-scented shampoo spewed down the pitched drive, across the sidewalk, and was pouring into the storm sewer in front of the building.

Norman began frantically sweeping the thick liquid into the drain with the push broom.

"Is there another broom you can grab or maybe get a hose to wash it down the sewer before Jack finds out?"

"Whoa, before Jack finds out? Norm, you need to go tell him what happened."

"No way. I'm not telling Jack!"

"Norm, if you try to hide this from him, he'll fire you. He double-checks the inventory anyway so he'll have questions, and besides, look at this mess. He's going to see it. Do you want to get caught hosing shampoo down the sewer?"

"It's better than me getting hosed! Just give me a hand, will ya?"

"I'll help you clean the mess, but believe me Norm, you can't pull a fast one on Jack. He's too sharp." I felt terrible for him but wanted no part of a cover-up. I wasn't about to risk my good relationship with my old boss. "Look, Norm, those barrels cost money. One of us needs to get Jack and explain it was an accident. I'll let you decide which one of us it will be."

"Would you do it? Would you go and explain it was an accident? He won't get mad at you."

"Oh, trust me when I tell you, Norm, he's going to get mad all right," I said, "but at least he won't fire you if you own up to the accident."

"I hope you're right," he said under his breath. I hoped I was right, too.

I found Jack in the office and asked him to step out into the shop. I explained there was a problem with one of the barrels, possibly a loose lid, and how it got away from Norman. Jack looked down and shook his head. I felt the beginnings of a squall in the atmosphere. We walked out together and found Norman at the curb, still sweeping the shampoo down the sewer. Norman froze at the sight of Jack, who gushed as forecasted.

"Jesus Christ," Jack started. "Why the hell did you stack them that high? Damn it, Norm! Use your goddamn head. And do you have any idea the kind of trouble we'll get into with the city for mopping that down the goddamn storm sewer?" Jack threw his clipboard to the ground.

By now, a few more workers congregated outside to watch the storm. I knew Jack's zip line was coming before he even thought about it. It was sort of a rainbow after the storm.

Then, sure enough, "The next person to *drop anything off this forklift* is fired on the spot!" I looked down to hide my smile. He scanned the small gathering and stopped at me. "Jerry, get on this goddamn thing and finish the job."

"Jack, do you want me to finish cleaning this up?" Norman asked.

"Clean what up, Norm? I didn't see any of this," Jack snorted.

"Huh?"

I translated. "Just get rid of it quickly, Norm."

"Oh, gotcha."

"All right, back to work, everybody," Jack ordered, picking up his clipboard before huffing away. I climbed aboard the forklift and anxiously eased the rest of the barrels to safety. Norm finished the job by hosing down the pavement.

I have to admit, Norm and I checked the sewer for floating bubbles the next time it rained – there were none.

Thankfully, Jack spared Norman's job as I had hoped, though he never regarded Norman as our *exclusive forklift operator* after this incident. Doc and I were put back on the shortlist of forklift drivers. Norman quit the factory on his own after only six months.

~~~

I finally met Jack's wife a few months later. Well, technically, I didn't meet her as much as I saw her the day she paid him a visit at the shop. The stress in his home life had finally boiled over. In plain view of a handful of people, she marched up to Jack sitting at his desk and gave him a loud and clear ultimatum that stopped production.

"Here's the deal," she began, hovering over him. "I'm only going to say this once, so listen very, very carefully. You can come home to be with our family right now and leave this smelly old place forever, or I'll leave here without you, and you can stay in this stinkin' place for the rest of your stinkin' life!"

Jack wisely chose the former and went home to his family. I was surely going to miss him, rants and all, but understood he made the right decision. The days of Kooper and the grunts squeezing the Walcott family from both directions had finally ended. Sadly, it was the last time I ever saw Jack. I wished him the best.

From my perspective, Doc seemed next in line for the job. He knew the factory better than anyone else and could have easily taken over.

"Will you take the job if Kooper offers it to you?" I asked. Doc was in good graces with the front office. So much so, he drove the yellow Porsche a few times.

"Not even with a ten-foot pole," was his response, although he oversaw the daily operations during the interim. I told you he was smart.

Mr. Kooper eventually hired a younger, calmer version of Jack. His name was Rudy. His face didn't have Jack's weathered gray look, at least not yet, but I wondered how long it would take before the grinds of this job would get to him too. Shortly after that, my friend Doc left the shop for a better full-time job. The old factory was never the same without Beto, Jack, and Doc.

Then it was my turn. I left a few months after Doc quit, right after entering the School of Education at Cleveland State University. What better job for a college student studying to be a teacher than a school tutor? It was another perfect part-time job for me. Still, I missed the convenient little factory just down the street. It served its purpose well and provided me with more valuable life lessons.

~~~

As strange as it sounds, Papa even missed the thick smell of sweet perfume that permeated my hair and work clothes, but not for the reason you might think. It was for the way people reacted to the scent I carried running errands in the company van. It didn't matter if I was at the airport, the hardware store, the post office, or just standing in a lunch line at a fast-food restaurant. The conversations were always about the same with your young papa.

"Excuse me. I don't mean to be rude, but is that you?"

"Is what me?" I would ask, knowing full well what they meant.

"That smell, that incredible smell. Is it you?"

"It sure is, I work at an incense factory."

"An incense factory? You've got to be kidding!"

BIG JERRY AND ANNIE

GENNARO, KNOWN AS JERRY IN AMERICA, was the good, strong man that raised me. Born in Ohio and brought up in Italy, he returned to America alone in 1930 to claim a piece of the dream. He moved into the home of his father's brother, Uncle Nick, in Cleveland. And that's where he met Anna – Annie to family and friends, who also happened to be the niece of his uncle's wife. The two families lived right around the corner from each other.

Annie was seven years younger than Jerry, so he patiently waited until she was in high school before asking her parents, Pasquale and Santa, permission for the couple to date. In those days, the female's parents had the first and last word in a daughter's courtship. Unfortunately, if a suitor didn't make the grade, the couple had little recourse. Jerry's reputation in the community as the strong, silent type with a kind heart was generally accepted and accurate. Annie said that's how she happened to fall in love with him. And while Jerry thought it might be an advantage to have his uncle already married into Annie's family, it had quite the opposite effect. Her parents adamantly denied permission because his surname differed from that of his uncle. No one in Jerry's family, including his father or Uncle Nick, could explain the discrepancy. Annie's parents wanted no part in any possible rumor mill. Case closed, despite desperate and repeated pleas against their ruling. "If you love our daughter, come back in five years, and we'll talk," was the final offer. Her parents remained unyielding. The surname mystery is unsolved to this day.

Yet we know this romance story didn't end here. On December 31, 1936, the young couple fled to West Virginia and returned to the neighborhood as husband and wife. Eventually, all was reconciled with Annie's disgruntled parents. As a matter of fact, they came to openly adore their son-in-law. The newly married couple even moved into the upstairs residence of her parent's house at 3320 Clark Avenue. There, in a two-bedroom apartment, the couple raised three daughters and me, Jerry Junior. *Big Jerry and Annie* eventually moved the cramped family into their own two-story duplex just around the corner on West 33rd when I was two years old.

Sometimes it's hard to break the cycle of old rituals. Ironically, my three older sisters, Anita, Sandra, and Linda, experienced a watered-down version of this old-world, courtship protocol. It included excessive curfews and constant monitoring. I know because I was regularly and involuntarily commissioned as a child chaperone for each of them – the designated nuisance.

~~~

My father was a talented man – a barber, a champion bocce player, a skilled musician, and a master with a trowel. He contracted many side jobs with his in-laws to build driveways, patios, garages, and sidewalks. And their ingenuity went beyond the common. Basements were another specialty, including the rare ability to excavate beneath existing homes to construct one. The men in my family also built small bungalows from scratch on Fulton Road near the corner of Memphis Avenue. And it wasn't unusual for them to travel to Florida and Arizona during the harsh Cleveland winters to build decorative stucco-covered cinderblock walls – beautiful and functional.

Big Jerry may have been that quiet type my mother fell for, but the rest of the family was pretty much loud and animated. I'm sure there were plenty of times when my sisters and I tried his patience. Although, we developed the skill of reading his still face, and knew when he had enough of our nonsense. He didn't have to raise his hand or voice toward us. His simple glance always sufficed.

He had his moments of acting just plain silly when the mood struck, which clashed with his macho persona, making him even funnier to us. Sometimes he would affectionately call me *guaglione* (wah-LYOWN).

It's a southern Italian slang term for a boy, roughly meaning *rascal*.

"Hey guaglione, let's go to the dump." If I had a tail, it would have wagged climbing up into his truck. He knew I loved riding there with him.

"Now? Can we go now? Can we, please?"

"Okay, okay, let's go. Climb in."

It meant he had a load of broken up concrete in the bed of that big, old, army-green '47 Ford dump truck. He might even let me sit on his lap and steer for a time.

The entire experience was like an amusement park ride. The truck's suspension was stiff and bumpy, the engine loud and whiny as he shifted through each gear. The inside of the cab had the distinctive smell of cement dust and leather. I loved how we loomed over all the cars on the road in that machine or *macchina* as he called it. I couldn't wait to grow up and drive the damn thing.

And the landfill was a mysterious place. Its vastness was unusual from my insulated urban perspective. The entire site consisted of mountainous piles of rubble and deep valleys of debris. There were flocks of birds everywhere scavenging for food. Funny how my first experience to the wide-open sky was at a dump.

My father would back the truck up to within inches of the cliff, pull the emergency brake, and then open his door.

"Now, you stay here. Don't come out and don't touch anything. *Capisce?*"

"Okay, Pop." The levers to activate the hydraulics were outside the cab. I had no intention of leaving the inside or touching any buttons on the dashboard. Looking down at that deep abyss was enough for me to scooch to the middle of the bench seat. Alone in the cab, I'd turn around to watch the bed rise through the small oval window. The entire truck shimmied and shook, and then loud clanging and banging ensued as the concrete chunks rumbled and tumbled out of the back. I'd cover my ears and question why the hell I ever agreed to go with him, at least at that moment. When it was all over, I couldn't wait for him to ask me to go back.

Ours was a comfortable relationship throughout my life. We never spoke very much, but then again, we never had to make small talk. Both of us were content just spending quiet time together.

Pop seldom turned me down for anything, so out of respect, I tried never to take advantage of him. Okay, most of the time. When I turned sixteen, I gave him some rational reasons why I needed a car, explaining how it would help me when I found a part-time job. I told him I'd be perfectly happy with something small and economical like a used Volkswagen bug. I was elated as hell when he agreed with me. It was only then I tried lobbying for something a little sportier. I had my eye on a flashy Opel GT. He was kind enough to take a look at it. He said it was "junk." It took six agonizing months before my dream came true because he had to find a super deal. He was always looking for a super sale.

Nevertheless, I'll never forget the day he rolled up the driveway in a big, old blue family sedan. It was a *'63 Ford Galaxy 500*. Sure, it was no chick-magnet, maybe by his design, but I still christened it the *Blue Streak*, just like the wooden roller coaster at Cedar Point Amusement Park.

~~~

Between laboring during the day, and all the side work, Big Jerry seemed busy all the time. He may have been the breadwinner and head of the household, but my mother, Annie, was in charge of the family's daily operations. She called the shots and seemed just as hardworking as her spouse.

Besides the natural maternal instincts all good mothers possess, Annie had two additional qualities making our happy home even livelier. It was her lovely singing voice and her silly sense of humor.

Our home had a healthy, melodic pulse. Ma loved to sing and was good at it too. She would belt out all kinds of songs in English and Italian. As a toddler, it was her lullabies. One of my favorites was an oldie called *Little Man You've Had a Busy Day*. It still sends me back whenever I listen to a version in my music library. No question, I was an Italian mama's boy. When the music wasn't live in our home, the Italian station on the radio or the record player sufficed.

Annie's signature song and most requested was, Mama, which she sang in both languages. It brought tears to my grandmother's eyes every time Ma sang that song to her. She joined the church choir later in her life, and when they weren't in the church's choir loft, members of the group volunteered their talents at nursing homes throughout town. I guess I was always proud of how she charmed people with her singing.

Then there was that wonderful sense of humor. Her quick wit and fast comebacks seemed to come naturally. Annie was also animated. When she was in a good mood, we all were too. In my teen years, I'd banter back and forth with her to see who would crack up first. She usually won. I still think of her as the Italian version of the comedienne, Lucille Ball.

I remember Ma racing up the driveway in the family car late one afternoon, then running into the house with a large, white paper bag. She had been gone all day with her girlfriends. It was minutes before Pop would be pulling in with the truck. Sure enough, the sound of his old macchina whining up the street meant it was just about suppertime.

In a matter of minutes, we were all sitting around the kitchen table as the oven timer went off. My mother pulled out a hot tray of crispy, golden-brown chicken legs, wings, and breasts, and then placed it on the table along with two side dishes.

Praise rang out around the table for her tasty chicken. Each compliment brought a bigger smile to her face until the final commendation brought an all-out belly laugh from her. We watched our family chef leap from the table to the garbage can where she removed a greasy cardboard bucket from the local fried chicken store. She put the chicken pieces on a tray and shoved them into the oven moments before we sat down. She was a delight.

To truly understand Annie, you have to speak of her selflessness. This included exceptional care for her elderly parents. My grandmother had a slew of ailments most of her adult life. She relied heavily on her only daughter, especially after my grandfather died in 1965. For nearly thirty years, Annie drove to Clark Avenue to give her mother daily insulin injections. I never heard her utter a single complaint when it came to famiglia – ever.

Annie's parents were not the only ones to rely on her. She was one of the few women in the neighborhood with a license to drive, so many of her lady friends requested transportation favors. The beauty salon, a doctor's appointment, and church services were the most popular destinations. Annie genuinely enjoyed helping other people.

~~~

We were a close-knit family that expanded over time. At one point, Anita lived next door with her family, Sandra lived upstairs with her family, and Linda was home with a visiting fiancé. Our house was the hub of it all.

My parents offered a standing invitation to dinner. All you had to do was show up. The number of place settings varied from day-to-day. At times, there was plenty of elbowroom at the kitchen table. Some days we sat shoulder to shoulder. Their generous offer extended to our visiting friends. Mangia. Mangia. Mangia.

Big Jerry and Annie lived happily together for thirty-eight years before his premature death in 1974. He went peacefully in their home. His passing devastated Annie, who was never really able to let him go, somehow always managing to work him into her conversations. Ma insistently stayed in that house another twenty-nine years before her peaceful death there in 2003.

~~~

A lot of living and loving took place in our home on West 33rd Street. Looking back, I still marvel at how casually self-sacrificing they were as parents. Now, Papa and Nana are in that role, so we try our best to live up to those high standards. Yes, it was damn good luck receiving all their blessings. Oh, and I had the good fortune of driving the old macchina once as a teenager just before my father sold it.

CROSSROADS

THE WORKFORCE WAS WAITING FOR ME right after graduating from West Technical High School. We were the last class in the Cleveland Public Schools to graduate in January. Now it was February 1971, and my initial plans for the future were incredibly underwhelming. The truth of the matter was I never really developed a strategy for post-high school life. So, I was going to do the next best thing and wing it, not really knowing the risks of having the future shape me rather than the other way around.

And believing in fate didn't do me any favors either. At the time, I just filled out a few job applications around my working-class neighborhood then waited to see what life had to throw at me. Would I become a butcher, a baker, or a candlestick maker? I'd let time answer that question.

Maybe a better question would have been when am I going to start looking up at life's road signs above my head. The head-down approach I was using might work well for bloodhounds, but it wasn't working out for me.

A perfect example of just *cruising life* was during

high school when I inadvertently placed myself in a major course of study that didn't suit me. I wallowed in the Industrial Arts program for an entire year, bored to death, before acknowledging the fact I had taken a wrong turn. I remained long enough to realize these vocations could manage just fine without me and vice versa, finally opting out at the next junction.

The days of lathes and welding equipment were over. I began working with a whole new bag of tools. As a business major, I was using account ledgers to balance finances and typewriters to create office documents. When high school was all said and done, I graduated from West Technical with quite an eclectic education.

An optimist might say the range of my experience was full-bodied and diverse, but a pessimist would quickly point out that a jack-of-all-trades is the master of nothing. Regardless, with my diploma in hand, I found myself standing at the next crossroad.

Just one week after filling out those job applications, a neighborhood factory called the house and offered me a full-time, second shift position. Their proposal was a confidence builder, and I eagerly accepted it. My new employer, *Reliable Springs*, hired me, of all people, to work on a variety of industrial machines that produce a wide assortment of wire springs, widgets, and doohickeys. They even gave me an impressive title. I was their newest *Set-up Operator Apprentice*. Imagine that!

Wait a minute. Did I just get a job in a goddamn machine shop? Yes, I most certainly did. So despite my move to the Business program in high school, I circled right back toward the direction I already knew I didn't want to go. This unfortunate turn of events got me thinking. Was this the future steering me toward an inevitable fate? Perhaps it was my destiny all along, and the sooner I owned up, the better off I'd be for it. After all, it's an honest wage, and I definitely could use the money. So why even resist? With little regard, I decided to continue down this pathway to see precisely where it led. However, as proverbial wisdom would soon point out, *"To go wrong and not alter one's course can definitely be defined as going wrong."*

This route took a hazardous turn from the get-go. My supervisor stationed me near a large window on the second floor of the building, left partially open to let the heat out generated by the busy machines. This location wasn't an unusual thing in and of itself. But the fact was the view from this window would provide the first of many potholes in what would soon become another bumpy ride.

My lofty perspective overlooked the company's parking lot, mostly empty on the second shift, but also the church property of Saint Rocco, just across the narrow street. And herein lies the problem. The churchyard and parking lot below were the exact locations of my entire teenage social life, or should I say my former teenage social life.

Rocco Boys! The neighborhood gang I spent every waking moment with for the past five years gathered right outside that very window – every, single, solitary, day!

Oh, the humanity! My wild and crazy lifestyle was right outside in plain sight, and all I could do at that point was watch over it like our heavenly patron saint. To add salt into this fresh, open wound, the boys literally taunted me from the parking lot below.

"Jer-ry, Jer-ry, Jer-ry." The boys chanted my name and whistled. "Oh, Jer-ry, can you come out and play-ay?" A car horn beeped until I appeared at the open window.

"Hey, there he is!"

"Pipe the hell down, guys," I yelled back as softly as I could. "You're gonna get me fired my first week."

"A toast, to the newest member of the working cl-ASS!" They raised their beer cans up at me. Someone shouted, "Buona fortuna, you poor stunad!" Then they all hooted, howled, and clanged their drinks together.

"Ha-ha, very funny. Now get lost, will ya? Some of us have to earn a goddamn paycheck." I closed the big window praying it would help mute the sound of the cars and the yelling and the laughter. It did, but I was still out there in spirit. I had a new gang to deal with inside the factory.

The four-to-midnight shift was a small crew of peculiar people comprised of a half-dozen older men, a chain-smoking woman named Dolly, and me. I felt ungodly out of place, not that it mattered. The wire-eating contraptions we babysat for eight-hours were spaced far enough apart to prevent any reasonable form of contact. I likened it to purgatory, convinced this was the place I would suffer for my wild, Rocco Boy ways, and any mortal sins that went unabsolved. Just how long could this penance last – thirty-five, forty years? Then a voice in my head answered, "This is what responsible adults do!"

Did I mention purgatory had a watchman? Calvin was the overseer of our poor souls. One of his responsibilities was to guide my spirit down the road fate had picked for me. Another one of his duties was to monitor and report my progress back to the first shift boss. Calvin was an exceptionally odd man. He was skinny and wore his factory uniform a size too big. Then his dark hair was so greased and parted it resembled a black, plastic helmet with a white scratch on it. His left eye pointed off at two o'clock, and he carried a pack of unfiltered *Pall Mall* cigarettes in his shirt pocket for easy and frequent access.

He spent time showing me the ropes whenever a piece of equipment needed setting-up that evening. Once finished, we'd mount a massive spool of wire onto its turntable and then thread it through. Most of these cursed monstrosities resembled colossal sewing machines.

As far as aptitude, I tried paying attention to Calvin's coaching but had trouble focusing on the work. It was painfully tedious. Still, Calvin was patient and kind, but

I'm guessing my questions made as little sense to him as his repeated instructions were to me. It gets worse.

The entire second floor was the size of a small school gymnasium. To conserve illuminating expenses, Calvin could only light the fixtures dangling above the stations in operation that evening. This mandate resulted in dim lighting and dark shadows throughout the old building, making this dismal place even drearier. It gets worse.

Each worker had a designated quota to meet on his or her assigned device, punching out these god-forsaken thingamabobs to the average tune of 8,000 pieces per night. The machines did most of the labor as they automatically measured, shaped, and snipped the wire. The finished product slid down a shoot toward the operator while activating a counter.

Paying close attention now was critical. On every tenth piece, the operator grabbed them up to bundle together on a separate, smaller mechanism. This one twisted a wire-band around the widgets in your hand with such immense force and speed – it was essentially the scarier of the two devices. Calvin warned me I could quickly lose a finger if I weren't careful, and I believed him. I winced every time the damn thing activated. I'll admit glancing at people's hands during the shift changes. I could only imagine the nickname the boys would brand me with should I lose a finger. Stubs, Captain Digit, Jerry Nine Nails. *Help me, Saint Rocco!*

The final step of this process was to toss the bundled gizmos into a giant drum. "Okay, one down, and 799 more bundles to go." Yes, it still gets worse.

Calvin occasionally appeared from the darkness to observe my performance by checking the counter against his watch. Then he'd scratch something down on a piece of paper and slip back into the shadows. Imagine Dracula with a clipboard.

I'm sure I was chronically delinquent in my production output since I seemed to have excessive machine malfunctions. An unscheduled stoppage jeopardized quotas, although I'm sure I was in some sort of grace period. Still, I must confess the breakdowns were welcomed distractions from the mind-numbing monotony.

When my shift ended at midnight, I'd walk home down Fulton Road passed the churchyard to see if any of the boys were still out loitering. It was empty most weeknights. If one of them happened to be there, he was usually getting ready to leave. After all, they all had first shift jobs or college in the morning.

When I got home, my mother might still be up reading the newspaper or finishing a nighttime television show. She'd ask if I wanted any leftovers before heading off to bed. I typically had a bite to eat and then caught some television before all the channels signed-off. The channels went dead overnight back in those days. After that, I would just lie in bed and think. Fate had created a new routine for me, consisting of eating, working, an old episode of *Tales of Wells Fargo*, and sleeping. Then repeat. My new existence living between being and non-being wore quickly on my young mind. This rough beginning to adulthood was very different from the one I had imagined. I wondered if this was what my elders meant by a daily grind.

~~~

I remember sitting alone at the open window one evening at work, eating my egg sandwich and feeling melancholy. Staring down at the quiet landscape, I realized *Purgatory Springs* was another dead end. It was time to face the facts. I couldn't go on for another month, let alone another forty years.

This wasn't the first time I felt this gloom and doom. The last time was in high school right before I mustered up the courage to meet with my guidance counselor – the day that changed my future. Then a revelation. Wait a minute! Why can't I do something like that again?

At that precise moment, I sat straight up, then literally jumped out of my seat. "I'm going to college!" I'm quitting this god-awful job and devoting all my energy to getting into the first college that will have me.

The prospect was nothing short of exhilarating, and I felt light as a feather. I wanted to tell anyone and everyone. Forget the details. I'd work them out later.

Reliable Springs had scared me straight into the path of higher learning. And this road had a bright, flashing sign!

I committed the next two weeks to the registrar's office at the Metro Campus of Cuyahoga Community College. Then without so much as a letter of admittance, I shared the news with Calvin. His reaction didn't surprise me.

"Yep, I saw it comin' all right," he said. "It's fer the best. I don't think ya was cut out to do this line-a work." He pulled a Pall Mall from his baggy shirt. "I could tell your heart was never in it." He lit his cigarette and dropped the lighter back into his pocket.

"I know that now, Calvin," I replied. "I hope I haven't created a problem for you."

"Nope," he answered. "There's plenty of folks looking fer work. We'll have someone in here by next week."

"How about if I stay until Friday? Is that okay with you?"

He agreed.

My last day couldn't have come any slower, but it arrived. I was a freshman by the spring quarter, commuting to college and working in a new part-time job with flexible hours. Ironically, it was in another nearby factory. This time, however, I worked in Shipping and Receiving with a couple of Rocco Boys. I even drove the company van around town. It was a fun way to earn spending cash.

~~~

Papa traveled forward, sideways, and even backward down this new road while being exposed to many new ideas and experiences. By remaining diligent, I eventually got to where I wanted to go. And the road signs to navigate my way around helped me get there. In all, it took five years to earn a four-year degree. Of course, a solid plan and an accurate compass are always preferable, but the long way is sometimes the only way to get someplace. Don't let it stop you. Papa will end this on another pearl of proverbial wisdom. "Perseverance is an attribute of the will."

THE "CON" TEST

I WAS ABSENT FROM MY TEACHING DUTIES for two days while recovering from whatever had me under the weather. I had a great teaching job at a small school in an eastern suburb of Cleveland. My eighth-grade American History class was near the end of the chapter and would have to wrap it up with a substitute teacher before the upcoming exam. No matter, the teacher's edition of the book contained extra notes in the margins and ideas for discussion topics. Plus, the sub had my weekly lesson plan to guide her through it all. There was nothing unusual about any of this, or so it seemed.

I was able to administer the test myself upon my return. The process was routine at that point. After each chapter, two or more, if the sections were short, we would review the information before examination day, many times in a game show format just for fun. Then, I would assess to see how well they understood the content.

The particular history book series I used that year included a booklet for the teacher that contained a multiple-choice examination for every chapter. There was a standard A to D choice for each question. The appendix of this booklet listed the correct answer to each item. Since these were the days before modern copy machines, I had a volunteer secretary type each assessment on a master ink sheet. Then, I used the master on the *mimeograph machine* in the office to make enough copies for all my students.

To grade the papers, I simply turned to the back of the booklet, found the exam chapter, and then ran my finger down the list of letters while checking off each question. I recorded the scores in my grade book.

This exam must have been too easy, I thought, or that substitute teacher was some sort of teaching savant. Over half of my class received a perfect score! It was possible, yes, but highly unusual.

Still, something wasn't sitting right with me. I could read people and developed a trouble-radar from growing up in the inner city with a large gang of boys. Honing skills like these were essential on the city streets. It gave me a kind of superpower that came in mighty handy in this profession of mine – a Teacher Extra Sensory Perception. And this *T.E.S.P.* is what kept gnawing at me. I tried to dismiss it as an overly suspicious nature, except I couldn't shake the feeling.

In the meantime, I congratulated my class's outstanding accomplishment during my absence.

"Nice job on this exam, everyone," I announced,

passing back the papers. "I just might be standing in front of a group of future historians."

"I studied hard for that test," a boy named Jimmy added. He was one of the perfect score students and an occasional mischief-maker.

"Well done, Jimmy, keep it up. You should all be proud of yourselves. Maybe I should be absent more often." Everyone laughed.

The next two weeks were devoted to studying the Civil War, one of my favorite periods to teach in American History. Everything was going according to plan as we approached the first examination on the subject matter. It was time to ask the volunteer secretary to type up the next chapter test when one of my better students approached me in the hallway after school.

"I have something I need to tell you," the teenager said, visibly unnerved.

The situation seemed urgent. "Come into the room, and we'll talk in private."

The student revealed an incident that occurred on one of the two days I was absent. At one point in the day, the teacher subbing in my room left the students alone for an extended period. During that time, one or more of the kids in the class went into my desk and removed the history exam booklet. They allegedly copied all the multiple-choice answers to the exams down and made them available to other classmates.

Okay, this probably explains the high rate of perfect scores from the last exam. The student wouldn't or couldn't identify the perpetrators, and I wasn't going to press the issue. I'd make do with the information provided to me.

"Thank you for being so honest," I said. "Let's keep this between us for now."

"Am I in trouble?" the teen asked.

"I don't think so. Why would you be? What was your grade on the last test?"

"B+."

"No, you're not in trouble."

"Phew! What are you going to do about it?"

"You'll have to wait and see."

Well, I'll be damned! My T.E.S.P. was right on the money. Initially, I wasn't sure how to handle the situation, at least not yet. We had a saying in my old Italian neighborhood. *Fool me once, shame on you, fool me twice, I'll kick your ass.* I wasn't about to let this go without some good old fashion street justice, but I needed to temper it with the student's best interest in mind. It had to be something that would scare the hell out of the guilty parties while teaching everyone a valuable lesson in general. I also decided not to make a federal case out of it. I would keep the school administration and the parents out of it.

Even with the surprising percentage of perfect scores,

I couldn't just assume an "A+" test score meant a student cheated. My plan had to be minimally invasive to shelter the innocent test takers from the fallout.

Since it was going to be nearly impossible to find all the culprits involved, I'd do the next best thing. Historians also have a saying. *Those who do not learn history are doomed to repeat it.* Yes, that's it. I would do absolutely nothing to stop history from repeating itself. Only this time, I would bait a trap.

What I devised would have made any con artist proud. I kept the same exam questions but shuffled the multiple-choice answers around, making sure none of them corresponded with the originals. Then, just to serve some cold revenge, I'd do a little conniving of my own. I rigged the original correct letters with some rather ridiculous claims.

The volunteer secretary typed my latest handwritten template and then mimeographed enough copies for everyone.

"Hey! You sure had some mighty strange information in this test," she said, handing me the stack of papers. "What gives?"

"Oh, I just thought I'd shake things up a bit, that's all. You know, to keep things interesting. I'll be customizing these history examinations from now on."

The next day I stood up in front of my students. "Here is the first test on the Civil War material we've covered the past two weeks. Now we'll see if everyone studied the same way as you did for the last exam."

"I studied even harder," Jimmy said, sounding very confident. "I'll bet you I get another A+."

"I like your attitude. Now we'll see if what you did pays off."

"So, do you wanna bet?" Jimmy asked.

"You mean you want to bet on this test?" I repeated.

"Yeah, we should," another student shouted. "What do we get for a perfect score? Everyone began weighing in with their opinions.

"Will you cancel history homework the next day?"

"How about for a week?" another one suggested.

"We should go outside and play kickball during history class," was another proposal. I occasionally took the kids outside to blow off steam as a reward for good behavior.

"You should bring in cupcakes or some treats for us."

"Okay, okay, pipe down, everybody," I said. "You're getting a little overly confident here. Now, if you're willing to make it more interesting, I say put your money where your mouth is."

"What do you mean?" Jimmy asked.

"It means Jimmy, I *will* bet with you, but you need a stake in the game too."

We hammered out an agreement before getting started. If ten students received a perfect score, I would cancel history homework for two days in a row. Plus, we would have a kickball game outside sometime the following week during our history period. However, I added a caveat. Anyone receiving a "D" or worse had to write a book report on a topic of my choosing. Also, anyone with a failing grade had to take the test home and have it signed by a parent. Everyone overwhelmingly agreed.

"Okay, then, we have ourselves a deal." I distributed the test and remained busy at my desk until the period ended.

"That was too easy," Jimmy boasted as I collected the papers.

"You sound very sure of yourself," I said, "but remember what they say, *you reap what you sow.*"

"Huh?"

"That means we often get what's coming to us." He looked at me sideways.

I'll admit I was anxious to rush home and grade the papers that evening. The results of my *con test* were bittersweet. Fortunately, or unfortunately, the *cheat snare* I set worked all too well. Almost half the class failed the exam. One student received a perfect score. Of the students that failed, most answers matched precisely to the original ones in the exam booklet. That means they didn't even bother to read the questions or those ridiculous claims I concocted.

In any case, these results would shed more light on the consequences of their actions than their knowledge of the subject matter. I would see to that. The following day progressed as usual until it was time for history class to begin. I removed the tests from my briefcase and held them up in front of the class.

"Okay, everyone, I have your first test scores on the Civil War in my hand. Once again, you have shocked me with the results." I paused for effect. "I'm so sorry to report there will be no pass on history homework. There will be no kickball game. Instead, there *will* be book reports and plenty of parent signatures." Then I passed the papers back.

"Apparently, some of you studied from a different book than mine. Let's review some of your understanding of the chapter. Here's one. Almost half of you think our janitor, Mr. Kern, ran the Underground Railroad back in 1853. The same students believe the first state to secede from the union was Canada. Oh, and those same students think the Gettysburg Address was 3320 Clark Avenue." Then I stared directly at Jimmy, who immediately looked away.

By then, everyone participating in the mass wrongdoing realized they were *oh, so busted.* A wave of disbelief washed over the classroom. Now it was vital for everyone to know – that I knew.

"Here's the strangest fact of all. If I had given the chapter exam in the booklet in my desk, the same students that failed would have all miraculously gotten a perfect score!" The room collectively squirmed. Checkmate.

Once I felt I had made my point, there was no need to press any further. I collected all the tests instead of sending them home as we originally agreed. I also let everyone keep his or her previous test score but averaged this one in with it. Then I created a little insurance policy for myself.

"These tests will remain locked up for *safekeeping* in case any of your parents ever want to discuss your history grade with me. I'll be happy to take them through this examination one question at a time while you explain your answers."

As far as the final bargain, students with a "D" or worse received the extra assignment of a book report. The topic of the paper was *Honest Abe Lincoln and the Importance of Trust*.

~~~

Admittedly, Papa's teaching methods weren't always conventional, whether it was with my students or my own children. The proper use of carrots and sticks is an invaluable art form. So is employing a gentle strength. And as far as street smarts go, well, President Lincoln said it best. "You can fool all of the people some of the time, and some of the people all of the time, but you can't fool a teacher with T.E.S.P. any of the time." All right, that's not exactly how it goes.

AN OFFER I COULDN'T REFUSE

BY MID-JUNE OF 1983, I had been working at SzarTech near Chagrin Falls for ten months. My six-year teaching career was regrettably over when I willingly immersed myself into a brand new, higher-paying career. The Information Technology industry had gone mainstream in the early 1980s, and the number of corporations seeking IT professionals was skyrocketing in Northeast Ohio. I hitched my wagon to this star by attending one of the computer schools that popped up across Greater Cleveland to meet the raging demand. The evening course ran from six to ten o'clock, three nights a week for ten months. I shared a ride and the classroom with my good friend Milo, a former social worker looking for a bigger paycheck the same as me. We grew up around the corner from each other in an Italian neighborhood on the near west side of town. This new job was going to rocket me out of debt.

The transition from education to this new field got off to a rocky start. It began with my surroundings, which proved to be a significant adjustment. My assigned desk down in a garden-level office seemed more like a sensory deprivation chamber than the bustling classroom I once took for granted. Now add all those lifeless bits and bytes I stared at all day. The silence drove me damn near crazy. It was a baptism by fire, but the saving grace was the considerable increase in pay, which was enough to appease me until my new manager, Alfie Buffone, entered the picture. "Houston, we have a problem."

The director of our department, Craig Richards, budgeted to expand our small staff of four. He started by hiring a second middle manager. Alfie was given one crewmember under his command. Of course, it had to be me, the newest member of the staff. I'll never understand what the hell Craig saw in this man. He was a wise-guy wannabe in a cheap polyester suit, sounded like a common thug, and practically bragged to me how he had sixteen jobs before landing this one. Alfie was cocky enough to admit most of them ended with his *involuntary termination*. I'll bet he left that part out of his interview. Moreover, it didn't take long to see he knew no more about computers than a rookie like me. My guess was Craig owed someone a huge favor.

Alfie seemed more enamored with being in management than doing his job. My Uncle Johnny used to say, *"There's only one thing worse than an asshole, and that's an asshole in charge."* Fortunately, I've dealt with

Alfie's type before growing up in the inner city, where you come across all kinds of people. My street smarts had him pegged in no time – a perpetual loser with a predictable prognosis. Only now, I had to deal with this baccala exclusively.

"Yo, Jer, you and me are doing lunch today," Alfie insisted one morning, "and I'm not taking no for an answer this time. No more excuses. You're coming with me today, end of story."

I turned him down so many times already that I ran out of reasons. I gave excuses like, I'm trying to save money by packing my lunch or making an urgent phone call at noon, or I was so busy I had to work through lunch. He knew I was stalling, especially since I went out to lunch with my work friends almost every day of the week. This particular time I decided the hell with it.

"Yeah, sure, let's do lunch." My new boss seemed elated as he scurried down the hall. What did I just do?

He was back at my desk promptly at ten 'til noon. I asked him where he wanted to eat, and he instantly identified a restaurant I'd never heard of before, but at that point, I really didn't care where we headed. He asked if I would drive as we entered the parking lot, and I agreed.

We pulled up to a small restaurant a few miles from work. It appeared to be a reasonable place to eat. I shut the engine off and pulled the keys out of the ignition as he grabbed my arm.

"There's someone here today I want you to meet. It's my father-in-law. Just so you know, he's a pretty important guy."

I didn't like the sound of this at all. "He's here?"

"Uh-huh."

"Here, waiting for us?"

Alfie nodded. "Yeah, he's inside."

"Okay," I replied. "And he's important?"

"He knows people if you hear what I'm saying. So don't screw this up." I believe Alfie just told me his family was, well, *in the family.* I was already regretting this decision, but to be honest, a small part of me was now very intrigued.

I entered the front door, scanned the room, and immediately zeroed in on a man seated in the center of a curved booth. He was wearing a dark suit and tinted horn-rimmed glasses. His gold bling and pencil mustache seemed a bit cliché. And the sides of his silver-streaked hair were styled up and back like the quarter panels of a '57 Chevy. Seated beside him was a young woman dressed to the nines. She was wearing a fancy dress and too much makeup. They were both smoking cigarettes and drinking martinis. I thought I was walking onto the set of a low budget B-movie.

"I'm guessing that's him over there," I said, tilting my head toward the booth.

"Yeah, that's Salvatore... Sallie."

"And he's married to your mother-in-law?"

"Uh-huh."

"I take it that's not her," I replied. I said it with a straight face.

"Sallie has a simple rule," he explained. "A man can have his fun as long as he's good to his family. We double date with lots of women all the time."

"You're kidding, right?"

"No, I'm not," he assured me, and I believed him. "Now listen, let me do the talking." That was not going to be a problem, I decided.

I smiled and shook hands with Sallie and his young *date*, Marilyn, as Alfie made the introductions. Neither seemed very happy to meet my acquaintance.

Alfie slithered into the seat next to his father-in-law so they could powwow. I slid in next to Sallie's Kewpie Doll.

"He works for me," Alfie proudly announced to Sallie, who smiled and nodded in approval.

Suddenly, I felt suspiciously like a prop as the two of them muttered about God knows what. Maybe I was supposed to be playing the part of Alfie's lackey driver. I pondered if Marilyn felt like a prop too. I could only imagine her role in this scene.

"Well, Marilyn, let's have a look at this menu. I wonder if the food's any good here. Have you ever eaten here before?"

"No," was all she gave me without making eye contact.

Her indifferent response irked the hell out of me. "So,

Marilyn, you guys headed to a funeral or something?"
That drew the reaction I was going for – a dirty look and
a plume of smoke in my face. At least I got her attention.
I ate my lunch in complete silence.

The ride back to work was also quiet. I made a vow
to myself never to eat lunch with this *asshole in charge*
again. And kept that promise.

~~~

Now it was August, and as I had predicted, things
were quickly going south for Alfie. The more he was
asked to do, the more his wheels wobbled, and the more
he opened his mouth, the more he stuck his foot in it. He
stopped me in the narrow basement hall one morning
after a closed-door session with Craig.

"You and me gotta talk," he said, visibly perturbed. "You
need to make a decision. It's either me or Tim." He was
referring to Tim Akers, the manager of computer operations
reporting to Craig. Tim and I got along well with each other.

"What are you talking about – me or him?"

"It's like this. Craig is pissed at me right now, so that
means he's pissed at you too. Got it? And he thinks Tim
can do no wrong."

"Wait. Why would Craig be pissed at me?"

"Cause you work for me. Your fate is in my hands –
that's why."

"And what does this have to do with Tim?"

"I know you're friends with that little bitch. I'm about to go to war with him. And guess what? I'm a goddamn battleship, and he's a little Chinese junket. So, after I destroy him, I'm gonna look at which side you picked to be on."

I tried to remain calm because my experience in the old neighborhood was never to let a bully see you sweat.

"Listen, Alfie," I said in a relaxed, quiet voice, "I'm not taking sides, and I don't want any part in your sea battle with Tim. Now, if you'll excuse me, I've got work to finish." I waited for a response.

"Okay. But just remember this," he said, pointing his finger at me, "if I go down in flames, I'm taking you down with me. All I'm sayin' is help me out here, or we'll both be looking for new jobs real soon."

My mind immediately drifted to a recent conversation I had with Milo, my old friend and night school partner. He was now working in the computer department at Arrow Distributors on the east side of Cleveland. He phoned the week before to tell me his manager was about to interview for another programmer and asked if he knew anyone interested in the position. Milo mentioned my name. All I had to do was update my resume, and Milo offered to hand-deliver it. I dropped it off at his house the night before last.

"Hey, are you even listening? Jerry!"

"What? Oh yeah, sure," I said. "You'll take me down with you. In flames."

"That's right!" Then Alfie turned and huffed away. I

headed straight back to my desk to call Milo. My resume was already in the hands of his manager.

~~~

Finding a job in this new field was not very difficult in the early 1980s once you had a little experience, especially with a college degree. Milo and I were the only college graduates in our night school class, which gave us a real advantage in the job market.

My interview at Arrow took place right around the time of my first anniversary at SzarTech. The posted job description included responsibility for all aspects of the Sales and Marketing, Sales Agent Information, and Payroll systems. My meetings with the department manager and the director were very comfortable conversations. I also talked with a few other staff members who spoke highly of the company and looked forward to the additional help.

"Why don't you go visit with Milo for a moment while I speak to the director," the manager suggested. I sat with Milo for almost a half-hour before returning to the manager's office. "Well, Jerry, I'd like to offer you the position right now," he said with a smile. "You would be a great fit here at Arrow." We discussed all the benefits and a salary increase of twenty-five percent. "Do you need time to think it over?"

"No," I quickly answered. "I'm happy to accept your offer. When can I start?"

"Terrific," he said, then looked at his calendar. "Can we say two weeks?"

"Perfect," I replied, "that works for me." This new position also helped to secure my future further. I celebrated the good news with my steady love, Judi Ruff, later that evening. Proposing marriage would soon follow.

~~~

Alfie showed up at my desk early the next morning. He had another run-in with Craig and was once again in a foul mood.

"It's time for you to start looking for that new job," he said.

"Listen. Is this you or Craig talking?" I asked. "Because up to last week, he didn't seem to have a problem with me."

"You and I are as good as gone," he answered. "Remember, we're a team. I have one foot out the door, and he just put a banana peel under the other one. I told you, if I go, you're gone too."

I delivered my two-week notice *to Craig* later that morning, which felt really good. He didn't seem very surprised. Nevertheless, he summoned Alfie to his office for another closed-door session in a matter of minutes. The door opened ten minutes later, and the sound of footsteps led directly to my desk.

"That didn't take very long," Alfie snapped.

"What didn't?" I replied.

"Cut the crap. You know damn well what!"

I snapped back. "Hey, you're the one that told me to start looking. I took your advice, that's all."

"But that quick?"

"They made me an offer I couldn't refuse." Alfie ignored my cynical reference to the popular *Godfather* movie quote. Instead, he marched out of my office.

We barely spoke over the next two weeks, until one morning, when we ran into each other alone in the noisy computer room. Mainframe computer rooms were loud back then due to the droning sounds of giant air conditioners, disk drives, tape drives, and impact printers. People had to speak over the noise. He leaned in close to my face.

"Are you gonna trash me in your exit interview?" he asked.

"What? No, I hadn't planned on it. Why?"

"You better not."

"What makes you think they're interested in you?" I asked.

"Listen, I don't need you bad mouthing me if they are. I'm warning you!"

"You don't have to worry," I answered. Although, up to that point, I hadn't given any thought to my exit meeting. But how would I respond if the interviewer asked about Alfie? To be perfectly honest, I was annoyed with Craig for hiring this idiot in the first place. Then he left me alone to absorb the brunt of all the stupidity. Besides, Alfie wasn't going to be my problem anymore. Let them clean up their own mess.

I stopped back into the computer room after lunch to pick a report off of the impact printer. I stood there staring at the green-bar paper scrolling up and out as the last few pages finished. The scheduled meeting with Personnel was in less than an hour. I turned around to check the wall clock. Alfie was standing right behind me.

"G-zus, you scared the hell out of me, Alfie!"

He stood there motionless for a moment as if he were making an important decision. "Here, take this," he said, and then shoved something into my hand. I looked down at what I was holding. It was a blue steel handgun. Now I stood there motionless. "Do you wanna know what that is?" he said, pointing at it. "I'll tell you what that is. That's a gun fired during a crime. It was a robbery."

I never even touched a revolver before. And now there I am standing in the middle of a computer room at work holding one.

"What the hell, Alfie?" I practically threw it back at him.

"I just wanted you to see it – and hold it."

"What are you up to?" I asked. Again, trying to keep my composure to deny his satisfaction. Honestly, he had me rattled.

"Well, I guess we both have our prints on it now, don't we?"

"What's that supposed to mean?"

"Oh, nothin' much, except now you and I have something in common. Remember that and watch what you say about me in that interview." I'll be goddamned. This *pezza di merda* was pressuring me into silence. Intimidating, yes, but you have to give him credit for creativity.

"Look, I told you I had nothing to say about you one way or the other." Except now, I almost wanted to unload about him at the meeting. I tore my report off the printer, and we left the computer room through separate doors.

∧

Of course, it was the first question out of the Personnel Manager's mouth. "Are you leaving because of Alfie?" She was the first person to interview me the year before, and instrumental in securing this job for me.

"Well, now, what makes you think that?" was my slightly sarcastic response. I decided to have a little fun with it.

"I knew it!" she said, closing the notebook in her hands. "To be honest, I never liked that guy and told Craig right to his face. And he hired him anyway."

I never went into great detail during the rest of the exit interview, especially the part about the gun. It wasn't necessary. By now, everyone there, including Craig, knew they had a mess on their hands. I washed mine of Alfie that day, thirteen months after starting working there. I never saw Alfie again.

Arrow Distributors was a completely different story. I had a long, enjoyable, and successful fourteen years with them, and worked with many fine people. I can honestly say not one of them ever once threatened me with a weapon.

~~~

Several years past before Papa ran into an old co-worker from SzarTech. We swapped stories about our time together and the people we remembered. I found out the company moved from Northeast Ohio not long after I quit. Eventually, I asked about my notorious former boss. Not to my surprise, job number seventeen ended in an all too familiar fashion for Alfie. And with this story, my dear family, Papa is reminded of an adage a Croatian friend once told me. "No man is ever a total failure, for he can always be used as a bad example."

SWEET JUDI

TECHNICALLY, THE FIRST TIME I MET HER was on a hot June afternoon in 1982. The girl with the sweetest smile I'd ever seen was literally ushered into my life. Yet, with the turmoil I was dealing with at the time, it was going to take an intervention, not a brief introduction, for me to see the obvious. Here's how it happened.

I was grading papers at my classroom desk, waiting for my junior high students to return from home. Class had already let out for the day at the small parochial school, but this afternoon was *Sports Club*, an after-school event I directed twice a week. I taught physical education in addition to all the major subjects. The program was an attempt to supplement the children's fitness since the private school had no gymnasium.

Sports Club was an outdoor-only activity, weather permitting. It was unlike gym class during the school day, which was mandatory, rain or shine. For gym time, we stayed indoors during bad weather. I had the kids push all the desks to the walls to make room for my planned activities. The difficulty of being in a classroom was trying to conduct gym class quietly. How do you play dodgeball quietly? The principal, Sister Agnes, would inevitably appear at my door to rein us back in. "Lest we forget, there are other classrooms to consider." She loved using the word *lest*.

Furthermore, all that activity generated quite a bit of heat in the tight confines of my room. It fogged up the windows, especially in the wintertime. And considering the building had no air conditioning and these were puberty-aged students working up a good sweat, things could get, well, overly ripe. I always opened the windows to air it out no matter what the season.

The end of the school year was fast approaching, and this would be my sixth and final year in education. I loved everything about my job, except, of course, the salary. A teacher's salary is not lucrative to begin with, but it's even worse in a small parochial school. When the opportunity fell into my lap to train in the computer science industry, I had to take it. Poverty had taken its toll, and I saw a way out.

To combat my financial woes, I attended night school for computer programming with my good friend Milo. We grew up together in the old Italian neighborhood on the near west side of Cleveland. Milo, a social worker, was in the same financial straits as me. What started as an investigation into a new field had mushroomed into a

480-hour certificate in *Data Processing*. This industry in Corporate America had erupted with new job openings.

The most pressing need now was to secure one of these jobs since I voluntarily chose not to sign next year's teaching contract without one. I don't recommend this practice, but I didn't sign knowing in good faith that I would break it. I just couldn't do it, not to a group of people who were so good to me. Only now, my loyalty had created a somewhat self-inflicted and finite deadline. My paychecks came the first of every month, and August would be my last one. I had to secure a new source of income starting in September to avoid the basement floor of poverty. So far, I had no bites on the multiple lines cast out in this job market. As pessimists would say, *no good deed goes unpunished.* Yet, I felt I was up to the task.

I checked my watch and saw it was time to clear off my desk and head to the equipment room before this afternoon's soccer match. Here comes that moment I said the girl with the sweet smile was literally ushered into my life. There was a voice at my door.

~~~

"Jerry, lest you be late for Sports Club, I ask you to please take a minute and meet Judi Ruff. She will be teaching here next year."

The principal was showing my replacement around the school. This new college graduate just signed her very first teaching contract for the following school year, the one I so honestly, or foolishly, let expire.

"Hi, nice to meet you," I said. "You'll love it here. It's a great place to teach."

"Hello, and nice to meet you too," she replied. "I can't wait to get started." We barely made eye contact as she surveyed my room. "Does this room always, uh, you know... It sure is hot in here."

"Oh, does it still smell? I can't even tell anymore. We just had gym class in here because it looked like rain earlier so I didn't take them outside. Sorry if it does."

"Oh, well, maybe just a little," she said, smiling at Sister Agnes.

Judi was tall, thin, and attractive, yet it was her sweet smile that I remember most of all – the kind that lights up a room and sets your mind at ease at the same time. Nevertheless, with so much on both our minds, neither one of us had any more to say to each other. Judi planned to scope out her new school surroundings, and the people she'd be working *with*, not replacing. My focus was getting through Sports Club, then heading back to my tiny apartment in Parma Heights to check the mailbox for any new job opportunities. And to continue the search. That damn September 1 deadline loomed over my head.

"Anyway, good luck to you," I said, with my hand on the light switch. "I'm sure you're gonna love it here." I turned out the lights.

"Yes, thanks." And with that, we left the room.

When soccer ended, I put everything away, locked up the equipment room, and headed home in my canary yellow, '76 VW Rabbit. One day closer to the end of the school year *and* my teaching career. It would be almost ten months before we'd meet again.

~~~

Once the school season ended, I was officially unemployed, and the pressure to find a new income source felt more intense than ever. I don't usually work without a safety net, but with no *Plan B* to fall back on, failure was not an option. At least now, I had all day to scour Northeast Ohio for a job designing and developing programs on a mainframe computer.

In the meantime, I had become quite efficient at conserving my expenses – keeping my apartment lit dimly in the evenings, cool in the winters, and warm in the summers. I had no choice in this matter. I was barely staying afloat. Luckily, there were plenty of diversions to keep me amused. Free things that I enjoyed most in life anyway, like playing sports, my guitar, listening to music, riding my bike, and just being with family and friends. My favorite, of course, was hanging out with my young son Gabriel when I had visitation. I was recently divorced, so spending time with him was always the highlight.

I dated someone for a short while, but inevitably got

dumped. She saw no future with a man in my position, a divorcee with monthly child support payments, and doesn't have two nickels to rub together. I guess I couldn't blame her when I think about it, though it seemed to fan the flames of desperation at the time. Those times were indeed a low point.

Then hope emerged from the ashes two weeks before the deadline. I landed an excellent entry-level job with a company called SzarTech, located just southeast of Cleveland near the charming little village of Chagrin Falls. They hired me as the fourth member of a programming team in the department, and the starting salary and benefits were substantially better than I had anticipated. Oh, happy days!

That's not to say there weren't any glitches in my transition. I quickly learned the environment surrounding computer programming was about as different as it could be from teaching. I went from a dynamic classroom to sitting on my ass all day in a dead quiet office. An electronic monitor and plastic keyboard replaced my lively teenagers.

A co-worker and I tried a portable radio once, but the director quickly kiboshed that idea. Despite our suit and ties, he felt it wasn't very corporate of us. Welcome to the dog-eat-dog world of profits and losses.

If that wasn't already bad enough, I sometimes found myself overwhelmed by the blast of all this new technology I had to absorb. It took months to adjust to this new world I willingly immersed myself into for the sake of the almighty buck.

These adjustments made the need to interact with my son, friends, and family even more crucial. I missed my old job at the school, and all those wonderful people I left behind – folks like my good pal, Danny Kern.

~~~

Danny was the janitor back at school and one of my best friends. We were about the same age, yet despite our different backgrounds and interests, formed an instant bond the first day we met. I called him *Bro*, which seemed to endear me to him. He called me the same. It stuck from that day forward, and this was decades before the term became obnoxiously overused.

"Hey, Bro-man, when can you look at that broken desk in my classroom?"

"It's next on my list, Bro."

We were down-to-earth guys from two different cultures.

My skillful friend loved race cars and motorcycles and was the first male friend I had with an earring. He was a genuine handyman, a jack-of-all-trades, and diligent about high-quality work. I also admired his steady composure. His calm demeanor reminded me of my father, which made him easy to be around.

Danny appreciated the strong Italian heritage I embraced, and my streetwise ability amused him. I think he enjoyed how I dialed it up or down at will, especially within the framework of our small school. You know, it's not easy to out-smart a teacher who can spot trouble from across the room.

Tess was Danny's kind-hearted wife that also became my good friend. She regularly volunteered at the school and church, helping wherever they needed her each day. The three of us often met in the teacher's lounge for coffee. Sometimes the three of us met after work for dinner or a beer and a game of darts, another one of Danny's hobbies.

Only now, I saw them both less since I left teaching. So I never turned down an invitation for one of Tess's home-cooked meals. It allowed the three of us to catch up on all the latest news.

One evening after dinner, while sipping our coffee and making small talk at the kitchen table, Tess cleared her throat and abruptly changed the subject.

"So, Jer, how's your love life been lately?"

I almost spit my coffee out. Danny scowled at his wife and then shifted his eyes toward me. "Sorry Bro, I told her not to do this, but she's going to do it anyway." He looked down at the floor, gently shaking his head.

"Hmm. Okay," I replied, looking back at Tess. "If you really must know, it's about as exciting as being chained to a desk in a dungeon all day, training a computer to sit, stay, and rollover. In other words, it's pretty goddamn boring. Thanks for asking." Luckily, my close friends know when I'm just being a smartass.

She laughed. "Listen. I've struck up a great friendship with the new teacher at school. I think you already met each other. Her name is Judi, and I want the two of you to meet again." She glanced at Danny, confirming they debated this topic earlier. He continued staring at the floor, scratching his head, and looking mildly annoyed.

"Well, I don't think so, Tess," I responded. "She looks maybe twenty-one, twenty-two years old. That's seven, eight years difference between us. What am I going to do with a kid like that? Take her to the circus and buy her a balloon?" Tess ignored more of my sarcasm.

"Judi will be twenty-three in May," she said, then added, "and she's a lot of fun, and she's pretty, and smart too."

"So tell me, Tess, what could she possibly see in an old divorced father like me, digging his way out of a financial crisis no less? She could probably have any guy she wants, so I don't think she'd give me a second look. And the funny thing is, I wouldn't blame her! As a matter of fact, I might think she was even a little *pazza* in the head." I mimicked twisting a giant, invisible screw in my temple. Tess waited until I stopped.

"Well, for one thing, she acts older, just like you seem

younger than you are! And another thing, she hears about you all the time at school. And it's all good stuff too, from the teachers, the parents, *and* the kids. I swear I think you'd be a good match for each other." I looked at Danny, now staring at the ceiling. "There, I said my piece," she insisted with certainty.

"Bro, you're sitting there all nice and quiet, hugging that coffee mug. What do you have to say about all this?" I smiled to let him know I was only having some fun.

"Just like I told Tess," he said, directing his comment toward her, "we're not here to play matchmaker for you, so I'd rather stay out of it. But since you're asking me, I'll tell you that I do like Judi too." He waited for Tess's eye contact. "Now, I think we should talk about something else."

We spoke no more about it that evening. Yet, over the next few months, Judi's name seemed to crop up in our conversations more frequently. Then one evening in early March of 1983, Tess nonchalantly stepped up her game.

"Oh, by the way, I had lunch with Judi today."

"That's nice. How's she doing?"

"She's good. She said she would be willing to meet you here at our house for dinner next week. I'm just saying, what's it gonna hurt? It's one short evening of food, fun, and good conversation, and we'll be here with you the entire evening. So what do I tell her?" Tess paused, waiting for my response, but what she didn't know was

I'd been considering this whole matchmaker thing for quite some time.

I didn't hesitate. "Okay, sure. I'm in. What time next week?"

~~~

It was cold and near dusk that evening on March 12 as I drove to the Kern's house in Garfield Heights. I passed a row of duplexes and parked my car across the street from their upstairs apartment. Approaching the side door, I glanced up at the lights shining through the windows. What the hell was I getting myself into this evening? The good news is I wasn't too worried since Tess assured me this was *not* a date. Although when I spoke to her earlier that day, she pointed out that, according to the Chinese Zodiac, *"Dragons and rats are perfect matches."*

"It's printed on all those Chinese paper placemats," she offered as evidence.

"Well, there you go," was my response. "I'm having dinner with a rat."

I got to the top of the staircase and knocked on one of the glass panes in the door. The curtain behind the glass swooshed briefly before the door opened. Tess greeted me as Danny held the door open behind her.

"Hello, Jer, come on in. Judi isn't here yet. Let me take your coat." Tess carried it into their bedroom and threw it on the bed.

"Hey, Bro, you want something to drink?" Danny asked.

"Sure, I'll have whatever you're having," I said, knowing it would be his usual, Wild Turkey and Coke. I followed them down the narrow hall toward the kitchen, stopping to admire a small, framed photo hanging on the wall. It was Tess and Judi sitting on a picnic table at some sort of outdoor campfire setting. Tess returned to the stove while Danny fixed my drink.

"Huh, so this is her," I said. "Must be recent, I don't remember this hanging here before."

"Yes, that's from a staff clambake last fall. Are you excited about tonight?" Tess placed a pot of water on the stove, and then looked at me. "Remember, it's just dinner with friends."

"Sure, sure, remind me again later if she shows up," I joked.

"Oh, she'll show, don't worry," Tess insisted.

"I'm not worried. Dragons aren't afraid of anything."

"Well, they shouldn't be," she said as we laughed. Danny handed me my drink.

"Hey, it smells delicious in here, Tess," I said. "What exactly are you cooking up for us?"

"We have pasta and meatballs with a salad, and I'm heating up fresh Italian bread in the oven. I know it's one of your favorite meals."

Ordinarily, I cringe whenever I hear my non-Italian friends are serving me their homemade pasta – only because my family has been cooking sauce every Sunday since the invention of the tomato. It leaves most of the competition tasting somewhere between hot ketchup and canned *SpaghettiOs*, although Tess was an excellent cook. The aroma of her sauce was making my mouth water.

There was a knock at the door just as Tess finished reciting the menu. She put her wooden spoon down and went to the door. Danny followed. I stayed in the kitchen because I wasn't sure what to do with myself until I began gravitating to the sudden burst of jubilation in the narrow corridor. But the open door spanned the entire small space, completely obstructing my view of the ongoing salutations. I ended up hidden awkwardly behind the door. I heard Tess ask Judi for her jacket to throw on the bed. It was an unveiling of sorts when Danny closed the door, allowing the four of us to see each other standing in a single file.

"Oh, Jerry, you remember Judi," Tess said, "Judi, Jerry."

"Hi, nice to see you again," Judi responded.

"Nice to see you again too." I reached around Danny to shake her hand. If there were any reservations about tonight's arrangement, they quickly vanished when she flashed that beautiful smile at me. We filed back into the kitchen where Danny made Judi a drink, and then we all chatted around the stove until the oven timer went off.

Tess's pasta dinner was delightful, and I made it a point to tell her so. It turns out she's part Italian. Va bene! The dinner conversation was equally delightful. As it turned out, the school provided the four of us plenty to talk about, and the dialogue was free-flowing, genuine, and fun. I was surprised by how soon dinner ended.

"Why don't you both go into the living room while Danny and I clean up," Tess suggested.

"Are you sure you don't want any help?" Judi asked. "Let me do *something*."

"No," Tess insisted. "We'll join you in a few minutes with some fresh coffee."

I followed Judi through the narrow corridor leading to the front room of the house. She sat on the couch, leaning her head back on one of the pillows.

"What an incredible meal," she said. "I'm stuffed!"

"Tess is a great cook," I added.

"They're both good people," she said, then patted the seat next to her in a gesture for me to sit.

"They sure are," I said, and sat down right beside her.

It was the first time we were alone together. I got her to smile a few more times before our hosts joined us with coffee. The four of us continued where we left off at dinner. Judi and I sat shoulder to shoulder the entire evening.

It was right around midnight when Tess stood to apologize for having to leave us. "Listen, guys, I'm so sorry, but it's been a long day, and I'm dead tired. I'm helping at nine o'clock mass in the morning, so I need to get some sleep, but by all means, please stay here for as long as you'd like."

"Yeah, stay, and I'll make us all more drinks," Danny insisted.

I know I wasn't ready to call it a night and I don't think Judi was either, so we took them up on the offer.

We talked almost three more hours until Danny stood up and wished us a good night. He had a few more nightcaps than we did, and the Wild Turkey had finally caught up to him. He insisted we stay as long as we wanted, so we put on a fresh pot of coffee and talked in the kitchen. Topics effortlessly flowed both ways. We spoke more like old friends than new acquaintances. It was almost 7 a.m. when we first noticed the sun rising.

"Hey, I'd better be getting home," Judi said, "since it's way past a respectable girl's curfew." We both laughed.

"Would you like me to drive you home?" I asked, thinking it sounded corny the second it left my mouth.

"No, no, I'm fine, really, but I should go." Tess had moved our coats into the living room before she went to bed, so I quietly grabbed them and helped Judi put hers on. "Well, thanks for a great time," she added.

"I had a great time, too, really. Will you give me your phone number, *lest* I call you sometime?" She got the reference and laughed.

"Oh sure," she replied, "but you'd better write it down *lest* you forget it."

I found a pencil and grabbed a napkin. We stopped at the door, looked at each other, and smiled. I leaned in and we had our first kiss. It was neither too quick nor too long, yet it was reciprocal and genuine, just like the entire evening. I walked Judi down to the '78 Chevy Camaro she drove and watched her disappear off into the sunrise.

I sat in my car, letting the engine warm-up. "What the hell just happened?" I put the car in gear and drove home with the song, *Suite: Judy Blue Eyes*, playing in my head.

~~~

I wasn't sure what the standard wait-time was for calling a girl after getting her phone number. There wasn't a guidebook for that, so for whatever reason, I chose to wait until Wednesday evening. I think I didn't want to come off too aggressive and scare her away.

Meanwhile, in the event she *would* see me again, I had to find somewhere to take her that would be low pressure, fun, yet impressive. The cinema was a standby, but I felt I could do better. It just so happened SzarTech leased a loge at the *Coliseum at Richfield*, an indoor sport and entertainment arena outside of Cleveland. They were very generous about giving tickets to the employees, especially to their golden boys in the computer department. That led to me reserving two tickets to a *Cleveland Force* game that coming Saturday. The Force was a professional indoor soccer team. I figured it was better than a movie because now we could talk as much or as little as we wanted, and sitting in a loge has a way of making you feel special. I went down to Personnel to pick up my two tickets. The woman reached into her desk drawer and pulled out twenty of them.

"Here, you might as well take them all," she said. "No one ever goes to these boring soccer games. I can't give them away." I stood there fixed on my fistful of tickets. "Oh, and here, take this too," she added, handing me a VIP parking pass.

Wait. What? Did I just score an entire loge for the two of us at the Coliseum *plus* VIP parking? I'm holding all the golden tickets to the *Willy Wonka Chocolate Factory* in my hands. We'll be together and alone in a private upper suite at Cleveland's premier sports arena. *Madonne!* It doesn't get any better than this if you're trying to impress a date. Now all I have to do is convince Judi to go with me.

Later that evening, I dialed the number on the folded napkin I kept. Just as the line started ringing, I realized I hadn't rehearsed what I was going to say. I decided to go with my gut and wing it. I mean, how hard could this be, right? When she picked up the phone, this is what spewed out of my not so smooth-talking mouth.

"Hey, so listen, I'm about to ask you to go out with me on Saturday. Don't answer yet. Now, I hope you say *yes*, and if you do, I'll tell you all about where I'm going to take you. However, if you *don't* want to go out with me, and this is important, just say you're washing your hair that night. I promise you I'll get the hint. We'll hang up as friends, and I won't ever bother you again. Honest. No hard feelings. So here it is. What are you doing Saturday night?"

"Hmm, well, okay. I *am* washing my hair on Saturday – but I'll still go out with you!" I pictured that beautiful smile on the other end of the line. I gave her all the details of our date, and she gave me her house address.

I pulled up to a small bungalow on Dunham Road in Maple Heights two-hours before the game started that Saturday. And being a gentleman meant going into the house to escort her out. It also meant meeting her parents. Her mother, Irene, wasn't home, but her father, Carl, was sitting on the couch reading the newspaper. Judi introduced me to him, and the three of us spoke for several minutes. He was kind and polite and made me feel at ease, just like his daughter. It must run in the family, I thought. When she was ready to leave, we said goodbye to her father, and the two of us drove off in my '80 Buick Skylark.

When we got to the Coliseum parking lot, I flashed my VIP parking pass at the man directing traffic.

"Take it anywhere right down the first row, sir, and please leave the pass on your dashboard. Thank you, sir, ma'am, and have a great time tonight." Now, this is the way to begin a memorable first date.

It was also a promotion night at the Coliseum. Camel

cigarettes were sponsoring that particular evening, so attendants were passing out free Camel baseball caps and a four-sleeve packet of cigarettes to everyone over the age of eighteen.

"No thanks, I don't smoke," Judi said to the man extending a packet toward her.

"She means thank you," I said, smiling at him.

"Oh, I mean, thank you very much," she repeated and looked at me. "Sorry, I forgot you even smoked."

"Hey," I said, quoting the company slogan, *"I'd walk a mile for a Camel."*

I showed our tickets to a loge usher who escorted us directly up to our private room. We took a moment at the door to browse. There was a cozy sitting area, a kitchenette, a stocked refrigerator, a private restroom, and closed-circuit television to watch the game while lounging. A glass wall overlooked the soccer field with reserved seating outside the loge if we preferred. Judi didn't care where we sat, so I chose to sit outside to people-watch and to see the opening ceremonies. We sat there most of the first half before heading inside for refreshments. My date was suitably impressed. Mission accomplished!

When the game ended, we watched the mortal spectators exit the building from our ivory tower. Neither of us wanted to leave, but it was time to go.

"So *Sweet Judi*, where to now?"

"Sweet Judi? Say, I kind of like that, but my eyes aren't all blue."

"True. I see some green, but there's enough blue in them for you to be my Sweet Judi. So what are you in the mood for next?"

"Gee, I don't know," she said. "How do you top this?"

"Well, at the risk of lowering my score on your *first date meter*, I'd like to take you to my favorite burger joint."

"And where is that?"

"*Manner's Big Boy*. I always get the Big Boy combo with a coffee." I paused to watch her reaction to my modest offer.

"I love that place," she said, "and I love coffee with my hamburgers too."

I wondered if she knew how many points she just scored on *my* first date meter. We drove to the restaurant on Pearl Road, sat in a booth, and ate our hamburgers with fries and coffees. I even smoked a couple of those Camel cigarettes. We seemed to hit it off no matter where we were and stayed there longer than we probably should have. Eventually, I drove her back home – a straight shot down Snow Road until it becomes Rockside Road, and then to Dunham. I shut the car off and walked her to the side door.

"By the way, do you want this baseball cap?" she asked, holding up her souvenir. "I don't look good in hats."

"I bet you do, but no thanks. You keep it here," I said.

"This can be my baseball cap backup site. I'll know where to come if something happens to mine."

"All right, I can do that."

We kissed our second kiss, and then I waited as she walked in and shut the door. The porch light went out as I rolled away. For some reason, I thought of Tess's dragons and rats. "I'll be damned."

~~~

I went on a pre-arranged blind date the following weekend. One of my older siblings had set me up with her girlfriend's younger sister before any of this started with Judi. Arranged with the best intentions, backing out at that point would have been awkward and rude. It turned out to be a dud, and I told Judi all about it. Fortunately, she understood, and we committed to being an exclusive couple very soon afterward.

Judi's birthday was approaching in May, and I wanted to get her the perfect gift. Again, without a guidebook, I decided the ideal gift for someone in the early stages of a promising relationship could be found somewhere in downtown Chagrin Falls. I took a long lunch one afternoon to visit all the little artsy boutiques. A pretty, petite vase caught my eye in one of the shop windows, and I knew I had found it. I presented my gift to Judi with a single budding red rose. She loved it enough to start a vase collection and proclaimed this piece as her first inductee.

Judi wasn't the only one that loved it, so did her mother, who was standing with us when I gave it to her. I think I earned a few brownie points with Irene, who, unlike Carl, remained reserved in my presence. I understood her apprehension toward me and accepted it with the hope of winning her over one day. It was a work in progress.

By August, we were having the time of our lives. One evening we sat down in Judi's living room after dinner.

"Hey, I have some interesting news. Do you remember my friend, Milo, the guy I went to computer school with? He called me today. He works at a place called Arrow Distributors near downtown Cleveland. Anyway, it turns out they're looking for another programmer, and he told his boss about me. The guy wants to see my resume."

"That's exciting. Are you going to send it to him?"

"I am, but I have to update it first. Do you have a typewriter?"

"Yes, it's a portable typewriter," Judi said, "and I'll even type it for you."

"Oh, can you type?"

"Sure, I can type. I had a full year of it in high school."

"Great! It's is in the car. I already penciled in the changes."

We sat on her living room floor as she typed – click, pause, click, pause, click, pause, click, pause. She finished my name in just under a minute. I watched her concentrate on my address. Click, and pause, and click, and pause, and click, and pause. I let her go for another thirty seconds.

"Okay, Sweet Jude, what are you doing?"

"What do you mean? I'm typing. Why?"

"Hey, I've got an idea," I said. " Why don't you put a pot of coffee on, and I'll take a crack at this." I had it finished by the time she got back with coffee and cake.

"Hey, how'd you do that so fast?" she asked.

"I guess typing on a computer keyboard all day will do that to a fella." We both had a good laugh.

By September, I was working at Arrow Distributors making even more money and receiving even better benefits. Judi and I became inseparable. It just didn't feel right leaving her every night to drive back to my empty apartment across town in Parma Heights. A significant change was on the horizon.

~~~

Now it was October, and I was still leaving her every night. Sometimes we would be at my apartment. These were the days before cell phones, in which case I would hand her an emergency quarter to call me from a payphone in case her car broke down. Then, I made her call me the second she arrived home, and we'd talk for another hour. We both knew where this relationship was heading, and the timing felt right.

243

We were sitting on the front steps of her parent's house just before dinner, watching the busy traffic pass by when I started another unrehearsed conversation.

"You know, Sweet Judi, we should get married. Do you wanna get married?"

"Yes," she said. "I'll marry you."

"Good. Let's tell your parents after dinner tonight. I'll ask for their blessing."

"Okay, that would be nice," she said. "Are you nervous at all, I mean about getting married?"

"No. What we have is so natural to me. I want it to stay this way forever. Are you nervous?"

"Nope. Not at all."

We sat arm in arm, sharing our thoughts on our near and distant future together until dinner was ready. My simple proposal and Judi's casual acceptance were that uncomplicated. What a perfect match.

When dinner was over, I offered my intentions to her parents and asked for their blessing. Both seemed genuinely happy – okay, maybe Carl a little more than Irene. He found a bottle of Asti Spumante in his wet bar, and the four of us toasted to health and prosperity. And we wasted no time setting a date for the coming summer of June of 1984. It felt so right, but we had one glitch.

Due to my previous marriage, we couldn't get married in a Catholic church. However, we found a nearby Lutheran church to perform the ceremony. To keep my accumulated brownie points with Irene, we promised to remarry in front of a priest, if and when, I could get an annulment. It seemed to appease her. We shopped for rings that week.

~~~

The Kerns were in our wedding party with Danny as my Best Man. Little Gabe wore a sharp blue suit with white shorts, handmade by Judi's mom. Our church ceremony was beautiful and flawless, but the reception at the Hilton Hotel on Rockside Road is what everyone remembers.

It began with a pre-reception social in the pool area, temporarily closed to the public to accommodate our wedding guests. Candles wrapped in live bouquets floated in the water as well-dressed waiters served hor d'oeuvres and cocktails poolside. Classical music played softly in the background. It was as elegant and impressive a setting as it sounds – for the first half-hour. That's when the real fun started.

A patron of the hotel missed or chose to ignore the *Pool Area Closed* signs and decided to join us. He wasn't going to let a large gathering of guests in formal attire or a gauntlet of burning wreaths floating on the water stop him from taking a dip in the pool. This middle-aged man disrobed himself poolside and began dog-paddling through the floating bouquets, extinguishing half the flames as the decorations bobbed their way to the outer edges. He quickly drew the attention of our now bewildered guests, who stopped mingling just to gawk. Friends and family began pointing and guffawing at the spectacle. Finally, one of the boys from the old neighborhood confronted him.

"Hey, buddy, what the hell are you doing? Can't you read? Do us a favor and get the hell out of the pool. This is a private party." The man treaded water as he listened but looked unfazed. "Look what you're doing to the goddamn candles. Get your ass out of there, now."

The man complied, but not until he propelled himself back to his original entry point. Judi and I were so engrossed in greeting our guests we missed most of the poolside excitement. Nevertheless, his appearance set the tone for the rest of a very lively, loud, and festive evening.

"This is the most fun I've had at a wedding," was the consensus.

"They don't get any better than this," others remarked.

"I'll never forget your *pool party* for as long as I live," was repeated.

To cap off the memorable occasion, two of our mutual priest-friends dropped in to show their support and wish us well. It was a meaningful gesture considering the circumstances. It especially pleased the parents of my new bride, scoring even more brownie points for their new son-in-law.

We kept our promise to Judi's family and remarried in

the Catholic Church when my annulment came through the following year. There was no congregation, no fanfare, no floating candles, or wedding crashers – just a simple ceremony in front of a priest at the altar. The Kern's were our special guests.

~~~

Today, my little sweethearts, Nana's vase collection has grown quite extensively. She has a marvelous assortment of beautiful glass and ceramic pieces from the many places we've been together in our travels. The very first vase from Chagrin Falls, the one with us from the incredible beginning, met its fate after a family pet knocked it to the ground, shattering most of it to bits. Too precious to discard, Papa salvaged the top half, which is still on display in our glass hutch for all to see. It draws the eye even more than it did before and is still our favorite.

TOEING THE LINE

CAMPFIRE STORIES have probably existed since the discovery of fire, making them one of the oldest forms of group entertainment. Traditionally, the best tales include storylines conjuring up ghosts and hobgoblins that appeal to the inner child in all of us. But this particular night, I was huddled together under the stars with adults that preferred a more controversial topic.

A group of co-workers was sitting around a fire pit on an outdoor patio in the early 1990s. We were all nursing drinks of one kind or another, and a couple smoked cigars. My colleague Jeffrey began telling a story about his immigrant yardman, who was recently pulled over by the police. The landscaper's taillights were out on the trailer towed behind his truck. When the officer ran the plates, they were registered to another vehicle. One thing led to another before discovering the man had entered this country illegally.

"So," Jeffrey sighed, "that's the last I ever heard of him. I tell all my neighbors it's why my grass looks like hell."

Laughter erupted among the circle of fire-lit faces as well as the darkness beyond.

"Was he any good?" asked a voice in the distance.

"Good? He was fantastic. And reasonable too. I sure do miss him."

"Serves him right," a woman named Lydia injected. "I hope he got all that was coming to him."

"You can't fix stupid," a man named Bill added in a plume of smoke.

"Why must they insist on breaking the law like that?" asked another faceless voice. "Why can't they just *toe the line* like the rest of us?"

More opinions ensued.

"It's how you're raised. Cheating is a learned behavior."

"Right, it's easier to scam the system. They have no decency."

"Call them what they are – criminals. We need more prisons."

"Takers is what they are, and guess who foots the bill."

"You've missed an obvious possibility," I added.

"Here we go!" said Bill.

"What did we miss?" Lydia asked.

"Yeah, what are we missing, professor?" Jeffrey quipped.

"Desperation," was my response.

"Desperation? So, that justifies cheating?"

"It doesn't justify cheating – it explains it."

"How so?"

"Well, for starters, people act irresponsibly sometimes when they're piss-poor broke and painted into a corner. They cut corners and shade the truth to make due. Poverty has a way of making honest, sensible people take risks and do things they wouldn't ordinarily do, even though they know better."

"I don't buy it," Jeffrey said. "That's no excuse."

"No? Have you ever talked with survivors of the Great Depression? I've heard their stories. People can get mighty resourceful when you've got nothing left to lose. My grandfather worked all kinds of odd jobs when the construction business collapsed. My family's old neighborhood in Cleveland was filled with good, decent folks hiding illegal stills in their attics and basements through those hard times. I learned my grandfather was one of them. And that was during prohibition. He and the neighbors helped each other out, doing whatever they needed to do to put food on the table until things eventually improved. You should be thankful if you can't relate to what I'm saying."

"Oh, and I suppose you can?"

"I've been known to take a risk or two back in the day, sure," I confessed.

"Go on then," Jeffrey said, "this sounds like a great campfire story, and it's coming from a guy who just received a stock bonus for the company's *Mapping Project.*

I can't wait to hear this." Everyone laughed again.

"Wait, you were on that project?" Bill asked.

"He was," Jeffrey answered, "and even had a clubhouse dinner and round of golf at the Chagrin Country Club with the bigwigs afterward."

"I said, *back in the day*," I repeated, "before I knew any of you. And my troubles don't even compare to my grandfather's or your landscaper's.

"Be quiet and let him tell his story," someone insisted.

~~~

So, I began at a time in my early adult life when money was a scarce commodity. It was 1976, and I was living in a tiny apartment in Parma Heights, a western suburb of Cleveland. My mode of transportation at the time was a '71 Volkswagen bus. I had a lot of fun in that little van, except in the cold winters, when it threw very little heat. It was also well past its prime. Automobiles back then rarely made it to 100,000 miles. If the mechanical failure didn't get you, the body corrosion surely did – I swear if you listened carefully, you could hear the rust eating away at the metal.

Still, it took me everywhere I needed to go, shuttling me between my part-time tutoring job at Walton Elementary School and classes at Cleveland State University. Plus I used it to go camping on the weekends. Yes, sir, I loved my *V-dub* bus, even after the engine blew on my way home from a night out with the old gang.

To make due, I went to my sister's house on West 33rd Street, where I stored a '59 VW Beetle in her garage. The previous owner had brush painted it jet-black, then added a giant white star on both doors. Once a *hippy-mobile* in the psychedelic sixties, it resembled nothing more now than a *sheriff clown car* at the circus. After high school, I bought the damn thing for fifty dollars so I could learn to drive a manual stick shift. Calling it a *junker* was being generous. I had to pump the brakes to stop, first gear was missing teeth, and it had a cracked windshield. The floorboards were so rusted I could see the ground below my feet. But it was free transportation, and this was no time for foolish pride. I charged the battery to get it started.

The broken-down bus sat mothballed in my apartment's parking lot until I could figure out a way of getting it fixed. Meanwhile, one of the tires went flat, and the license plates had expired. I knew it was only a matter of time before someone complained to the lease manager. I just didn't have the time or money to do anything about it until my old pal, Beto, gave me hope with a possible way out.

He became friends with another Clevelander named Chris when he was in the military. The two remained army buddies after they got out. Chris began showing up in the old neighborhood hangouts with Beto.

Chris was a bashful guy with blondish hair, a brownish beard, and round wire-rim glasses. I didn't know much about him until Beto told me we shared something in common. We both drove VW buses. Beto also pointed out that Chris did all of his own mechanical work, and suggested he might be willing to check out my engine.

Thankfully, Chris agreed and came to my place one evening for a look. I explained what happened the night I drove down Big Creek Parkway a quarter-mile from my apartment.

"I was rattling along just fine in fourth gear when suddenly the whole damn bus backfired with a hard jolt. The engine stalled, and I coasted to the side of the road. One of my neighbors helped me push it home the next day, and it's been sitting here dead as a doorknob ever since."

"We won't know too much until I get inside for a look around. I can't work on it here in this parking lot. Is there somewhere we can tow it?"

"Well, there's always my mother's house in the old neighborhood. I'm sure she wouldn't mind if we towed it there. The question is – how?"

"I could tow you if we had a tow chain," Chris suggested.

I knew there was one at Ma's house somewhere. My father died two years earlier, but his tools were still scattered in the garage, basement, and shed. Chris drove me to my mother's house to check it out.

"She uses the right side of the garage," I explained,

"but we can park the bus on the left side of the driveway."

"That works for me," Chris replied.

"Now all we have to do is find that tow chain.

My father was a collector of sorts. He seemed to have at least one of every gadget, gizmo, and doodad on the planet. It took us a while to rummage through all the drawers, shelves, and boxes, but eventually, I found the rusty, old thing.

Chris arrived at my apartment the following day. We took turns hand pumping air into the flat front tire before attaching the link chain to our buses. Eight feet separated our bumpers.

"Keep your window rolled down so we can yell to each other," I advised. "My battery is dead now, too, so I can't use the horn to get your attention."

"All right. Then you won't have emergency flashers either."

"Correct."

"And where are your license plates?"

"I threw them on my front passenger seat because they're expired."

"Hah! What's next? No brakes?" Chris joked.

"Not even funny," I said, "but I bet they're rusted tight from sitting here all this time." We jumped into our vehicles after a short discussion on the safest route to Ma's house. It was about seven miles. Chris watched through his rearview mirror as I reminded him to roll his window down by giving him the universal hand-cranking gesture. He acknowledged with a thumbs-up.

The first tug on the chain freed the rust-frozen brakes with a sonic boom, and a neck-whipping lurch forward. I tapped the brake pedal a few times to make sure that wasn't the next surprise. They were fine other than a loud, scraping sound. I assumed the worst was behind me as I rolled down the apron of the parking lot.

The first two miles went smoothly. Then I looked into my rearview mirror to see flashing lights. There was a Parma Heights police cruiser on my back bumper. It's always a sinking feeling whenever it's you.

I tried beeping at Chris until I remembered the battery was dead. "Chris! Pull over," I yelled out the window. He glanced back at me and headed to the curb. The officer sat in his car for the longest time before finally stepping out. I watched him approach my open window from the side mirror.

"Afternoon," he said, with no emotion. "Do you know why I pulled you over?"

"I'm sure it wasn't for speeding," I said, hoping he'd smile. He didn't.

"You have no license plate on the back of this vehicle. Why not?"

"Oh, I have it. It's right here," I said, grabbing it off the passenger seat. "I didn't think I needed it since I'm not technically driving."

"Wrong!" was his response. "*Technically*, when I see a vehicle rolling down the road, I expect to see a plate." I didn't know if that was the law or not, yet I wasn't about to challenge him. He scowled at the plate in my hand and pointed at it. "That thing isn't even valid anymore."

"I know, sir. That's why I took it off."

"Uh-huh. And why didn't you buy new ones?"

"Well, I ah, I wasn't gonna spend money on plates just in case I ended up junking this thing." I pointed at Chris. "He's gonna look at the engine and tell me if he can fix it or not. If he can, I'll buy them."

"Again, it doesn't work that way," he replied with no expression. "Why aren't you using your emergency flashers?"

"My battery is dead."

"Okay. License and registration."

I frantically rifled through my glove box with no success. Christ, are you kidding me? This traffic stop had gotten off on the wrong foot. I knew I had to stop ruffling this man's feathers.

"Sorry, sir, the registration isn't here. I thought it was in my glove box. I don't know where else it could be." I was digging my own grave!

"Let me see your driver license," he said, wafting his index finger at me.

"Oh, okay, I know I have that for sure." It was a victory, albeit a small one. I managed to fish it out of my wallet. "So is it a driver license or driver's license? I hear it both ways all the time." I tried to lighten the mood – still no smile.

"It says *driver license* right across the top. Look at it."

"Oh, yeah. I'll be darned," I said, handing it over.

He studied it for a few seconds. "Stay in the vehicle," he ordered and walked back to the cruiser. I glanced up at Chris, who looked back at me from his side mirror and smirked. I shrugged my shoulders. The officer returned with more questions.

"So, where do you think you're headed?"

"Um. We're going to my mom's house."

"Where does she live?"

"In Cleveland."

"Where in Cleveland?"

"West 33rd Street, near Sackett."

"Why are you going there?"

"Cause that's where he's going to take apart the engine."

"And who is that?" he said, tilting his head toward Chris.

"That's my friend, Chris."

"Chris who?"

"Chris... Chris... I have no idea. He's just Chris to me."

"He's your friend, and you're letting him tow you to your mother's house to take your engine apart, and yet you don't know his last name?" Now even I'm thinking I sound suspicious.

"Yes, well, that's true, when you put it that way. I swear this is my bus. I know it sounds fishy," I said, "but it's because we just recently met. I mean through a mutual friend. Like I said, he's just going to look at the engine for me... at my mother's house... you know, to see if he can fix the engine. Just like I said." I finally stopped babbling.

"Uh-huh. Stay in the vehicle," the officer repeated once more. "I'm going to go talk to *Chris with no last name.*"

"Yes, sir," I nodded, "I'm not going anywhere."

I stuck my ear out of the window to listen in on their conversation. I only heard the officer's side of the discussion with my soft-spoken friend. The officer asked him for his driver license and registration. He followed up with an inquiry about me.

"So, who's the guy you're towing back there?" He asked while reading the paperwork in his hands. Chris muttered something back. Then I heard, "Jerry who?" I knew how Chris was going to answer that question. The officer stopped reading and looked up. "He's your friend, but you don't know his last name?"

This is where I stopped listening altogether and lit a cigarette. Questions began swirling around in my head. How will I pay for a tow to the impound garage on a broken-down bus I couldn't afford to fix? How sorry is Chris feeling right about now for agreeing to help me? Is that old clown car going to become my permanent means of transportation?

Then my next thought really scared the hell out of me. What if Chris is somehow in trouble with the law? How the hell would I know if he had any warrants out for his arrest? They'll probably throw the goddamn book at both of us. I squirmed in my seat as the officer headed back toward me. I crushed out my cigarette and clutched the steering wheel.

"Okay. I shouldn't do this, but I'm letting you go," the officer said, returning my license.

"Huh?"

"I'm not a betting man, but odds are you'll never make it to West 33rd, and the next guy's not going to be so nice."

"It's only a few miles."

"You do know the Second District station is right on Fulton Road, right?"

"No, sir. I mean, yes, sir. We already talked about taking back roads."

"Yeah, well, good luck with that," he said. "Now get going before I change my mind." Finally, a slight grin appeared in the corner of his mouth.

"Yes, sir, thank you, sir." I waved Chris forward, and he nodded back. I adjusted my rearview mirror as the bus lurched forward again. Chris inadvertently towed me straight down Fulton Road. I crossed my fingers and lit another cigarette, passing the police station. We arrived safely at my mother's house minutes later.

I met Chris at Ma's house whenever he was available

and managed to scrape up the cash to buy replacement parts. He really knew his way around an engine, while I functioned as his enthusiastic assistant. It turned out one of the valve heads snapped off, causing quite a mess inside the engine block. Chris drilled a hole in it, strung a cord through, and hung it from my rearview mirror. I paid him mostly in lunches, dinners, and an envelope of cash. He had me back on the road within a couple of weeks.

~~~

There were immediate questions around the fire pit when my story ended.

"Did you keep the old V-dub?"

"Whatever happened to the Beetle?"

"Whatever became of Chris?"

"I kept the bus one more bone-chilling winter. After graduation, I found a teaching job and saved enough money for a downpayment on a used car with heat. I sold the old Beetle for thirty-five dollars. Chris, Beto, and I are still good friends."

~~~

Like the famous Greek storyteller, Aesop, Papa was asked if there was a moral to my bond fire fable. I had to think carefully for a moment before answering. "Towing the line can be a poor choice." Papa's response went right over the heads of Jeffrey, Bill, and Lydia.

RUFF AND READY

HOW MANY CREATIVE WAYS can you turn down a request from your new father-in-law without disappointing him? All he wanted to do was introduce me to the game of golf. Hitting the links was Carl Ruff's favorite pastime for at least as long as I've known him, which was right around the time he retired. It was a game he watched and played as often as possible on any day of the week.

The problem was I had absolutely no interest in the sport. None. Zero. I didn't know the first thing about golf and was happier for it. I couldn't tell a wood from a wedge, or a birdie from an eagle, although I knew which end of a putter to hold from playing miniature golf. And the thought of watching it on television was unbearable. *"I'd rather watch paint dry,"* was my wisecrack comeback if anyone mentioned it – anyone except Carl. He was a kind-hearted man, and I never could bring myself to disparage something that brought him such joy.

"It's a beautiful day to go hit some balls at the driving range. You should come with me," Carl would always suggest. "You don't know what you're missing." He'd mention it almost every time he went to hit practice balls. I was surprised he still asked me after turning down his invitations so many times.

"I have a lot of chores to get done," was a standard answer. It was a legitimate excuse.

"I'll help you afterward if you come."

"No, you go, but maybe next time." I used that one a lot too. Okay, maybe that's why he asked so often.

The fact was I did enjoy spending time with him. He was always an easygoing, positive, glass half full kind of guy and a perfect elder role model. Every young man should be so lucky. Next time did come, and this time I surprised him as well as myself.

"Yeah, sure, let's go. Why not?"

"Really?" He looked shocked as hell and pleased at the same time. We drove to Shawnee Hills Golf Club down in the Bedford Reservation, just a few miles away from his house on Dunham Road. I set up next to him so he could share his clubs with me. We each hit a bucket of balls.

He also shared some of his favorite golf tips. Truth be told, I had a good time despite spraying balls all over the range. It was enough fun for me to accept his invitation several more times over the next few weeks.

That's when he started suggesting something new, repeatedly. "We should go play nine holes."

"Oh, I don't think so," I said. "Spattering shots all over

the range is one thing, killing someone with a golf ball is quite a different story." He laughed, but I was truthfully self-conscious about my gross inability to control my golf shots.

"You know, Shawnee Hills has a nine-hole par-three course. It's one of the best in Northeast Ohio. The longest hole isn't even two hundred yards long, and the course is beautiful. We'd have a lot of fun," he said, "and we'd finish in an hour and a half." He was so determined.

"I have to cut the grass."

"I'll cut the grass tomorrow while you're at work."

"No, you go, but maybe next time."

"Okay, next time then." He was also very patient.

Meanwhile, at work, some friends at Arrow Distributors joined the company golf league. They had such enthusiasm for the sport. Golf was always the hot topic around the water cooler, and at lunch, especially during the golf season. All I could do is sit and listen. It made me want to become part of the fun and excitement. The next time Carl invited me, I accepted his offer.

"That's great! I have an extra bag. I'll add some clubs, a few balls, and some tees, and you'll be all set to go." I was as nervous as he was excited. "You're gonna have a lot of fun. You'll see."

"Yeah, I'll see," I replied.

"It's a weekday evening, so there won't be many people there."

He was correct much to my relief. There weren't many golfers to accidentally bludgeon, or for me to humiliate myself in front of that evening. Carl was also right when he said the course was beautiful. Lush, green trees lined the rolling fairways, the greens were like carpeting, and the surroundings were genuinely peaceful. From what I gathered, this wasn't typical for a small public course.

To be clear, the aesthetics did absolutely nothing to help my pathetic game. I hacked the course all the way around, shooting double, triple, and even quadruple bogeys on the first seven holes. Worm burner, duck hook, shank, duff, and mulligan were new words introduced into my vocabulary that evening. On the bright side, I never had to yell *fore*, since the ball rarely flew high or far.

As expected, Carl remained encouraging the entire round. Sighting feedback like *just take the shot over, great three-putt, we don't count whiffs*, and my favorite, *kick it away from behind the tree*. If you're going to hack your brains out on a golf course with anyone – let it be Carl Ruff.

I teed up on the eighth hole. The weather was picture perfect. The wind was calm, and the view spectacular. If only I were having fun, I thought.

My drive on number eight was my best shot off the tee. Sure, it was short of the green by thirty yards, but it flew up in the air and landed in the middle of the fairway.

"That was a beauty," Carl said. "Now chip it up and one putt for par."

"Stranger things have happened."

I shanked my second shot badly. We watched it scream along the ground to the right with enough pace to hop right through a group of trees like a scared jackrabbit. The ball finally dropped dead somewhere on the ninth hole.

"What were you saying about par?" I asked.

Carl laughed. "Just take a long club like your four iron, play it back in your stance and punch it through the trees. This is one shot you *want* to keep low."

"Uh-huh."

"Just relax and do what I said. You can do it!"

When I found my ball on the other side of the trees, it was resting in the rough, several yards in front of the ninth tee. Unfortunately for me, a foursome was waiting there to tee off.

"Son of a bitch!" slipped out from under my breath as I approached them.

"Go ahead and play it," one of them said.

"Are you sure? I can wait."

"We're going to be here a while with these slowpokes in front of us."

"Yeah, lucky me," I muttered.

I just got used to hacking the course in front of Carl, and now there's a gallery to watch me make a real chooch of myself. This should give them something to laugh about, I'm sure, unless, of course, the ball ricochets off a tree and beans one of them. I had the sudden urge to go home. Why the hell did I ever agree to come to this goddamn place in the first place? I'm just going to do whatever Carl said and then get the hell out of here.

I looked at the green through the trees, glanced at the enthralled onlookers, settled over the ball, and took a swipe. I let go with a low laser shot, remarkably missing every tree trunk along the way. It took a few bounces in the clearing beyond just before jumping up onto the green. It rolled another twenty feet, hit the flagstick, and dropped into the hole. Par! I stood zoned-out for a few seconds until the sound of applause and cheers brought me back. It was my crowd of four. I turned toward them, still slightly dazed.

"Man, that was beautiful!"

"The shot of the day for sure!" someone said.

"That takes years of practice," I heard another say.

"What club did you use?"

"Uh... I uh... I used a four-iron," I remembered.

"Huh, a four-iron. That's not an easy shot any day of the week!"

"Tell us how you played it."

"Well... I played it back in my stance, then punched it through." I replied, parroting Carl's instructions.

"Yeah, well, I'm going to remember that advice."

I'll admit there was a bit of a swagger in my step heading back through the trees toward the green. Carl was on the other side when I got there.

"Well done! That was a real *whopper-do!*"

"Thank you, thank you," I said, waving to an imaginary crowd as I picked the ball out of the cup. Of course, it was back to reality on the ninth hole, but I didn't mind since I was still glowing from my miracle shot.

"So, what are you doing tomorrow?" I asked Carl as we packed our clubs into the trunk of my car.

"All it takes is one good shot to bring you back," he said. "Looks like I just found myself a new golfing partner."

We returned two days later. In the meantime, Carl gave me more tips along with a paperback he called his golfer's bible. I wore out the pages referencing it so often. I also subscribed to a golf magazine.

Before long, I had my own golf equipment and joined the company league. In time, I became an avid golfer and even helped to run the company league and the annual outings. My golfing buddies and I played all the time.

I golfed throughout Northeast Ohio over the next ten years, and never went on another family vacation without my clubs. I even attended golf-specific excursions to Myrtle Beach. And through my job connections, I had opportunities to play at several elite clubs, including Chagrin Country Club, Quail Hollow Resort in Concord Township, and Firestone in Akron.

But my favorite private club was not nearly as prestigious. It was right at home. I counter-sank a few tin cans in the ground and laid out a course on my one-acre property. My three children and I had some great tournaments in the front and back of our house. Those were the best.

When Carl and I weren't out on the links, we enjoyed watching the PGA pros on television together. He also joined me on league night periodically and was quite a big hit with my coworkers, who often asked to play in our foursome.

~~~

So you see, dear family of mine, your papa enjoyed countless rounds of golf, and many included my father-in-law, Carl. I'm happy to report he played the game through most of his eighties until it was no longer possible.

Papa is grateful for my many blessings. Among them are Carl's gentle persuasion, patience, and encouragement in introducing me to his favorite pastime. If there is a heaven and it has golf courses, I know my very first golf partner will save me a spot in his foursome.

BUILD YOUR OWN FAIRYTALE

ONCE UPON A TIME, long, long ago, my beautiful June bride, Judi, and I embarked hand in hand on a new chapter in our lives. It was a humble beginning, to say the least, so I was determined to prove myself as the latest member of her family. And my work was cut out for me too. After all, I had no money to show for the six years I taught at a parochial school in an eastern suburb of Cleveland, not on the small stipend I received once a month. Now throw in a difficult divorce and child support for my precious baby boy. Hell, I was grateful for their civility.

Nevertheless, there was no doubt in the blind trust Sweet Judi placed in me, and I was sure her father, Carl, backed me too. The rest took a more cautious wait and see attitude. I was determined to succeed, and my new computer technology career was just the tool to help me do it. It wasn't going to happen overnight, but I was sure we would build a storybook life together.

To save a little extra cash before our wedding, I left my apartment in Parma Heights to move into the tiny suite above my mother's home on West 33rd in Cleveland. It was a simple move considering all I had was a few sticks of furniture, a touring bicycle, and a stuffy old mattress to throw on the floor in the bedroom.

At that point, the old house, as well as the neighborhood in general, had fallen on hard times. My parents missed the opportunity to migrate to the western suburbs, along with most of their family, friends, and neighbors. And there was no budging my mother from her home after my father died.

"This is where your father and I lived for thirty years," she argued, "and where we raised our children and where my husband died. I'm not leaving here – ever!"

My move back to West 33rd was just a small piece of a larger plan hatched with Judi's parents. They were moving to Virginia temporarily after our wedding to be closer to their other daughter. Since the move was not permanent, they offered us their small bungalow on Dunham Road in Maple Heights rather than leave it abandoned. This plan was a win-win for everyone. However, it required Judi to stay with me in my *not so humble abode* for a few weeks until they packed and moved. She didn't even bother to bring any belongings with her.

A few unexpected snags in the plan pushed our move-in date back, from July to November, and with this delay came an extra dose of life in the inner city for my suburban bride. This new experience was a real eye-opener for her.

"Jerry, what's a hoe around here?" she asked one evening.

"A hoe? In what context?"

"Well, I saw graffiti sprayed on the factory wall around the corner this morning. It said, *Mary Jane is a hoe, h-o-e.*"

"Oh, a hoe. Just somebody trying to call Mary Jane a *puttana*," I explained. "The Language Arts aren't always a top priority around here. Remember, Dorothy. You're not in Kansas anymore. And are you remembering to keep your car doors locked like I asked you?"

"Yes, I am. I don't suppose clicking my heels will get me home any faster."

"We'll be there soon enough," I said.

"And what's with the television reception around here? These rabbit ears can only pick up a couple of channels, and they're fuzzy."

Our television reception was iffy, but as it turned out, it didn't matter. All the action, drama, and comedy we needed were right outside our window.

"Hey, Jude, whatcha' watching?" I yelled from the front window of our bedroom one evening. "Anything good?"

"I'm not really paying attention. Some new show. I think it's called *Miami Vice*. Why?"

"There's something out here you'll pay attention to."

During our four-month stay, we witnessed a midnight fistfight in the middle of the street, a car crashing into the home across the road, and the house three doors down burning to the ground. November couldn't have come too soon, but we never forgot where we started together. There was nowhere to go but up.

~~~

The little bungalow was terrific. It was built shortly after World War II, along with most of the other homes on the street. Judi's parents were one of the first residents to move into the new neighborhood. They kept it looking like new, too, and even added an in-ground pool to the small backyard. Judi and I threw some fun pool parties back there.

I taught at a private school in Maple Heights for six years, but it was my first time living on the east side of town. Judi was teaching for the city school district at that point. Her new classroom was literally two minutes away from home, and my former schoolhouse wasn't far away.

We found ourselves living amongst her current and my former students. That meant running into them and their parents every time we ventured out around town. It might sound like an uncomfortable arrangement for some people, but we always found it enjoyable.

For instance, we threw a big party one evening when three of my former students showed up to invite us to a little pizza shop on the corner. Another former student of mine was playing in a band there. These young men were all in high school now and stood eye level with me. Judi and I marveled at their sincerity and couldn't resist the thoughtful invitation. We left our own party to join them for a half-hour.

Then there was the time I received a telephone call from a friend of ours. Neal was a young, fun priest. We both played guitars and shared an interest in folk music, never turning down an opportunity to jam at get-togethers with friends.

"Hey Jer, it's Neal. Can I use your pool for an hour?"

"Uh, okay. Can I ask why?"

"To show some kids how to flip a capsized kayak."

"Jeez Neal, that sounds awfully dangerous."

"I'm taking a group of students kayaking next week," he explained, "and I don't want any accidents."

"So you're gonna tie them into a kayak and capsize them in our pool?"

"Well, yes... but that's why I have to show them how to flip themselves upright. They'll tap the side of the kayak if they're in danger."

"Are you sure you wouldn't rather teach them to juggle machetes in our garage?"

"That's next Tuesday. Seriously, it's okay. I'll be in the water the whole time with them, I promise." He pulled up twenty minutes later with four kids in his car and a kayak strapped to his roof. Judi and I watched them the entire time holding *our* breath. I'm happy to report no one drowned.

Living at ground zero also meant anonymous motorists honking at me from the busy road as I mowed the front lawn. I wasn't sure exactly who it was most of the time, but I always waved back.

Life was good in Maple Heights. And in between all the spontaneous visits, fun, and excitement, Judi and I began hatching a plan for a new and challenging project that consumed us for the next two years.

~~~

The project started unintentionally in December of 1985 as we drove to a Christmas party hosted by my IT director from Arrow Distributors. He lived in Far Hills Estates, a development in a place called Concord Township. It's thirty-five miles east of Cleveland in Lake County. Neither of us was familiar with this area, which explains why we got lost in the dark. We traversed the entire town until I stopped at a gas station in Painesville for directions. The attendant set us back on course.

"At least we got to see Concord," Judi exclaimed, "and from what I can tell, it's a pretty town. I'd love to see it again during the day."

"Yeah, I was thinking the same thing," I said. "Although it seems so rural. I haven't seen a traffic light since we left Painesville. Hey, maybe they don't have electricity out here."

"Or maybe it's just a quaint, rural town off the beaten

path," she countered. "Would you ever consider looking for a house around here?"

"I might," I replied, "but I have this notion to build a house on a pretty plot of land someday. And I want us to design it from the ground up."

"Are you kidding? We don't know anything about building houses."

"Yeah, but I know where we can learn," I suggested.

"Hmm, okay, you have my attention."

So, I shared my idea as we drove to the party, and from that day forward, we committed ourselves to find the right spot to build a custom home. As much as I considered leaving Ohio, I knew we never would, not with a beautiful, young son to help raise in town. A suitable piece of property somewhere different in Northeast Ohio was the next best option.

We started weekend expeditions to look for this suitable piece of property, scouring Greater Cleveland in every direction. Getting lost was all part of the adventure, just like I did as a kid on my bicycle.

Meanwhile, we spent hours on the phone with the two most knowledgeable people I knew on the subject of house designing. It was my Uncle Johnny and Aunt Hedy. They were professional artists, designers, and builders of almost everything imaginable; homes, furniture, sculptures, drawings, and paintings – you name it. Despite living hundreds of miles away, they willingly educated us over the phone and through the mail on the principles of form and function – roof types, building materials, plumbing configurations, window styles, and where to efficiently place them. They also explained the three most important factors to a desirable homestead – location, location, and location. All this information gave us the confidence and determination to find the right place to build our home.

One day on a weekend excursion eastward, we found ourselves lost in farmland somewhere outside of Lake County near Thompson. I eventually turned the car around and headed back west on a quiet and scenic country road. The sign read, SR 86. The quiet ride abruptly ended when something caught Judi's eye.

"Stop the car! Did you see that sign we just passed?"

"What sign?"

"Back there. It said, *'For sale – one and two-acre lots for executive homes.'* Turn around. Turn around and go back to that street!"

"Okay, okay, but where the hell are we anyway? Are we even in Ohio for God's sake?" I joked.

"I'm not sure where we are right now, but I really like it around here."

I spun the car around as Judi referenced the map she was holding. The new street wasn't even on the map, but once we realized we were in Concord Township, it suddenly didn't seem all that distant. Of all places, we were minutes away from Far Hills Estates!

The brand new road was a cul-de-sac paved atop a plateau shaped like Florida. Most of the parcels lined one side of the street. The other side was lined with trees and cliffs with not enough land to build. The acreage below was a reserve owned by the Lake Metropark System. A covenant prohibited any building on the cliffs whatsoever. One house occupied this entire grand ridge.

We drove slowly up and down the quiet street and eventually parked the car to walk the parcels. Some had sold signs, but not all of them.

"That does it! I'm calling tomorrow," Judi said eagerly.

"I hate to burst your bubble now," I warned, "but please don't get too excited. You know we probably can't afford to live on a street like this one."

"You don't know that, and it won't cost anything for me to find out."

"Okay, just don't get your hopes up is all I'm saying."

The next day over dinner, Judi told me all about her conversation with the developer. The location was far enough from city life to be affordable, and there were six lots left from which to choose.

We signed the papers on the hood of our new '85 Toyota sports pickup truck in front of our future homestead. Judi and I stayed afterward to walk *our* land. I picked up a rock the size of a bocce ball and showed it to my co-property owner.

"This is our rock," I told Judi, "and upon it, we shall

build our home." We laughed and took it home with us.

I bought a large pad of graph paper to sketch out house plans using all the information we learned about home construction. The rooms whirled around and around on the paper, changing shape and size over the following months. Compromising was vital in the design and not always easy. And our limited budget loomed ever-present, pulling us back to reality whenever we crunched the numbers.

I'm telling you there really must be something about Italians and building! I had a blast, and with only a few sheets of paper left in the pad, and the remnants of a new eraser, we agreed on an affordable design.

To me, the next phase of the planning process was the most exciting challenge, which was constructing a three-dimensional scale model of the house. I made it from a sturdy white tagboard, complete with a removable roof and second floor.

When finished, we had a small, white prototype to study. The concept became substance. I set the little house on a table. We got down eye level, then peered across the two-story living room, up at the loft, into the den, through the dining room, along the kitchen, and down the hallway. It was easy to imagine standing inside the white, full-sized home. We even set the tiny structure in a clearing on the property to see how the sun moved across it.

Judi and I carried our house plans and the model

to meetings with several different builders. A two-story living room was not very common at the time, so one builder shied away altogether, saying it would be too expensive. One said it was a bad idea with all the open wasted space. Another gave his estimate way over our budget.

The second last builder caught our attention with his opening comment as he reviewed our plans. He built quality homes but was not a custom builder at the time. He expressed an interest in seeing my drawings and the model since he was looking to get into that market.

"Wow, you're going to save a lot of money on this two-story living room."

"Really? Go on," I said. His observation was encouraging.

"That's four-hundred square feet of floor space above your living room you won't be paying for." Hell, I was starting to like this guy! We talked for two and a half hours. By the time we finished our meeting, we knew we had found the right guy.

Building a new home, especially a custom home, requires open and well-defined communications between the builder and the owners. So if you're going to get what you asked and paid for, expect some intense conversations from time to time.

Judi and I crossed town to the construction site as often as possible to minimize complications, but not often enough. Most issues were minor to moderate. However, two monumental oversights caused setbacks when the cathedral ceiling trusses were nailed in over the guest bedrooms instead of the master bedroom. Thankfully, we got there the day before they started roofing. They had to tear down what amounted to two-thirds of the trusses and swap them. Then we dodged a second disaster by preventing the wrong ceramic tiles from being used in the kitchen, dining room, and hallway. That mistake cost us another week and a half.

One Sunday afternoon, we found all the doors in the house locked. Builders often do this when the finish-work begins inside. Yet I managed to slip in through an unlocked basement window and used a ladder to climb up the stepless staircase. I opened the sliding glass door in the living room for Judi. Then the most peculiar thing happened to us once we were inside. I closed the door and turned around. Judi was already frozen in a hypnotic gaze. All the white drywall was up.

It was déjà vu. We peered across the two-story living room, up at the loft, into the den, through the dining room, along the kitchen, and down the hallway. Only this time, we weren't peering through a miniature scale model. This time, we were standing inside of the actual white, full-sized house. It was eerie and awesome at the same time.

"Are you as freaked out as I am right now?"

"Uh-huh."

~~~

After a few months of mutual concessions with the builder and a couple of knockdown, drag-out arguments, they completed our house. I'm not sure who was happier to part ways. The final walkthrough took place on my birthday in 1987. It was the largest gift I had ever received! We moved in the following week as other homes continued to spring up along our new street.

To be honest, it took a few months for two city slickers like us to get used to the blackness of night and the sound of silence in the evenings. Where were the rumbling trucks, car horns, and streetlights of Maple Heights? Where were the screeching tires, sirens, and passing voices of Cleveland?

"Hey, are you awake?"

"Been awake for the past hour. Just as I'm about to nod off, that damn owl starts up with all that hooting again. Do you hear it?"

"Oh, I hear it all right! I don't know what's more annoying, the total dead silence or the near-total dead silence. Am I right?"

"Exactly! And we have to work tomorrow."

"I'm turning on the outside lights."

"How 'bout I find a radio station for some background noise?"

"Please, and thank you!"

And it didn't stop there. We found ourselves living with more than just pigeons, sparrows, and robins. Suddenly, there were bats, owls, hawks, falcons, wild turkeys, and species of birds we never knew existed before. So many, in fact, I bought a book to identify all of them.

There was also an abundance of woodland creatures like deer, rabbits, snakes, coyotes, and red foxes living among us, or should I say we were now living among them. The topper was the occasional bear alert. Bear alert? What good is a B-B gun during a bear attack?

~~~

Nana and Papa eventually settled into our new surroundings. Nana's parents moved back to Ohio and bought a condominium in the adjacent city. My mother-in-law even grew fond of me. We made our house a home and expanded our loving family. Some of you reading this now are proof of that! It's true what they say about time flying when you're having fun. Over three decades have passed, and our time together keeps us smiling. Like a fine wine, life remains full-bodied for the couple with humble beginnings. That rock I picked up after signing the papers on the hood of our truck is still on display in our glass China cabinet. And as most good fairytales go, they all lived happily ever after...

THE CURVE

WE SAW MORE THAN OUR FAIR SHARE of accidents living near the top of a hairpin curve on Route 86 in Concord Township, Ohio. Carved around the side of a steep rise, it was so severe the sharp bend obstructed the view of oncoming traffic in both directions. Thank goodness for the secure guardrail wrapping around the outer berm, shielding vehicles from the certain peril below. Accidents were so dreadfully common it seemed everyone in the vicinity knew someone with a horror story related to that treacherous stretch of road. We locals referred to the sight simply as, *the Curve*.

Hell, the sound of screeching tires and crumpling metal could be heard from our house a quarter-mile away.

"Uh-oh, there goes another one!"

"That sounded like a bad one."

"We'd better get down there and have a look. Someone might need an ambulance." Not everyone had a cell phone toward the end of the twentieth century.

It was always a version of the same story. Driving

westbound from Leroy Township, you advanced at the legal speed of 55 mph. A quarter-mile before the curve, the speed limit dropped to 35 mph and then again to 15 mph as you passed a yellow warning sign of a truck on a steep downgrade. That's when you entered the curve, veering right around the inside of the blind bend.

If you ignored some or all of these warnings for any reason, you have forfeited your control. You are about to experience a frightful adrenaline rush and the sinking feeling of helplessness. Standing on your brakes is instinctive. Anyone driving long enough knows the panic I'm talking about here.

At this point, you're looking at three possible outcomes.

The best-case scenario means it was your lucky day. You may or may not have crossed the centerline, but managed to regain control of your vehicle with no harm done. You were the blind squirrel that found a big, old acorn. You were allowed to carry on about your business and should buy a lottery ticket.

Were you having a *somewhat* lucky day? Then crossing the centerline and scraping along the outer guardrail was highly probable before regaining control. What was essential here is you didn't involve anyone else in your little fender-bender. You did minor harm to your vehicle as well as your ego. Of course, the damage was compounded if you were pulling a trailer. I witnessed a speedboat and even a small mobile home teetering on the guardrail. In both cases, a secure trailer hitch prevented the plunge over the cliff.

This middle scenario was prevalent based on the perpetually fresh paint streaks smeared along the battered rail. Car pieces and broken glass scattered on the berm was another telltale sign.

I saved the worst-case scenario for last. You were heading westbound, moving much too fast at the curve, and lost control. Except in this situation, you were about to involve oncoming eastbound traffic. Some poor motorist traveling up the hill is about to learn more than they ever wanted to know about you. They were simply in the wrong place at the wrong time. That lousy day most likely included law enforcement, ambulances, and fire trucks.

And it is here where my story gets personal. The year was 1994, and I just returned home after leaving work early. My wife, Judi, and I had an appointment with our son's kindergarten teacher at the elementary school. Judi's parents picked him up after school and took him to their house in Mentor. They already had our two-year-old daughter Zanni. I was waiting for Judi's return home so we could drive to school together. According to my watch, she was late. That's when the house phone rang.

"Jerry, I was just in an accident," Judi said, audibly shaken. She was calling from our first-ever mobile phone.

"What? Where are you?"

"I'm at the curve."

"What happened? Are you all right?"

Her voice quivered. "The car is all smashed up and my head's bleeding."

"Christ! Do you need an ambulance?"

"They just pulled up. I have to go now. Can you come to get me?"

"I'm on my way!"

I jumped into my car and sped off. My neighbor later told me she knew something was up by the way I raced down our street. When I got there, our '88 Honda Accord was pinned against the guardrail by another car. The Accord's left front fender and bumper were severely crumpled. The driver's side windshield was cracked, possibly from Judi's head. The other car had equal damage plus liquids streaming from its undercarriage. A small crowd of onlookers had gathered. I approached a county deputy examining the new skid marks.

"Excuse me. Where's the driver of the Honda?"

"She's in the back of the rescue truck."

I found Judi seated inside as two EMTs tended to a gash on top of her head. Blood covered her face and hair.

"Is she all right?" I asked.

"I'm fine," she answered.

"She's going to need an X-ray or two, and some stitches. We're taking her to Lake East Hospital in Painesville if you'd like to follow." I did.

After Judi's X-rays in the ER, a nurse escorted us to an area behind a curtain. Judi explained how it happened while we waited for the doctor.

The other car flew around the curve, crossed the centerline, and hit her head-on. It was the textbook, worst-case scenario, and the latest testimonial for the need to address our version of Deadman's Curve.

Eventually, the doctor entered with a local anesthetic to numb Judi's wound. After a few minutes, he began probing around her scalp with his fingers.

"What are you doing?" I asked, trying to make small talk.

"Searching for glass fragments inside the injury before I stitch her up."

"This seems pretty routine for you," I said.

"You'd be surprised the things I do around here," he answered. "This is like taking a break for me."

"I'm just glad I don't feel any pain," Judi added.

"We'll give you something for pain when the local wears off," he said. "You'll feel something by then." He calmly closed her wound like darning a sock, and after more casual conversation said, "Well, on to bigger and worse things. You're going to be fine." He wrote a prescription and disappeared.

The nurse finished dressing and bandaging Judi's stitches as a deputy sheriff asked to enter. He told us a truck towed our Honda to a salvage yard and suggested we call our insurance company to help us with the arrangements. He was also holding a clipboard stacked with papers.

"Oh, two more things before you leave," he said, looking at his notes. "The lady that hit you had an outstanding warrant for her arrest. We've taken her into custody."

"G-zus! Was she injured too?" I asked.

"She's all right. We have her here now getting checked out along with her passenger."

"I heard there was a man with her."

"Yes, that's correct."

"I also heard someone say he may have pitched something over the cliff just before you arrived."

"We heard that too," he replied. "There's an officer at the scene right now investigating. No doubt, it was something like drugs or alcohol."

"What's the other thing?" I asked.

"What's that?"

"You said there were two more things. What's the other thing?"

"Oh, yeah, that's right," he said, looking down at his notes again. "She doesn't have insurance."

"*Schifosa!* Why am I not surprised?"

"It'll all be in my final report."

I called our insurance company when we got home. I hate paying for those pricey insurance premiums but was thrilled the uninsured motorist clause covered the costs. We never heard any more about the deadbeat driver or her suspicious passenger. It was probably better that way. The police and our insurance company took care of all the details, while I focused on Judi and securing a loaner vehicle.

The insurance company gave us the option of having the Honda fixed or declared totaled beyond repair later that week. The body shop informed us the cost was right on the bubble. We chose the check because of the Honda's age and high mileage, then used the money as a down payment on a brand new, economical '95 Saturn, which was a huge mistake. The car mysteriously leaked when it rained, causing the driver seat to dampen. The dealer didn't know how to repair it, so who took that car depended on where you were going and the weather forecast. We dumped it two years later.

After things settled down with the accident, I penned a lengthy letter to the trustees of the township imploring them to do something regarding the curve. It was read aloud in a televised meeting. I imagine they added it to the tall stack written before mine. Still, I'd like to think it was *the final straw* because they took action soon afterward.

Judi came home very excited one day. She pulled into the garage, beeping the horn of our '97 Dodge Caravan. I thought it was to carry in the groceries.

"Guess what I just saw?" she said, stepping out of the

291

car. "I was coming westbound from Leroy and noticed a row of yellow signs with black arrows warning of the curve ahead. They really catch your eye."

"Hey, maybe my letter did some good after all, huh."

"Yes, maybe this is the answer to the problem. Go check it out!"

I immediately hopped into my car and headed down toward the curve. Sure enough, just as Judi said, a row of bright yellow signs alerted me of the treachery ahead.

"Finally," I mumbled.

Just as I felt a tinge of pride and accomplishment, I entered the blind turn to find a car stopped on the outer berm. It was facing the wrong way, and the car's emergency flashers were engaged. The driver was out of the vehicle, picking up side molding torn from his car. The fresh paint-streak on the guardrail matched the color of his car. Yes, this was his somewhat lucky day.

Once I knew everything was fine, I turned my head driving by so he couldn't read my lips. Upon my return home, it took some doing to convince Judi I was telling her the truth, the whole truth, and nothing but the truth. I penned another letter to the trustees that night. It began, "What you're about to read is a story I couldn't make up if I tried..."

I don't know if they ever read it aloud on television, but what I do know is the accidents continued on the curve. Then, finally, with enough pressure from the community on the state and local governments, a state-funded undertaking solved our dangerous problem for good.

~~~

The state purchased and demolished a string of homes in that vicinity, making way for a construction project that straightened the curve out into a safe, low-graded, gentle bend in the road. But seriously, who wants to refer to it as, "the gentle bend?" We all still call it the curve. Nevertheless, the first step in solving a problem is identifying that there is one. Since then, I'm happy to report that Papa hasn't written any more complaint letters... at least recently.

THE JEEP CREEP

OH, THE LENGTHS WE'LL GO TO for the things we want badly enough. Here's a confession for a lie I once told to get what I selfishly craved. Although, in my mind, it was a mere venial transgression according to my understanding of how the Roman Catholic Church rates sins. I'm guessing worth one Our Father and one Hail Mary – two tops. Hear me out.

When it was time for a new family vehicle, I knew exactly what I was looking for this time – I was on the prowl for a Jeep Cherokee. It met the three requirements my wife Judi and I needed. Four-wheel drive for the rough Cleveland winters, a high view of the road, and at this point in our lives in 1992, room enough for our expanding family. We just had our second child together. That's three kids for me.

Our peppy little '85 Toyota sports pickup truck had become obsolete. It had only two of the three boxes checked; four-wheel drive and a high view of the road. But the tiny cab only had two seats, which was a significant inconvenience for a family always on the go.

It was quite a different story before we had children, back when we first built our home on a one-acre wooded lot in Concord Township, Ohio. I lost count of the number of trips I took to the county dump hauling cleared debris off the property so we could landscape. Likewise, it was invaluable for transporting the new bushes, flowers, and decorative trees from the numerous nurseries in Perry and Madison just east of us. Even the couple dozen bails of hay to cover the grass seed I planted once we groomed the ground.

No matter, with three kids in the picture, we needed a second *family* vehicle now besides our '88 Honda Accord.

Money is always a factor for any growing family like ours, so we had to be financially sensible on our next vehicle purchase. Sure, I looked at the brand new Cherokees, but they were too steep for our budget. If I were going to scratch this Jeep itch of mine, it would have to be on a late-model used one, dramatically narrowing my search. Jeep Cherokees were hot commodities at the time, so finding the right one was not going to be easy. Nevertheless, like Jason pursuing the Golden Fleece, I was a man on a mission to make this happen.

Then early one Sunday evening while driving through the city of Mentor, I noticed something out of the corner of my eye. It wasn't much, but enough for my *Inner Cherokee Detector* to go off. I swear I just spotted one sitting in the customer parking lot of a Chevrolet car lot. What caught my eye was the absence of a license plate. I suspected it might be a recent trade-in by the thick, dried mud caked along both sides of the attractive, red body. This particular dealership sold new trucks but also had a large inventory of used cars with many different makes and models. I just had to go back for a closer look! I pulled into the lot and parked nearby.

It was a '91 Limited Edition, meaning it came with some *extras*. Thin gold pinstripes ran along the doors and quarter panel, and the four, cross-spoke aluminum alloy wheels had matching gold trim. The interior was dark gray leather. It was only a year old, so I assumed it was probably a one-year lease. A logo stenciled on both front doors made it evident this was a commercial lease. In classy, gold script lettering it read, *Exclusive Homes*, a local homebuilder. That would explain all the mud. Personally, this was still the prettiest vehicle on that entire lot.

I cupped my hands to my temples and pressed my face up to the driver's window to see the odometer. It registered less than twelve thousand miles. Upon further inspection of the leather interior, I was pleased to find it was spotless inside. The cherry on top of this discovery was the limited edition's interior upgraded sound system and anti-theft alarm. Guess what? I just found my family's next car.

I looked around to see if anyone was still inside the

showroom to have it unlocked for me. Unfortunately, I would have to wait a day since it was Sunday evening. I circled it a few more times, looking for dents or scratches. Incredibly, there were none. The worst I could find was a nail in the front left tire. I suppose a vehicle driving through construction sights all day is entitled to puncture a tire on occasion. Monday after work couldn't come quick enough for me.

Just as I was about to leave, a car rolled up behind me. A man about my age stepped out and began circling the Jeep like a goddamn vulture.

"This sure is a beauty," he said without making eye contact. I didn't like the sound of that and wanted to tell him to get the hell back in his car and beat it. I remained calm and civil.

"I guess it's all right."

"Yes, I've been looking at these Cherokees," he said. "Is this yours?"

"Nope."

"Looks like a company vehicle," he said, pointing to the sign on the door.

"Yep, that should tell you everything you need to know," I said, desperately hoping he would bite.

"What do you mean?" he asked. Thank you.

"Well, think about it. Who really takes care of a work vehicle? No one I know! Am I right?"

He shrugged his shoulders and nodded. "I suppose."

"Yessiree, this old workhorse got whipped hard and put away wet every day, I'll bet. Probably never saw the inside of a garage or had an oil change. Just look at all that mud caked over this thing. It's been used, abused, and now discarded. I mean nobody in their right mind trades a car in after just one year unless you're hard on them. It's like a disposable vehicle for these companies that lease. Beat the hell out of it, then go get the next one."

"Good point," the man said, and then looked in at the odometer. "Eleven thousand and change. Not bad."

"Not bad? Are you kidding?"

"What, you don't believe that?"

"I'm just saying. Eleven thousand miles? Come on. Look at the condition of those tires and tell me that makes sense. They have twice the wear."

Of course, working in a tire store as a teenager, I knew a little about different kinds of tires. Standard touring tires are durable and make for a comfortable ride. This Jeep came equipped with sporty, high-performance tires, used for gripping and handling the road, not longevity. Now I had to see if he knew anything about tires.

"You know you're right," he said, squatting down to take a closer look. "Do you think they monkeyed with the odometer?"

"I can see you're a man that can't be fooled," I replied. "It's one of the oldest tricks in the book. We both know those tires were brand new a year ago. Now I'm not

299

saying they did anything wrong, but it's not very hard to disconnect the odometer cable and reattach it when you bring it back. I knew plenty of guys that did that in my old neighborhood. One thing's for sure. There are plenty of questions surrounding this bucket of bolts. Oh, and by the way, the left front tire has a nail in it too."

"So you're not interested in it?" he asked.

"Who me? Hell no, I wouldn't think of it," I said, smirking, "but I feel sorry for the poor sap who is."

I hoped my reverse sales pitch planted enough doubt to stop him, or at least slow him down until I could get back there the following night. "Well, good luck with your search," I said, climbing back into my pickup truck. I was so excited to get home and tell Judi all about our next family car.

Okay, what do you think? Am I a Jeep creep or an evil genius? In all fairness, I was there first, protecting my claim. Besides, all's fair in love and war, and this beauty had me smitten.

~~~

The following evening I drove straight to the dealer from work and asked Judi to meet me there. She brought our two babies. The Jeep was nowhere in sight. I carefully scanned the used car lot. Nothing. Where the hell is it?

"But I drove by yesterday and stopped," I said to the salesperson. "I walked all around it. There was a red Jeep parked right over there in that spot."

"Hmm. We don't have any Jeeps around as far as I'm aware."

"Are you sure? It was all muddy. A red Cherokee with 'Exclusive Homes' printed on the sides."

"Oh, the Cherokee? Right, I forgot. I was thinking of a *jeepy Jeep.* You know, a Wrangler. I'm sorry. Yes, it came in on Saturday. The owner of Exclusive Homes leases a brand new vehicle from our company owner every year. He has a Jeep dealership too. The guy picked up a new Chevy truck from us yesterday."

"And where's the old Jeep? Is it gone already?"

"What? No, no. They have it back in the shop for inspection. They're cleaning it up. It'll be ready for the used car lot by tomorrow." Thank you, St. Rocco!

I had him take it out of the garage to show Judi, and then we took it for a test drive. By the time we returned, I was dying to take it home but had to put my poker face on to get the best possible deal. I used what my father taught me about buying cars. He was a master haggler, always starting the negotiations out by asking, *"How much for this junker?"*

"So, what did you think," the salesperson asked when we returned.

I started with a shrug of the shoulders. "Eh, it's just okay. Rides a little stiff," I said. "And those tires are shot. I'm wondering if it ever had an oil change. Can you even get the signs off the doors without ruining the paint job?"

"Oh, sure we can. Our body people are terrific. They'll peel them right off, and then buff the entire body out until it shines like new. It'll look as good as the day it left our Jeep dealership. We'll service the whole vehicle for you."

We haggled back and forth for another thirty minutes as Judi paraded our children up and down the showroom to keep them quietly entertained. Finally, she approached with one in her arms and the other holding her hand.

"I'm not sold on the whole Jeep idea for a family car," Judi said, in front of the salesperson. "I'd much rather have a van. But if you're going to pursue this thing, they better give us a helluva deal." She looked at the man and began with a barrage of facts and figures. My wife schooled him on everything from depreciation to trade-in value to finance loans. He barely got a word in edgewise. When he did, she countered-punched like a pro. It was a scene worthy of any godfather movie, watching my enforcer batter him into submission while I sat there quietly giving him the *malocchio*, the evil eye. She ended the negotiations with, "And my kids aren't riding in a car with bald tires!"

"I'll have to go talk to my manager for an offer like this, ma'am."

"Well, go talk to your manager," Judi repeated. My tag-team partner turned back toward me. "We should take these kids home now. We can go look at the van I want tomorrow." Then, without letting the salesperson see, she smiled and winked at me.

"Oh, right. Okay. Why don't you take the kids and I'll finish up here. If the manager wants to make a sale tonight, I'll sign the papers right now." Judi walked out of the showroom. I turned to the salesperson. "Looks like I'm either buying this Jeep from you right now, or I'm getting a van tomorrow." He excused himself to find his manager.

I'm not sure if we met my father's level of negotiating skills, but I did sign the papers that evening. They even put four new touring tires on it for us. I picked up the Jeep that week and christened it, *Big Red*.

A few weeks later, Judi and I ran some errands in Big Red with both of our kids in the back seat. I pulled into a small shopping center on Mentor Avenue and parked directly in front of a store with a large picture window. The kids and I stayed in the car as Judi entered the front door.

She immediately began talking with a middle-aged couple on the other side of the glass. I didn't recognize them, but they seemed to be having a friendly enough conversation, occasionally looking out the window and gesturing in our direction. The man smiled at me as he and his wife exited the store. Judi returned with some interesting information.

"You'll never guess who I just met in the store," she said.

"I saw you talking to that couple, but I didn't recognize either one of them."

"And you wouldn't," she replied. "Those were the owners of Exclusive Homes. They saw the Jeep when we pulled up and watched me get out. He knew right away that it was his old Cherokee. They told me everything about it."

The couple confirmed how they leased a new vehicle from the same dealer every year and raved about how wonderful the Jeep was for them. They assured Judi our new automobile was well taken care of and garaged every night. He only used it to drive locally from one work site to another. The woman said the farthest she ever drove it was to Columbus and back once, less than 400 miles.

I thought of the man I misled at the car dealership that Sunday evening and felt remorseful. Okay, maybe not that much. I was much happier learning how well the Jeep was taken care of by the previous owners.

When I traded it in six years later, Big Red looked as good as the day I drove it off the car lot. I enjoyed it so much that I bought a brand new one, a '98 Cherokee that I dubbed, *Black Beauty*. It was black and beautiful, and yes, I could have been more creative with the name.

~~~

Papa and Nana owned many vehicles during our lifetime together. Teaming up to buy a new car was always a sort of competition for us. It never mattered if it was a car or a truck, a sporty convertible, or classy sedan. All Papa did was take his enforcer, your nana, down to the dealership for the best deal.

A GRAVE DISEASE

DRASTIC TIMES CALL FOR DRASTIC MEASURES, which is why I was on my way to University Hospital near downtown Cleveland for a medical procedure involving radioactive iodine. Doctors had finally given my illness a name. They called it, *Graves' disease*, named for the doctor that first described it back in 1835.

Initially, my primary care physician, Dr. Waggard, diagnosed my red, puffy eyes and blurring vision as allergies and prescribed antihistamines. I told him thyroid disease ran in my family and requested a test. He asked me to give the prescription a chance for the next few weeks, so I went along with his recommendation.

It was then my metabolism began racing out of control, triggering some very concerning symptoms. Signs of hand tremors and extraordinary irritability ensued, followed by overheating. I unintentionally dropped fifteen pounds. My wife, Judi, and the kids watched as I routinely shoveled snow and chopped wood outside in the dead of winter in short sleeves. In the wink of an eye, scary bouts of double vision began interfering with my ability to read, watch television, and even drive.

I was an energetic forty-two-year-old in 1994, in the middle of a very happy, hectic life. My young family was enduringly active and needed my full attention. I was also nurturing an Information Technology career dialed to full-throttle. An experienced Systems Analyst designed and developed software, which meant staring at a computer monitor for hours at a time. I also chaired meetings and managed projects. There wasn't any slack in my daily calendar.

Yet this new predicament surfaced that required my undivided attention. I referenced a medical encyclopedia we kept at home, which seemed to confirm my own diagnosis. These symptoms, in layman's terms, pointed to a thyroid *on the fritz*. I returned to the doctor's office for another consultation, only this time, insistent on a thyroid level test.

The look of concern on Dr. Waggard's face after re-examining me was apparent. He excused himself abruptly to rush across the hall to his office. I watched through the open door as he grabbed a large hardback off the bookcase and skimmed his index finger up and down the pages. He returned by popping his head into the exam room.

"Stay put, please. I'll be right back." There I sat, alone in the exam room, perched on the edge of the table, coming to terms with the fact that this was not going to end well. The stagnant wait-time triggered yet another intense bout of irritation. Dr. Waggard eventually returned with an ophthalmologist named Dr. Welsh, who briefly introduced himself before lifting my jaw to study my face.

"Yes, he has a hyperthyroid," the eye doctor concluded with reasonable confidence. "The *lid-lag* is a telltale sign. Watch him blink. One lid lags behind the other. There, do you see it? Unmistakable. More than likely, Graves' disease brought it on. We'll need to run some tests to confirm it."

A *hyper*thyroid, again in layman's terms, is one *stuck in high gear*. It produces an excessive amount of the hormone thyroxine, and it was responsible for the lengthy list of problems I was experiencing. The nastiest, by far, was the damn double vision. The muscles and tissues around my eyes were gradually swelling and hardening, causing my eyes to twist and bulge. This complication does not necessarily affect every hyperthyroid patient, yet my double vision was coming on like gangbusters. Moreover, mine grew so severe it placed me in the top five percent of total cases. Imagine that, I had beaten impossible odds at something in life, and go figure – it had absolutely nothing to do with winning the lottery.

Who's got time for any of this bullshit? But I guess my lifestyle didn't matter to this disease. We must play the cards dealt in life, like it or not, and I was holding a crappy hand. At the time, I never appreciated when my old Italian grandmother said, *"If a you no lucky in gambling, then you be lucky in a love."*

Dr. Welsh referred me to one of his colleagues that was an eye surgeon specializing in a wide range of eye disorders. Doctor Bernard's reputation preceded him as a leader in his field. He once told me he was *the James Brown of ophthalmology.* Singer James Brown held the title of hardest-working man in show business. And I can attest to that claim because I visited his office once a week for six months running as he closely monitored by optic nerves. Patients from all walks of life packed his waiting room.

The threat of blindness was a real possibility, but not imminent. Yet, I could never get Dr. Bernard to reassure me of this fact. He was not a man to mince words and quite the contrary to warm and fuzzy. Still, I felt there was a sympathetic side in him somewhere dying to get out. After seeing each other as often as we did, an open relationship eventually developed between us. We spoke candidly to each other.

"I can see you're not going to tell me I'm going to be fine."

"If I told you losing your sight could *not* happen, and then it did, you'd say I was some kind of quack. You'd want to sue me."

"Only for your poor bedside manner."

"Your optic nerves are being traumatized."

"So most patients with Graves' disease go blind."

"No, I didn't say that."

"So most of *your* patients with Graves' disease go blind."

"I didn't say that, either."

"Then, some of your patients go blind from it?"

"Now you're putting words in my mouth."

"Then tell me how many of your patients went blind from this."

"None of *my* patients went blind from it."

"So, we can say some people do go blind from it, but none of yours... yet."

"It's possible to go blind when optic nerves are compromised. Yours are."

"You Doctor, are one helluva stubborn man."

"I was thinking the same about you."

"Doctor B, do you know what I do for a living? I study patterns, analyze configurations, and use deduction to find bugs in logic. I think I've gotcha here. Throw this hungry bloodhound a bone."

"All right, already. You'd be *my* first patient to go blind from Graves' disease, but as long as you're under my care, you're going to keep coming here, and I'm going to keep a very close watch to see that you don't become the first. And if things don't improve with initial treatments, we're going to have a serious conversation about a serious eye surgery somewhere down the pike."

"Thank you. See. That makes me feel better! Now was that so damn difficult?" We both smiled. It was like pulling teeth, but he threw me a bone, albeit a small one. And judging how close to the vest he was playing this, it was the best I was going to get from him. Underneath all the banter, two things were clear. I had confidence in him, and he knew I was distraught.

Week after week, Bernard's staff administered vision tests to compare with my baseline scores. They even snapped a photo of my eyes each time to keep a visual record of the physical changes.

The keen vision I once took for granted was unquestionably gone. I found myself wearing corrective eyeglasses with a prescription that changed on average every three months. But these spectacles did absolutely nothing to alleviate the two of everything I was experiencing. The solution? A light-bending prism affixed to my right lens. A medical assistant shaped the flexible piece of plastic with scissors, which adhered easily to the glass. It reduced the problem of double vision, but not completely. The see-through patch wasn't very subtle looking either, but this was no time for vanity.

Prisms come in calibrated degrees of thickness to meet the different levels of severity. I knew this all too well by the time I needed my fourth one.

"Wow, I never ordered one this thick before," the nurse said as she filled out the paperwork. Again with beating the frickin' odds, I thought. "And the thicker ones are less transparent," she added. "You're nearing the max." She was right. Any thicker would be like trying to look through wax paper.

This impairment was also a new level of stress and exhaustion. Driving was becoming a challenge. To combat the double vision, doctors suggested patching one eye while I maneuvered through the streets. It was much harder than I imagined, and going to take some getting used to, especially during rush-hour traffic. I struggled to track movement, judge distance, and perceive depth. It took every ounce of my being to concentrate at sixty miles per hour. I'll admit there were times when I pulled over to the berm to rest for a few minutes. It's precisely why I let Judi drive me to the downtown UH campus that particular morning for a scheduled procedure that had me asking, *"You want me to do what?"*

A thyroid scan confirmed my diagnosis. It helped the hospital doctor, an expert in nuclear medicine, determine the amount of radioactive iodine I had to ingest orally to deactivate my thyroid-gone-wild. I would have a *hypo*thyroid once this nuclear martini stopped it from functioning. At least there are medications to control low thyroid levels. Unfortunately, this wouldn't repair the damage already done to my eyes.

The hospital did not store the radioactive material, so Judi and I went to lunch while waiting for my dosage to arrive. When we returned to the office, a nurse escorted us to a laboratory room to wait for the specialist.

The doctor walked in and immediately turned toward Judi. "Okay, you have to leave the room now," he said while donning a lead vest and a face shield. "You can stand right behind that door with the glass window to watch. I'll join you in a minute." Judi wished me well and darted out of the room.

Then he turned toward me. "All right, are you ready?"

"Any chance of you drinking this stuff while I stand behind the glass window?"

"Relax, this is all precautionary," he said, slipping on thick rubber gloves and picking up a set of long metal tongs. I was standing just a few feet away as he opened the door of a small lead vault. It contained a little glass vial. He stretched to reach it with the tongs and carefully lifted it out, set it down on the table beside me, and inserted a straw.

"Okay, when I leave the room, I want you to suck the contents out of that vial through the straw. I'll signal you through the glass when to start. You have to drink every drop, so I expect to hear slurping. Any questions?"

"Other than are you joking? No."

"You'll do fine," he replied, heading toward safety. Once behind the glass window, he signaled a thumbs-up. "Okay, go ahead."

I looked at Judi, rolled my eyes, and slurped it all

down. Afterward, he gave me strict instructions for the following five days.

"No swapping fluids with anyone and wipe down the toilet after each use. Do you have children?"

"Yes, two young kids and a teenager."

"Don't touch them for a few days, not even to sit on your lap. Questions?"

"G-zus, do I glow in the dark now?"

"No, but you might set off any Geiger counters lying around the house," he joked.

From that point on, I officially needed an endocrinologist to measure and manage my thyroid hormone levels. That's when I met with Dr. Wisen, a recommended doctor about my age. I had a good feeling about him.

Now that we nipped the problem at its source, we needed the disease to run its full course before focusing on the eye damage left in its wake.

The massive amounts of corticosteroids I consumed to reduce the swelling in my eyes had bloated my face into the shape of a soccer ball. Regrettably, it didn't have the intended effect. That's when Dr. Bernard decided to take this fight to the next level by prescribing something more radical called, *orbital radiation therapy*. Small doses of radiation can relieve the swelling in some patients with thyroid eye disease, TED for short. So, it was back to UH, this time to the Ireland Cancer Center for a two-week bout of radiation treatments. Each visit was one to two hours away from my job, so I made my appointments late in the afternoon and went straight home afterward.

The UH campus covered several city blocks, so the parking lot where I left my car was at least a five-minute hike from the cancer center. I walked over a bridge connecting two buildings, down several corridors, up a staircase, and down an elevator before reaching my destination. It added an extra fifteen minutes to my first visit, and probably the second one too.

I checked in, took a seat, and began to peruse the waiting room covertly. I remember feeling a bit trivial while sitting among all the cancer patients. I'm not saying my problem wasn't serious, but I did see my situation as *a glass half full* for the first time. They called me after a short wait.

"Mister, uh, mister, uh..."

"That's me. I'm Jerry."

"Sorry about the last name thing."

"Jerry is fine."

To begin treatment, they needed to make a form-fitting mask to lock my head down to the table. It would prevent any movement as they bombarded radiation to specific locations around my eye sockets. I laid flat on the table as one of the technicians placed a hot, wet plastic-mesh shroud over my neck and head. They made sure it draped snuggly on my skin. Once it dried and hardened, the technician peeled it off and cut holes out for my eyes using a utility knife. She placed it back over my face, only this time it was clamped down and locked to the table. Whoa! The mask was so tight it was impossible to move my face muscles.

The first thing that crossed my mind was, "What the hell would I do in an emergency evacuation?"

"Are you okay, Mr. Jerry?"

"Mm-hmm" was the best I could answer.

Next, they lowered a giant machine over my face and excused themselves from the room. Here we go again, first scans, then radioactive iodine, and now frickin' radiation beams! This gadget fired pinpoint magical rays at the muscles and tissues around my eyes. There was no pain involved in the process, other than the discomfort from that damn mask. After several minutes of this new kind of weirdness, my first radiation treatment was over. Once they removed my mask, it was labeled with my name and placed on a shelf with others. Then I was formally released from captivity. Everyone there was exceptionally kind, but I was still glad to be free of that crushing head shackle.

Then, just when I thought all the absurdity was left behind, another kind of weirdness followed me to the elevator doors. I had the eeriest feeling people were staring at me. They didn't smile or frown. It was more of a sideways glance until I looked back, then they'd turn away. Keep in mind, I was used to curious, indirect looks because of the peculiar prism on my glasses, but these once-overs seemed a bit more obvious. I told myself they were pity stares for a cancer patient and wanted to assure them I wasn't one. But how do you begin that conversation? I kept my head down in the elevator.

Leaving the elevator, I continued my trek back through the maze that got me there, except the glances continued my way. I felt the looks in the corridors, down the staircase, and over the bridge connecting two buildings. Now how the hell did these people know I came from the cancer center? I posed this question to Judi when I got home.

"It's that wild imagination of yours," was her explanation.

"I don't think so. It felt real, almost creepy."

"Then it's stress. You're letting your irritability show."

"You think?"

"Yes, I know so. Try relaxing. Smile a little more and lighten up a bit."

I thought of the furled lines developing between my eyebrows from a yearlong squint and remembered a co-worker telling me I always look pissed.

I conceded. "Maybe you have a point."

"It will be different tomorrow. You'll see."

But it wasn't different. It happened the following day as I left the cancer center. Despite a conscious effort to lighten my mood, smile, and nod more at passersby, I sensed those same subtle, glancing peeks. I briefly mentioned it at dinner but didn't belabor the point. After all, this entire ordeal with my eyes was just as stressful for Judi as it was for me. I didn't need to add my paranoia to the mix. We both needed a break, so I dropped it.

This puzzling sensation of stares remained unsolved the entire first week of treatment until I returned to my car in the parking lot one evening. I sat still for a moment to prepare for another mad rush-hour drive home. I took a deep breath, removed the heavy frames off my nose, and turned the rearview mirror toward my eyes.

There it was, plain as day. The answer to this bizarre mystery was clearly and quite literally plastered across my face. The mesh mask binding me so tightly to the table left a deep, bright red, crisscross pattern etched over my forehead, nose, cheeks, and chin. It looked like I slept face down on a fishnet hammock. I just sat there alone in the parking lot and laughed. Judi never said anything because the marks vanished by the time I arrived home during the thirty-minute ride. I shared my discovery with her over dinner, and she joined me in another good laugh at myself. It was nice to find a little humor in an otherwise miserable situation.

I wish I could say the radiation helped my bulging, crooked eyes after the two-weeks were over, but it did very little. In fact, I don't think it helped one bit.

My weekly appointments with Dr. Bernard continued after the disappointing outcomes from the steroids and the radiation. Then one day, he shared his final plan of attack. It involved an operation to remove bone and fat around my orbits to enlarge the eye sockets. This surgery is known as, *an orbital decompression*. It would reduce the bulging. The good doctor explained how we had to wait for the thyroid medication to stabilize my erratic eyes before we could proceed, unless, of course, my optic nerves were in danger. He specified that this operation was only the first of more to come.

In the meantime, he wanted me to meet another associate surgeon who specialized in the muscles of the eye. Muscle surgeries would hopefully restore my single vision after the decompression. At this point, I joked, "I'll try anything once."

~~~

Now enter Dr. Tivor to the team. Dr. Bernard would perform the decompression operation, setting my eyes back inward, so that Dr. Tivor could realign the muscles around my eyes. He compared it to adjusting new headlights on a vehicle. I was now in the hands of three skilled eye doctors and an endocrinologist. The four of them conferred with each other on occasion.

It was quite an impressive team of doctors working together to get me back to normal – or as close to normal as possible. They told me just having single vision straight ahead and downward to read was realistically par for the course. That was the goal of my super team. Shifting my eyes left, right, and upward would always have limitations. I accepted the prognosis.

Then just before Christmas in 1996, after carefully examining my optic nerves, Dr. Bernard informed me it was time. The extensive and delicate operation took close to eight-hours. I remained hospitalized for several days with patches over both eyes while being judiciously sedated. The only thing I can recall from that stay was hearing voices of the kind spirits tending to me. One, in particular, had an unusually calming effect. I later found out it belonged to an elderly African-American nurse.

"Okay, baby, let me fluff your pillow for you now. That's right, my darling, lift your head, you're doing just fine, sugar." Her angelic voice brought such comfort.

They had me home by Christmas, though I didn't see much of it. And knowing I wouldn't see much of anything for a spell, I bought an electric guitar before the surgery. It was a Christmas present to myself while I convalesced at home. Music was a hobby that didn't require vision. Reading, TV screens, and coaching my son, Zach's indoor soccer team, were activities definitely out of the question.

Once things began to improve, I stayed home alone with my young daughter, Zanni, still too young for kindergarten. We had a wonderful time playing music, watching cartoons, and eating our lunches together. I made our sandwiches cut into different shapes each day for her amusement as well as mine. Her favorite activity was ironically playing *the match game*. Try hunting through rows and columns of cards looking for matched pairs with double vision. In my case, it was two-pairs. No matter, our father-daughter quality time was a treasure.

I was relieved to hear Dr. Bernard proclaim the operation a success. There was no longer any foreseeable danger to my optic nerves. Now it was time for Dr. Tivor to do his thing.

~~~

Right off the bat, my new eye doctor warned me not to expect too much from this next surgery. He said this one was an initial adjustment to bring me *closer* to single vision. We could make more calibrated alterations to the eye muscles in the third operation. Nevertheless, he assured me the master organ of the human body, the brain, would work overtime to make things whole once more.

"Your brain wants single vision back as much as you do," he stated, "so if we can get those muscles close to where they need to be, it will help in the fight."

He was correct about my second eye surgery. The results were, unfortunately, underwhelming. On a positive note, they downsized the thickness of my prism, so I suppose this battle was a small victory in the war waged against this disease. The truth was it left me discouraged. This whole ordeal had worn my patience down to a nub. Yet the fight must go on.

The third hospital trip was the last battle of the war, and this one had a *unique twist*. A pun you'll soon understand. An explanation of the procedure gave me hope while sounding like it came out of a torture chamber from the Dark Ages.

Dr. Tivor planned to use dissolving stitches on the muscles surrounding my inner eyes just as he did in the prior operation. This time, however, he'd leave five inches of the suture thread dangling outside my eyeballs to physically tug while I read an eye chart in a follow-up office visit. Take a minute to let that sink in – strings protruding out of your eyes so someone could yank them while you sit there looking across the room. Who in their right mind consents to an operation like this? Me. Despite his admission that many patients opt-out of this procedure.

Judi drove me to his office a few days after the surgery. There, a nurse gave me a mild sedative to swallow before the doctor entered the room.

"Can I have a few more of those pills?" I joked.

"Sorry, one's all I'm allowed to give you."

Dr. Tivor walked in and greeted us while dimming the lights.

"You have to leave now," he said to Judi. Here we go again, I thought. "Believe me. You don't want to watch this."

When we were alone, I asked, "How badly is this going to hurt, Doc?"

"Well, I won't lie to you. It's not going to be pleasant, but I'll do this as quickly as I can. You must try to relax and focus on the large 'E' on that eye chart on the far wall."

Granted, I've never gone through the agony of childbirth, but I'm going to go out on a limb and guess the pain I felt at least rivaled the miracle of quintuplets. He repeatedly gripped and pulled the goddamn catgut as I fixated on the chart across the room. Better or worse? Better or worse? Better or worse? Finally, after a few minutes of what felt like hours, he stopped the tug-of-war and snipped away the exposed thread. Disappointment soon followed as my vision was no better.

"Keep in mind there's been a massive disturbance in and around your eyes," he explained. "This is going to take some time. You have to be patient. Once the swelling goes down, we'll see how much things have improved. And don't forget, your brain is fighting for you too. Things will get better." I must admit I preferred his encouraging bedside manner to Dr. Bernard's.

It was another leave of absence from work. Two weeks past, and I was still wandering around with that goddamn prism plastered to my glasses. However, I did improve enough to start driving again finally and was able to take Zanni to and from preschool.

Then one day, just as I was leaving to pick up Zanni, my eyes started acting strangely, and not in the right way. The double vision was worsening. "Christ, what now?" By the time I stopped at the first traffic light, my vision had deteriorated. I removed my glasses and began blinking my eyes. The two red traffic lights above me suddenly became one. That's when I realized the prism was causing the double vision this time. I peeled the prism off my lens just before the light turned green.

The emotion I felt the rest of the drive was somewhere between sheer joy and total panic. I held my breath in fear this development was only temporary. Once in the preschool parking lot, I immediately called Judi at work on my first-ever cell phone. This news couldn't wait.

"I'm sorry, but she is teaching in her classroom right now. May I take a message?"

"No. I need you to interrupt her right now," I insisted. "This is her husband." When Judi picked up, I started with this, "Ready for some good news? I'm looking at the light at the end of the tunnel, and there's only one!"

~~~

Twenty years went by before bumping into Dr. Bernard. He stared at me intently as we spoke. I knew he was admiring his work. Eventually, he buckled.

"Hey, mind if I take a picture of you?"

"No, Doc," I replied. "Go right ahead." Two decades later and the hardest working man in ophthalmology was still going strong.

Dr. Tivor moved out of state a year after my last surgery. I wish him nothing but good fortune.

I still see Dr. Wisen for my annual thyroid checkups. We joke how we've grown old together. He's an extraordinary physician.

Dr. Welsh, the first doctor to diagnose my illness, retired after my twenty-fifth annual visit. He is another exceptional physician. The day I met Dr. Welsh was the last time I ever saw that primary care doctor.

~~~

To this day, Papa still has limited peripheral vision, but I make do. And those furled lines on my forehead are still there too, only now they make me look like a grumpy, old Italian man. But the truth is I'm very content in this stage of my life, even when you think Papa is scowling at you.

And what about my young, active family now? Well, we've all grown older, though it feels like they never let me slow down. Maybe that's what is keeping Papa young at heart.

MAID OF THE MIST

NIAGARA FALLS WAS ONLY A THREE-HOUR DRIVE from our home in Concord Township, Ohio. Imagine living so close to a famous wonder of the world, and yet we seemed to take it for granted. By the mid-1990s, I had been there several times in my life, and so had my wife Judi, but this would be a completely new experience for our two young children. Our son, Zach, was almost eight, and our little daughter Alexandra, Zanni for short, was five. The family was taking a mini-trip in our brand new Dodge Caravan. We also invited Judi's parents along as we headed east for a fun, autumn, get-away weekend.

It was an easy drive through Pennsylvania to New York that warm Saturday afternoon, and back in those days, it was just as easy to drive across the border into Canada. The three-hour ride went by quickly, especially playing games along the way to pass the time. After registering into our hotel, we headed over to the falls for a quick preview before going to dinner.

The next day was filled with marveling at the

magnificence of this natural wonder from the observation decks. We even stood behind the falls in those human-made tunnels and strolled along the Great Gorge. When the kids had their fill of water attractions, we visited the famous Tussaud's Waxworks Museum and shopped for souvenirs. We did everything we wanted to do, everything except for one major attraction – the Maid of the Mist.

"Jer, do you think we have time to take the boat tour?" Judi asked. "It would be a great experience for the kids."

"I was thinking the same thing."

The Maid of the Mist carries passengers up the Niagara River, from the calm waters near the Rainbow Bridge, passed the American Falls to the swirling, misty waters of the thundering Horseshoe Falls.

"Could we, please, please, please," Zach begged.

"I ain't goin' on no boat," Zanni insisted.

"Why not, Zan?" I asked.

"Cause I won't go," was her firm and only reason. I suspected she was frightened.

"Well, let's just wait to see what everyone decides."

The adults looked at each other and smiled. Everyone wanted to see the falls from this unique perspective; everyone except Zanni, and I knew she would love it too, given a chance to experience it. I walked through a few more gift shops with the family before checking my watch. Judi and I had to work the next day.

"We should go now if we're going to do this," I said to Judi.

"Do what?" Zanni interrupted.

"Go on the Maid of the Mist."

"I'm not going. I'm not going!" She began tearing up.

We took turns explaining how safe it was and how fun it would be, but Zanni would have no part in it. I finally had to go into *dad-mode*.

Now I can't speak for everybody, but in most Italian families, dad-mode has three settings – loud, louder, and dead silent. Loud is the standard setting. It's what the family is used to experiencing. Loud requires no skill.

Louder is very useful in situations requiring immediate results, especially in emergencies. Louder is a no-nonsense tone perfect for ending any talkback. It's not one to overuse, or it loses its dramatic effect. So use it sparingly. Louder also requires no skill.

The dead silent mode is unique, perfect for developing a child's intuition by sharpening their self-awareness skills. It's an unsettling, obscure, deadpan stare as the lower jaw slightly protrudes. Done correctly, it will provoke a child to question, "What am I doing wrong right now, and how can I fix this?" It may require some practice but can be developed over time, although Italian fathers seem to be naturals in this mode.

However, I used the classic American approach on this day – *Father Knows Best*.

"Okay, Zanni, let's walk everyone down to the water, then you and I can just watch them from the pier."

"I'll go, but I'm not gettin' on a boat."

"Okay. Hold my hand."

When we got to the ticket booth, Judi bought a handful of tickets while the rest of us watched a boat filled with passengers taking off.

"Let's walk down with the family so we can watch them waiting in line," I said to Zanni. "Then, we'll stand where we can wave to everyone once they're aboard."

"Okay, but I'm not getting in line."

"All right."

We reached the end of the pier and stopped at the back of a line of people waiting for the next boat to arrive.

"This looks like a line," Zanni correctly observed.

"Well, if we wait here in line with them, we can talk until the boat comes. We'll be close enough to see Zach's face when he gets on board because he's going to have so much fun – you know, without us." Zanni looked up at me, so I gave her a wide grin.

"But I'm not really in line," she insisted.

"Okay. You're not really in line."

We watched an approaching boat dock. I saw another opportunity as passengers covered in mist and delight disembarked.

"Boy, oh boy, Zan, they sure look happy," I said. "Look at that brave little kid with his parents right there. I bet he'd go again if they let him." She watched as the boy skipped along next to his family. She kept silent.

As the line inched forward, we confronted a man distributing blue waterproof ponchos.

"How many?" the man asked.

"Two, please," I answered with Zanni listening.

"What are you doing?" she asked.

"I'm taking ponchos. The man thinks we're in line, so I had to take them."

"Okay, but I'm not putting that thing on."

"Think of all those people that got off. I didn't see one unhappy face."

"They were all wet," was her response.

"Only their ponchos were wet. They were nice and dry underneath."

When we got to the gangplank, our family began boarding. I reached for Zanni's hand again.

"Zan, let's go aboard with them," I said. She scowled and stopped dead in her tracks.

"You're taking me on this boat ride, aren't you?"

I kneeled down at eye level with her. Now comes the moment of truth.

"Would I ever do anything to hurt you?" She looked down, lightly shaking her head in response. "Okay, so if you always trusted me before, I want you to trust me now." Her lower lip quivered. "We have to get on now, Zan, there's a line of people behind us waiting to have fun." Judi and I each extended a hand, and the three of us crossed the gangplank.

"Tell you what," Judi said, "let's go stand right in the center, away from all the sides."

The family walked to the middle of the boat and donned our ponchos.

"I want to see the water," Zach said. Judi's parents escorted him to the side railing. Judi and I kept Zanni busy by reminiscing of all the fun we had during the day. We asked questions and rambled on about anything that popped into our heads to keep her distracted.

The boat jostled and whistled as we left the pier, and the passengers began waving goodbye to those next in line. We started in calm waters just as the brochure mentioned, which soon became too dull for Zanni. Her eyes shifted toward the river.

"Where's Zach?"

"Do you want to move a little closer to the water?" Judi asked. "He's right over there looking over the rail with your grandparents. He sure looks excited."

Zanni grabbed my hand and pulled me in tow toward her brother. Before long, she was peering over the side on her own. The mist thickened, and the sound of rushing water grew louder as we approached the Horseshoe Falls. I moved closer and grabbed a handful of her poncho out of instinct.

"Easy does it, Zanni-girl," I warned. It's what I often called her.

"I'm okay, Daddy. Look, the water's gettin' foamy. Let's go to the other side." She turned and ran to the opposite side of the boat. We chased behind. "Look, it's foamy here too," she said, leaning over the side.

"Please be careful, Alexandra," Judi said, laughing. She looked at me and shrugged her shoulders. "Apparently, Zanni isn't scared anymore."

"Dad, can I touch the water?"

"No, you may not!"

"Do you feel the wet on your face?" our fearless daughter asked. "It feels cold."

And not surprisingly, Zanni asked if we could stay on the boat and go one more time. We opted to head back home.

~~~

All of Papa's children grew up to become successful adults. Zanni-girl is a brave, strong woman, and an excellent mastered educator. Of course, I still have to go into dad-mode now and again when she's trying something new and needs a little extra coaxing. But all I really have to say is, "Remember the Maid of the Mist."

THE PLANE TRUTH

"THE TERRORISTS HAVE WON," a stranger exclaimed to passengers seated around us as we sat motionless on the tarmac. Several people on the plane nodded in agreement. It happened shortly after September 11, 2001. After that day, the fun had pretty much been sucked out of air travel forever.

In the prior century, most folks considered commercial flights to be a pleasant adventure. Some might even go so far as to say a little exotic. You reserved a seat on a plane, boarded the flight, and then ate, drank, and even smoked your way across the skies. All the while, an attentive crew of flight attendants overly pampered you with pillows, blankets, and moist towelettes.

And flying was practically as uncomplicated as public land transportation. There were no excessive security barriers or extreme policies infringing on the appeal of a bustling airport. Nevertheless, my wife, Judi, and I were about to find out just how bad things had changed.

We packed lightly that morning for our extended

summer get-a-way weekend. We were off to see relatives living in horse country near the beautiful foothills of the Smoky Mountains in North Carolina. John and Hedy retired to the quaint little town of Tryon sixteen years earlier. Their resort-like home rested snuggly between a rolling patchwork of meadow and a forest of loblolly pines. The four of us were always close. We visited each other as often as our hectic schedules allowed.

Tryon is roughly 600 miles from our home in Cleveland. The closest airport to them was forty minutes away in Greer, South Carolina. The picturesque airport was Greenville-Spartanburg International.

"We look forward to seeing you," Aunt Hedy exclaimed from their speakerphone that morning.

"And she's been cooking up a storm all week," Uncle Johnny added. Aunt Hedy was an excellent cook and always made my favorite dishes when we traveled down to see them.

"We'll call you after we land and rent a car," Judi said. "We should be there for dinnertime."

The direct flight we once enjoyed took about four-hours, door-to-door, but was no longer available. We needed a connecting flight now, usually through Charlotte, which added another two hours. Still, the extra time to see family in the warm, sunny south was worth every minute.

We arrived at Cleveland Hopkins International a

couple of hours early to an obvious situation inside the terminal. Two long, menacing lines filled with hundreds of travelers stretched toward the security corridors – a telltale sign that this was not going to be a typical commute. I had never seen the terminal so packed with people.

"I hope those aren't the lines through security," Judi said.

"We're in big trouble if they are," I replied.

The check-in line was also unusually long, but they finally tagged our one bag and verified our boarding passes. "You're leaving from gate E28. Have a great flight," bid the woman at the counter.

"Please tell me those aren't the lines to get there," I said.

"I'm afraid so," she replied, slightly wincing. "Either one. Take your pick. For some unknown reason, things got backed up. The one on the left looks a little shorter."

We queued-up like everyone else and stood for over an hour, inching ever so slowly toward the gates before it became clear that we were now in a time crunch.

"We're not gonna make our flight," I said to Judi.

She was thinking the same thing. "Stay here." And before I could say any more, my determined traveling companion started walking up the long line that curved in toward the restricted area. I watched as she marched to the front of the line and approached one of the security agents. The woman stood as they spoke.

After their brief discussion, Judi turned to someone in line and began another conversation. A few seconds later, she looked my way and waved me forward. I was hesitant to leave my place in line, so I shrugged my shoulders as if to say, "What's going on?" She repeated her action, this time more animated. I reluctantly walked out of line toward the security entrance.

"I asked the security lady if we could cut in line, so we don't miss our flight," Judi explained, "and she said as long as everyone else in front of us gave their permission."

"What? I'm supposed to ask fifty people if we can cut in front of them?"

"Well, that was her solution until this kind young lady said we could stand in front of her. So, I accepted." She pointed to a young woman wearing a Kent State University sweatshirt standing nearby. She overheard Judi's dilemma and took pity.

"That's right. It's okay," the college student repeated. "Just get in right here in front of me."

I wondered what the people behind us were thinking but not enough to decline the offer. We cut in line and exchanged pleasantries with our young savior, thanking her several more times as we inched our way into the restricted area. As it turned out, her destination was Charlotte too.

After zigzagging our way three more times to the baggage X-ray machine, we heard an announcement over the loudspeaker coming from one of the gates in front of us. "This is the final boarding call for flight 6739 to Greenville, South Carolina. Gate E28."

"My god, that's us," Judi gasped. "We're still not going to make it!"

The departing gate was a good city block away. I grabbed my shoes and the rest of my belongings from the X-ray conveyer belt.

"I'll make a run for it and stall them," I said. "Just get there as fast as you can!" I turned and left without her.

Do you know how you see people running frantically through the airport, and you think, *"Poor shmuck, better you than me?"* Well, this time, I was the poor shmuck. A young man sprinted by me as I jogged down the corridor. "There goes another one," I supposed. He turned out of sight at gate E28. Hopefully, he bought me some time.

Arriving at the gate, I tried explaining the long lines behind me to the attendants, but they seemed indifferent to the situation. So I put my backpack down on the floor, retied both of my shoes, and then fished around inside my stuffed backpack for the ticket that I knew was tucked inside my pocket.

We boarded the small jet together after Judi arrived out of breath. The good news was our assigned seats were the first two in the front row, next to the door.

"Last on, first off. What a relief!" I joked as we buckled our seatbelts. We both took a deep breath. "Look at all this legroom. I can stretch my legs straight out."

I quickly pulled my feet back under me as the stewardess reached for the door's handle to close it. That's when I realized someone was missing.

"Uh-oh, where's the girl?" I asked Judi.

"Who?"

"The girl... the girl from Kent State. Where is she?"

"Oh no, she didn't make it," Judi said, cupping her mouth. "She let us cut in, and now she's missed her flight. I feel horrible."

Just as I was about to plead with the flight attendant, our college heroine shot through the door. We exchanged a high-five.

I naively turned to Judi. "This trip can only get better, right?"

~~~

We were about twenty minutes from Charlotte when the pilot picked up the intercom. "Ladies and gentlemen, this is your pilot, Captain Ray speaking. We have confirmed there is bad weather ahead. It is currently not possible to land in Charlotte at this time. Several tornadoes have touched down near the airport. Hundreds of severe storms are currently causing delays throughout the southern states. The bottom line is we are being diverted to the nearest safe airport just as a precaution. We don't know how long the delay will last, but I will keep you updated. For those of you with connecting flights in Charlotte, there will be someone at the gate to help you once we arrive. I'm sorry for the delay, but your safety comes first. Thank you."

A chorus of sighs and mumbles swept through the cabin. I wasn't the only one annoyed by the bad news. Now we're going to sit someplace, who the hell knows where, and waste more precious time. Then, a glimmer of hope.

"Ladies and gentlemen, this is Captain Ray, again. I just received word that we will be landing at the Greenville-Spartanburg Airport in South Carolina. They are expecting us in about thirty-five minutes. Thank you."

Judi and I looked at each other. Did he just say what I think he just said? Are we landing at our final destination? The attendant standing three feet in front of us joined the jubilation. Her name was Pearl, according to her badge.

"Guess what, Pearl? That's our final destination," I said. "We're going to be in Greenville two-hours ahead of our schedule."

"I know," she said with a snicker, "I saw it on the passenger manifest. And I'm going in to tell the captain about it right now. I'm sure they'll let you off when we get there."

"What about our luggage? It's one suitcase. Will that be a problem?"

"No, it's just a matter of pulling it out of the luggage compartment."

I was highly skeptical until she returned ten minutes later with an encouraging message from the pilot. "Captain Ray said they'd pull your bag out once we land and get settled."

"I take back every bad thing I ever said about your airline," I said, teasing Pearl. "You're the best attendant in the world." She snickered again.

~~~

We touched down at GSP as schedule and taxied the runways for a few minutes, before rolling to a dead stop. The engines shut off, and the cabin air quickly began warming up inside. Pearl opened the cabin door to a gush of fresh air. It was hot Carolina air, but at least now it was circulating. Then she re-entered the cockpit. I leaned forward and looked out the open hatch. We were nowhere near any building.

Suddenly, a convoy of police cars encircled our isolated aircraft a hundred yards away. Some of the officers got out of their vehicles. Others remained inside. All of them began speaking on their radios.

"Well, this doesn't look very promising," I said to the attendant upon her return.

"The pilot will be out shortly," she replied in a quiet tone. "He wants to talk to you personally."

"Here we go!" I said to Judi. "We're not getting off this goddamn plane." My new admiration for the airline evaporated into the southern heat. A minute later, the cockpit door swung open and out stepped a uniformed man in his late forties.

"Hello, are you Jerry and Judith?" he asked, politely.

"Yes, we are."

"Hi, I'm Captain Ray. Say listen, I'm really sorry about all this, but I just spoke to security, and they're not letting anyone off this plane. It's for the protection of everyone."

"I made that deduction the minute you shut the engines down out here in the middle of nowhere," I replied. "What's with all the security out there?"

"They're making sure no one enters or leaves the plane."

"Well, I guess that's that," was Judi's response. There was no need to pursue this any further. I understood no one on the plane had any control over this situation.

"Then there's the weather," Captain Ray added, in an attempt to appease me. He took out his smartphone. "Let me show you the satellite view in this area. The Carolina's alone have already reported over a hundred tornadoes today. The tower here says we must be ready to depart at a moment's notice. I'm sorry. I know it doesn't make any sense." He was genuine.

A voice interrupted our conversation from across the aisle. "The terrorists have won!" A man had been listening to our discussion along with everyone else within earshot.

"They've won," someone else repeated. Several heads nodded in agreement.

"Well, that may or may not be true," I said, "but they're the one's in charge." I pointed to the law enforcement surrounding our aircraft. The captain wisely remained silent.

"Thank you both for at least trying," Judi said to Captain Ray and Pearl. "We appreciate the effort."

The pilot returned to the cockpit to await his orders. The attendant closed the hatch about an hour later. We eventually taxied to an open runway and flew to Charlotte in order to catch our connecting flight back to, you know, the Greenville-Spartanburg Airport.

Of course, we missed our connection in Charlotte due to our unscheduled stop at our final destination. Are you with me?

The impromptu layover cost us another five-hours. Wasted time we can never have back. We made it to Tryon by nightfall. Aunt Hedy warmed up our cold dinners, and the four of us had another beautiful North Carolina visit together. Happily, the return trip home was uneventful.

~~~

Ever since that trip, whenever your old Papa stands in a long security line at the airport, I can't help but wonder if those passengers were right. Did the terrorists win? Then Nana usually tells me to relax and drags me to a seat near the corridor where we can sit together and people-watch. There are plenty of oddballs to observe at an airport. I enjoy making up stories about them to entertain Nana. It helps to pass the time.

DEARS IN HEADLIGHTS

I WAS ABLE TO RECALL THE ONCOMING headlights after my wife, Judi, finished telling me how the story ended. The entire incident happened so fast it was over as quickly as it began. No one in the car was injured, and that's all that really mattered to me.

My dear family and I were returning home from a nearby party late one Saturday night. It was an outdoor summer festivity, hot, and muggy. A minute from home, the blasting air conditioning was just beginning to cool down the car. I was driving my beloved red, '91 Jeep Cherokee. So beloved, in fact, I referred to it as *Big Red*. Judi was in the passenger seat next to me. Our kids, Zach and Zanni, aged nine and six, played a word game in the back seat.

It happened as we cruised up the narrow, winding hill leading to our house in a rural area of Northeast Ohio. It's a quiet and desolate country road, especially in the black of night. A route we so often travel, I never gave the steep ravine to our right a second thought, especially with the brand new guardrail safeguarding us from the abyss below. The drive had been, up to this point, uneventful. There was no bracing for what happened next.

In an instant and without warning, a dark, ominous shadow rose from the cliff like a black tidal wave. It appeared to loom over Big Red for a moment until the ghostly silhouette maneuvered effortlessly away onto the narrow berm, avoiding a collision. Now it looked to be floating on thin air alongside us as we continued forward at the legal speed limit. Suddenly, a dreadful thud boomed against the front passenger fender before I could react. Judi screamed, and the children gasped.

A large stag had leapt over the guardrail, panicked, and then careened off my freshly polished front fender. Now it was nowhere in sight. I quickly checked the rearview mirror but saw nothing in the darkness behind. We reached our street by that time, so I signaled left and coasted homeward. Everyone began breathing again and responded at the same time.

"What was that?"

"What just happened?"

"Aren't you even going to stop?"

"It was a deer, it hit us, and why bother," I answered. "Everything is fine. You can all relax."

"I can't believe you hit a deer," Judi said.

"Yeah, well, technically, he hit me, not the other way around. And it only grazed the side of our car, that's all.

I'm sure he's already long gone. Besides, we're home now. We'll make sense of it here."

I failed to admit my concern was more for Big Red than the damn, bushwhacking buck. I pressed the button on the garage door opener as we pulled up the driveway.

"Well, I'm going back to check on him!" Judi said, walking straight to her car.

"Ooh, can we come with you, Mom?"

"Yes, get in kids," Judi said, without ever taking her eyes off me. "Are you seriously not coming?"

"Yes, I'm seriously not coming." That's when she mumbled something about a deer and a jackass.

After watching them drive back into the darkness, I turned my attention toward Big Red. To my delight, there was no damage, no blood, not so much as a smudge as far as I could see. I smiled. "God protects small animals and idiots," I said to myself, and then waltzed into the house to watch television until my dears returned.

Almost twenty minutes passed before I decided I'd better see what was keeping my family. Clearly, I hadn't shown much compassion towards the animal or the situation in general. A little guilt was beginning to creep in, so I rose from the sofa as I heard Judi's car pulling into the garage. I walked out to greet them, fully expecting to hear how there was no trace of the woodland creature. Instead, Judi sprang from the car visibly shaken.

"Uh-oh, is everything okay?"

"Yes, but, oh my God, this is way too crazy!" Judi said. "If I gave you a hundred chances, no, a thousand chances, you'd never guess what happened."

"I'm all ears," I replied, glad she was no longer annoyed with me. The kids ran into the house while I stood in the garage with Judi as she began telling a tale so incredibly bizarre it sounded like pure fiction. Except I knew my wife would never make up a tale this far-fetched.

Upon her arrival, Judi encountered a man standing beside a parked car on the roadside. His high-beam headlights were fixed on a large stag straddling the median. Both man and beast appeared locked in a motionless stare-off. The stranger broke his concentration long enough to glance over his shoulder, then quickly turned back. Judi stopped behind the vehicle and switched on her hazard lights.

"Kids, stay in the car," she ordered.

"Awe c'mon, Mom, I want to come too," Zach pled.

"Absolutely not, wait here with your little sister!"

Judi left the car and cautiously approached the frozen man, stopping just behind him. The Good Samaritan broke his trancelike silence without ever turning his head to look at her.

"I was driving down the street when this big red Jeep heading toward me hit this deer. He didn't even stop. Can you believe it?"

Judi shifted her eyes toward him and then quickly

focused back on the deer again before she responded. "He doesn't appear to be injured," she answered, deliberately ignoring his reference to our Cherokee.

"I hope you're right," was his response. The stare-off continued.

"He's going to be fine," Judi said.

"Yes, I think you're right. It's stunned, that's all," the man said with a sigh of relief. "If we go now, he'll leave too." The man turned toward Judi, blinked for the first time, and nodded with a grin.

And here's where it all went to hell. At that very moment, a speeding sedan interrupted their quiet departure. Unfortunately, the petrified animal remained bewitched by the man's headlights.

By now, you've guessed the outcome. Judi and the stranger watched in horror as the vehicle sealed the deer's fate that night. The startled motorist attempted to swerve away, but it was too little, too late. He stopped the car for a moment but only checked for damage before getting back in and driving away. Can you believe it?

"I gotta go. I've got kids in the car," Judi said to the stranger, cajoled into another speechless trance. She took a step backward, turned, and scurried to her children, leaving the scene as she first saw it. Well, not quite as she first saw it.

Thankfully, little Zanni was strapped into the back seat of the car and spared the gruesome sight. Her big brother wasn't quite so fortunate. Zach experienced the entire fiasco in full-living color from the front passenger seat.

Now I was the one standing like a dear in headlights after Judi's account of the incident. "Is... is it dead?"

"Oh, trust me. It's dead," she assured me. I shut off the garage lights as we entered the house. Judi paused in the hallway to finish her thought. "You know what, Jer, I feel terrible. We need to do something about this, right?"

"Are you kidding me? What could we possibly do now? You do realize it's after midnight," I argued, again catching myself sounding insensitive.

She ignored my tone. "I don't know. How about calling the sheriff's office? I mean, there's a large dead animal sprawled all over the road out there. It could still cause an accident. Would you do that for me, please, so I can sleep tonight?" She tilted her head, made a frowny face, and I caved.

"Oh, all right." I did my good deed for the day by picking up the phone and alerting the sheriff's department of the massive roadkill.

"That's right, officer. No damage to any vehicles. Just the deer in the road."

"Is it dead?"

"According to my wife and son, without a doubt."

"Do you want the carcass, sir? If so, it's yours for the taking."

"Uh-uh, no, thank you," I answered. "I'm just reporting this so nothing else happens over there tonight."

"And we appreciate that. We'll send someone to check it out. Have a good rest of the night." And with that, my penance was paid in full.

The next morning, Judi hopped back into her car to check out the scene from the night before. Her final report was not nearly as dramatic. The road was clear of all deer and dumbfounded strangers.

~~~

Papa used this opportunity for another life lesson the following day at dinnertime. I asked the family what each thought the moral should be for this story. The kids both agreed you should always look both ways before crossing the street. Nana said it's best to let your conscience be your guide. My take-away was that sometimes ignorance is bliss. Each has its merit, but here's one I think we can all agree upon – It's never a good idea to stare... Sorry, I couldn't resist!

MORE THAN A GAME

WHEN I LEFT TEACHING to break into the new world of computer technology during the early eighties, it left a void in me that needed filling. I had developed an appreciation and a passion for education back in college when I tutored children for three years in the Cleveland Public Schools. The following six years were in my own sometimes overly crowded classroom. It was a career filled with energy and excitement.

Suddenly, I find myself trapped in a quiet office all day, speaking *computerese* to a cold box of wires and circuits. I've gone from one end of the communal spectrum to the other. The pay was lucrative enough to keep me there, but I needed something to replace the human connection I'd grown accustomed to from the previous era. I took up golf and let it consume me, but realistically, where was all the organized chaos?

So, I jumped without hesitation to coach a co-ed youth soccer team when it presented itself in the mid-1990s. In addition to teaching in the classroom back in the day, I taught physical education and directed an after-school program called Sports Club. Soccer was one of the activities we played, so the game was already familiar to me.

Coaching soccer began when my son Zach turned five, and Judi signed him up for an Under-6 team. I drove him to his first practice at Kruger Park in Mentor, where we introduced ourselves to Coach Glenn. I offered my help in any way he saw fit, and without hesitation, he turned to his small team.

"Hey everyone, I want you to meet Coach Jerry." It took me by surprise, but I was more than delighted. It felt like Sports Club all over again. An old passion revived. I jumped headfirst into the bits and bytes of a sport the world calls *football*, and its most dedicated fans refer to as, *the beautiful game.*

After our daughter Zanni turned five, I added head coach to the mix. It was the beginning of year-round sports for my immediate family with soccer as our flagship activity. I found myself crisscrossing from one squad to the other and back again – indoor, outdoor, practices, league play, and tournament games filled our family calendar.

Of course, we couldn't have done it without Judi coordinating our hectic schedule. She helped out wherever she could, supporting our children, their teams, and me, making this the best possible experience imaginable.

~~~

Zanni's earliest co-ed recreation teams performed incredibly well, despite my inexperience as a head coach. To compensate, I combined my teaching knowledge with my understanding of system configurations to organize the bedlam typically found on a youth soccer field. As our opponents swarmed around the ball like bees to honey, we focused on a simple formation. I used imaginary boundaries on the field with an emphasis on passing the ball to open teammates waiting to receive it *away* from the beehive.

Practice sessions began routinely enough with technical training to develop dribbling, passing, and shooting skills. And the team learned all the positions on the field and their purpose. But I dedicated a portion of time to some very elementary tactical instruction by dividing the field into three lanes stretching from goal to goal using colored saucer cones. I named the center lane, *"the driveway."* I encouraged players to stick to the side of the field assigned to them but stressed the driveway was there for everyone. There was one special request for the magic center strip. Players must avoid drifting off the far side unless they found it necessary. After all, this is a game requiring fast and free decision-making. This tactic allowed every position two-thirds of the field length to operate.

I also trained the defensive backline to move in-sync with each other. It's a basic soccer tactic where the closest defender goes to win the ball while the other defenders shift behind in support. Drilling the term *"windshield wipers"* as a word association was my mantra. We rehearsed it repeatedly – back and forth, and back and forth, again and again like the wipers on the family car.

Association is a building block to learning. So are fun rewards and penalties, referred to as *carrots and sticks*, which are used to reinforce it.

Finally, on game days, I'd crouch down in front of our goal with the team huddled behind me. We visualized how the driveway was still there, stretching down to the opponent's goal, only now *invisible*. Some swore they could actually see it. While I was down there, I used my dry-erase clipboard to sketch each player's assigned position. Of course, every child had equal playing time in all games and tried each position, including the goalkeeper.

My harshest critics believed my strategic campaign went overboard, claiming U6 was too young to teach these concepts. The results proved otherwise. We basked in praise of spectators, referees, and opposing coaches for the synchronized effort. The team went easily undefeated that season, both outdoor and indoor.

The following fall season, the club president advised me he received calls from parents inquiring about my team. Some wanted on while others accused us of stacking the talent deck. To me, it was purely reducing the game down to its lowest common denominator.

Regardless, the club appeased our accusers by passing a new rule to shuffle all but three players on every team. Only the system worked again, producing another perfect season, indoors and outdoors. By the third season, I received all but three players with no soccer experience. The undefeated seasons were over, but still one helluva run.

In the travel league years to follow, the close-knit families of our teams were fantastic. Our loyal supporters trekked from game to game, and tournament to tournament, making the entire experience worth all the effort.

Woven into the travel league era came middle and high school soccer. I was fortunate enough to coach teams at those schools too.

Eventually, Judi and I watched our children play soccer in college. Attending university games was an entirely new level of excitement for me. And it took some getting used to being the proud parent cheering from the bleachers.

Zach's college soccer career at Ashland University was noteworthy. He received an athletic and academic scholarship. During his sophomore year, the men's team was nationally ranked in the NCAA for division two and went undefeated during the regular season. He also had the most team minutes of play recorded that year. That year was incredibly exciting.

I remained coaching, playing, and learning during that time. One of my favorite experiences was attending clinics organized by coaches from the Italian youth squad of A.C. Milan, my favorite professional team at the time. I drove my family from Cleveland to Maryland one summer weekend when Italy's Milan played England's Chelsea in a summer tour of the United States. I'll just tell you it's a super soccer fan's dream weekend.

I coached high school soccer for six consecutive years before returning to club soccer as my coaching career wound down. Eventually, I hung up my whistle and clipboard about the same time I retired from my computer profession. In all, the soccer community had given me twenty meaningful years on which to reflect. There are more keepsake memories than I'm able to recollect, but when pressed to give my favorite, two in particular jump out at me.

~~~

The first happened very early on with Zanni's powerhouse U7 co-ed team. It was a winter session, so we were playing on a small indoor field. As usual, the halftime score was lopsided enough in our favor for me to place restrictions on scoring more goals in the second half. These constraints varied to keep the players thinking as they sharpened their skills.

For example, I might say they could only touch the ball twice before having to pass it to another teammate. Or the player dribbling into the penalty area had to find someone else to take the shot on goal. Sometimes I asked them to score a goal using his or her weaker foot. I knew which foot each player favored. I often incorporated new skills into the restriction.

However, this particular day, I chose a new second-half challenge. Only Adam could shoot on goal. They were to bring the ball downfield and then pass to their teammate Adam. His job was to get into a position to receive the ball and shoot on goal. All of my players were very excited about Adam. He was the only player that didn't score a goal during the earlier fall season. He was neither the fastest nor the most skilled player on the team, but he tried hard and attended every practice and game.

When halftime ended, the players took the field and kept their eyes peeled on our target player. I was so proud of everyone doing his and her best to make this happen for him. Still, Adam was having great difficulty scoring his first goal – *ever*. I pulled him out for a short rest and a drink of water, then put him right back into the game. The parents soon caught on to what we were doing and began cheering for him every time he touched the ball. I watched his mother's face in the stands as people yelled his name. She was so excited and nervous at the same time. I was too.

It happened with only a few minutes left in the game. Adam received a pass and scored. The entire place erupted in celebration as if he just scored the winning goal in a World Cup match. Even some of the parents from the opposing team stood and applauded for our *player of the match*. Adam's teammates all congratulated him as he beamed with joy. It took me a minute to compose myself. After all, Adam was dealing with *cerebral palsy*. This feat was a team accomplishment on multiple levels and a top contender for my best coaching experience ever.

~~~

The other nominee for favorite coaching memory happened toward the end of my soccer career. It was a U14 team from the inner city of Painesville comprised almost entirely of Spanish speaking boys. A couple spoke no English.

I took an immediate liking to this group, which had everything to do with the fact that they reminded me of my own youthful years growing up in Cleveland's inner city. Like my old Italian gang from back then, these kids were good-natured, high-spirited, and street smart.

Most had exceptional ball skills and a good understanding of the game. The boys got along well and supported each other, but they lacked two critical components of play that stifled their potential.

The first was sharing the ball. Individually, they were

a joy to watch when it came to juggling, dribbling, and shooting. Yet, despite these required foot skills, they collectively lacked the mindset or at least the desire to pass the ball. Their emphasis was on flashy footwork with a *dribble 'til you lose it* mentality.

The second was defense. Most of the boys seemed to feel protecting our goal was the backline's job exclusively. "Maybe you'd like a seat in the bleachers to watch the game," was something I'd say to grab their attention. "The name of the game is 'score goals', but defense wins championships," was another one of my favorites.

I'm not sure what caused this widespread epidemic, but I can speculate it had something to do with practicing for hours alone. No matter, teamwork became my top coaching priority to unlock the potential I saw in them. Selecting the right activities to address their needs lasted all pre-season and beyond. I began to see positive results through repetition and the correct proportions of carrots and sticks.

My next major issue involved logistics. The intercity travel league we were part of had teams from all across Lake and Geauga counties. Frankly, I had a parent problem. Very few adults were showing up at our games, especially the away games. The parents of my players had good reasons for not attending. I knew most had jobs requiring long hours away from home, but now it was up to me to find a way to transport them. They were working so hard. Game-day was their reward.

Fortunately, one of the fathers that did attend games volunteered his services. He owned a full-size utility vehicle, and together we hatched a plan. Players needing a ride game day gathered at the home of a boy living near the center of town. The two of us piled everyone into both our cars. Problem solved. In the past, I resisted transporting players for safety reasons but took a chance for these boys. The players and their parents seemed grateful.

I must admit I enjoyed chatting with my players about various topics unrelated to soccer on our way to and from games. They'd ask me questions like did I go to college, where I worked, and how much my house and car cost.

Each one had a great sense of humor, teasing me about what to do if the police pulled me over *"with all these immigrants in your car."* It both surprised and impressed me. Immigration was a touchy subject then, and they were very well aware of it.

Most of the boys communicated fine, but for the few that had trouble with English, I had a secret weapon.

Clemente, my assistant coach, helped me direct the players to stay focused and organized during games.

"Coach Clemente, tell the midfield to push up and join in the attack!"

He'd call them by their numbers. "¡Ocho – Arriba! ¡Nueve – Vamos!"

"Clemente, please remind Tico this is a *team* sport and to pass the ball!"

"¡Tres, pase el balón – por favor!"

"Get back! Get back and support!"

"¡Hola – Defensa – hola!"

Judi attended some of our games. The boys would ask her to look after their valuables while they played. "Thank you, Mrs. Coach's wife," one of them would say.

The boys received many compliments on their entertaining style of play. I continued drumming combination play and team defense into everyone's head throughout the season *ad nauseam*. The team responded by presenting me with another undefeated season at the end of my career.

The only downside to that exceptional year was witnessing, first-hand, occasional slurs aimed at my Spanish speaking team. The comments came from opposing players and even some adults frustrated by our talent. I dealt with these incidents as they arose and admit the cutting remarks made winning just that much sweeter. I am proud to have coached these boys to this day.

~~~

Now, during Papa's retirement years, I still have a passion for the sport and enjoy sharing it with people who feel the same way I do. Watching matches gives us something to discuss when we get together. I still love playing too, although my body puts limits on how often. One of my biggest thrills is playing alongside some of the young men and women I once coached as children. Better still is playing together with my own kids. This beautiful game is a global phenomenon bringing people from all walks of life together. I can only hope I've given back as much as I've taken from a sport that is so much more than a game.

ANNE'S KITCHEN (EULOGY)

ANNE'S KITCHEN was the center of our Italian-American universe. It's where our family lives played out every day. I can testify to this fact as the youngest of Anne's four children and her only son. Our home had an open-door policy for everyone. No invitation was ever needed. You just showed up to a welcome of hugs and kisses. It was Grand Central Station with all the comforts of a warm, happy household.

Anne's kitchen is where the feasts were prepared and served. And the fragrant aromas changed from spaghetti sauce to bakery to fresh-brewed coffee. It's where we sang songs and played live music. Wild card games often sprang up spontaneously around her kitchen table. You could even get a kitchen haircut from her husband during the sing-a-longs or between shuffles.

Sometimes there was just casual conversation in Anne's kitchen as the "Italian Hour" played in the background on the clock radio perched on the stove. Some of those discussions were spoken all in English.

Others all in Italian, but most were a harmonic symphony of both languages.

The same was true for her chats on the only phone in the house – the kitchen telephone fastened to the wall. My sisters and I loved teasing her when she was speaking Italian on the phone. We only spoke English, so it was fun trying to guess what she was saying, and even more fun mimicking her words and gestures. She'd wave to shoosh us but then laugh at the same time, which only encouraged more of the same.

Anne had a fantastic sense of humor and could always take a good joke or prank, and was just as eager and capable to dish one out. Sometimes I think all we needed was that one room in the house.

Her kitchen was also the place to console and be consoled. And where we solved problems over a banquet of food and drink. Somehow that kitchen table always brought people together.

It was when her husband, her true love, passed away that everything changed forever. From my point of view, it was really the day the music died, along with everything else in her kitchen. Sadly, my mother grieved until her death twenty-eight years later.

~~~

As Papa reflects on her profound influence in my life, I've come to realize that her precious gift to me is everything that I wish for all of my family, present, and future. It's the priceless time spent eating and singing together, laughing and crying together, and just being with each other. Consider it a regift that can be traced back directly to what went on in that kitchen – Anne's kitchen.

WELL DONE, GRANDDAD (EULOGY)

WHAT A MAGNIFICENT LEGACY he leaves with us, this man from Maple Heights, Ohio. I met Carl Ruff on my second date with his beautiful daughter, Judi. At the time, I never would have guessed the inspiration he would become in my future. There was an instant bond between us, though I was neither the first nor the last to feel it. I noticed how my friends and family were also comfortably drawn to Carl when I introduced him. I suppose that's why so many people besides his family called him, *Granddad*.

He was a masculine figure, athletic, and active his entire life. In his teens, he lettered in football, basketball, and track at Maple Heights High School. One of his peers told me Carl was tough as nails on the gridiron, yet always extended a helping hand to an opponent after knocking him down. And it took over a quarter-century before someone broke his pole-vaulting record. Carl was also a popular student in high school, enough to be elected class president his senior year.

Of course, some may have mistaken his easy-going style with people, especially loved ones, as indecision. I knew better. He got exactly what he wanted because his family's happiness was his reward. What a chivalrous and simplistic way to go through life.

I had several father figures in my life. My dad was one, of course, but he died when I was only twenty-two years old. As a young man, I was fortunate to have three terrific uncles to spend time with whenever we could get together. Yet, after I married into Judi's family, Granddad was the one to emulate. I was admittedly streetwise and brash like many young men with my background. Nevertheless, I knew if I could be more positive, patient, and accepting like him, than maybe one day, I could fill that role – a monumental task for sure. I'm still trying.

To recall just a few stories isn't easy for me since Granddad and I worked and played together for three decades. There are many memories of family time, especially home projects. I'll only mention two.

~~~

Months after Judi and I built our home on a large wooded lot, Carl and his wife Irene, his true love, helped me prepare the yard for landscaping. We built bonfires to burn some of the cut and piled brush, but loaded much of the debris into the bed of my pickup truck. I lost track of how many truckloads we hauled to the local dump.

WELL DONE, GRANDDAD (EULOGY)

Carl developed a case of poison ivy that was so severe I had to take him to the emergency room after showing me the affected areas on his limbs. He insisted it wasn't so bad, except I remember sitting with him behind a hospital curtain as a nurse unwound the soiled gauze protecting his arms and legs. I watched her expression slowly morph into a squeamish squint. We both laughed once she left the room. I congratulated him on grossing-out a trauma nurse. If that wasn't funny enough, the attending doctor thanked Carl for sharing the worst case of poison ivy he had ever seen in person. It finally cleared up over time with medications. After that, we ribbed him about wearing gloves, long pants, and long sleeve shirts whenever he worked in the yard. He took it well.

~~~

Then there's golf, which he introduced me to early on in our relationship. We played hundreds of rounds together. It was just the two of us at first until I gained enough experience. After that, we often met up with my friends, who were always happy to see him.

Anyone that knew Carl well knew he disliked profanity. It was a little strange to me since I grew up where cursing rolled off the tongue naturally. Yet, as avid golfers can attest, it's the one sport capable of testing a saint's patience. I can proudly boast of being one of the few, if not the only person to have had the pleasure of

371

hearing old Granddad cuss aloud. He was quick with an *"aw gee whiz"* or an *"oh nuts"* and even the occasional *"darn it."* However, on that afternoon, standing in the middle of the fairway together, his seven-iron let him down. We watched as his ball rocketed out of sight into the deep woods. He turned to me calmly and let go of the most perfectly formed *"damn"* that I can still hear. He stretched it out for a second or two and then ended it with a smile. Coming from him made it hilarious. We had another good laugh and another fond memory. And just for the record, *"Ain't that a whopper-do,"* was his signature expression.

I've heard it said that every young male needs an older man to let him know how he's doing for himself and his family. It's a kind of paternal cheerleader. I had the privilege of spending lots of quality time with mine, and I can only hope to be as good as the one I had in my corner.

~~~

Yes, it's sad he's gone, but he'll never be forgotten, not as long as Papa is around. I can't help feeling anything but happiness whenever I'm reminded of him because of all the goodwill he left behind. It says something compelling about the man. And maybe most importantly, I see that part of Carl in my children who he helped raise. Well done, Granddad!

ANGEL, FIRST CLASS (EULOGY)

HERE'S A HYPOTHETICAL QUESTION for you to ponder. Do you know anyone you would nominate for *Angel, First Class*? I'm talking about a special someone you know personally and believe with certainty will receive his or her heavenly wings the first day they enter the pearly gates. My oldest sister is, without a doubt, my nominee. My money is on Anita.

Anita consistently demonstrated genuine goodness for as long as I've known her. And because we met the day I was born, that means my entire life. Her random acts of kindness toward people – family, friends, and even strangers, were instinctual and plentiful. She was the poster child for morality. No exaggeration.

These qualities may already be enough to merit those heavenly wings. However, what clinched my endorsement is how she performed these deeds while battling a mounting bag of chronic illnesses hindering her lifestyle from childhood. Yet somehow, Anita managed to carry on every day as if nothing were wrong. She flourished in life despite it. Where this courage came from, I have no clue. And there is more.

Along with this subtle humility for others came a fantastic sense of humor. Now add a pinch of silly and a dash of nutty. It made her so much fun to be around. Ask anyone that was close to her. I guarantee they'll have at least one testimonial of her kooky personality. In my family, we referred to them simply as, *Anita Stories*. Here is a perfect illustration of an Anita Story.

~~~

At one time during her working days, Anita was a PBX operator at Lutheran Medical Center on Cleveland's near west side. A good phone operator at a hospital must be quick, courteous, and above all, knowledgeable about the medical facility to properly transfer calls to the appropriate departments. You could say operators are the first-contact representatives of the medical center. Anita had been at it for many years and was considered a veteran. Fielding calls were matter-of-fact for my big sis until the day she received a phone call that was anything but routine.

"Lutheran Medical Center, how may I direct your call?"

"I'm not sure," a weak voice responded on the other end of the line. "I need help getting there to my appointment next week. How am I going to do that?" Anita immediately recognized it was an older woman.

"I'm sorry sweetheart, you say you have an appointment

next week, but you can't get here?"

"Yes, next Tuesday morning at nine-thirty. I don't drive anymore, and I have no one I can call. What am I going to do? I'm all alone."

As they spoke, it became evident to Anita that this person was also confused. She needed extra special attention. What department was Anita supposed to direct a call like this to anyway? It's not really in the switchboard operator's handbook.

So Anita did what Anita does best. She got personally involved by asking where the woman lived. It was not too far from the hospital.

"Give me your address, and I'll come to get you on Tuesday," Anita said.

"Are you sure? I don't want to put you out," the woman replied.

"It's not a problem at all. I will come to your house and get you."

"But how will I get home?" was the woman's next question.

Anita thought for a second. "Well, I can take you back home too."

"Do you promise?"

"Yes, I promise."

"Bless you, my dear, bless you." Anita scribbled the woman's address and phone number down on a piece of paper.

After they hung up, Anita opened her pocket calendar to pencil in the appointment on Tuesday. It was then she realized Tuesday was her day off.

What now? I know what our angel did – she came through on her promise. Anita woke up early Tuesday morning, drove into Cleveland from Olmsted Falls, picked up a total stranger, waited for her in the doctor's office, and then drove the woman back home. That's what she did.

It wasn't easy pulling this charitable deed out of my humble, sister-chauffer. Anita didn't want or need the limelight for her actions. Of course, it's precisely what you'd expect from an angel. We had to pry them from her.

~~~

Once Papa put all the pieces of this amazing and amusing deed together, we had ourselves one more "Anita story" to add to the collection. And what a helluva story it is. She was a remarkable sister, daughter, mother, wife, and friend, not to mention a fantastic role model and human being. Just think what a wonderful world it could be if the rest of us exercised even a fraction of this selflessness. Therefore, it is my honor and gives me great pleasure to respectfully nominate my big sister, Anita – Angel, First Class.

EPILOGUE

To my beautiful family, present, and future,

Papa wants you to remember that we come from a proud, loving, and passionate people. I consider myself fortunate to be deeply immersed in this Italian American culture. In turn, it's my pleasure to share some of the traditions with my twice removed *Americanized* children.

One of my favorites is Sunday mornings in an Italian household. There was nothing more comforting than waking up to the sound of music from Italy, and the aroma of tomato sauce permeating the house. It not only let me know it was Sunday but also defined who we are as a family.

Nowadays, I supply the Sunday morning Italian music while your British-German nana, outstanding with any Italian recipe, does the cooking. "Stir the sauce" is something you'll hear throughout the day. And although it's optional, dipping chunks of fresh Italian bread into the simmering *sugo* is honestly irresistible.

My dear ones, it is my fondest hope that you will sit

down in front of whatever modern device you have at your disposal to preserve some of your memories for the generations that follow. Who knows, if enough of the family participates, we could end up with an ancestral library one day. In any case, I hope your journey back in time fills you with the joy and satisfaction that mine did for me. And I can tell you in no uncertain terms – from where I'm presently sitting, the voyage passes quickly.

Remember to let your subtle vibrations be a positive influence on those around you. It may give them something to write about someday. *Salute!*

PAPA loves you!

GLOSSARY

Some words and phrases the way I use them...
Baccala (bahk•kah•lah') – Dried salted cod/a foolish person
Bambini (bam•bean'• nee) – Children
Bocce (bawt'•chah) – Italian variety of lawn bowling
Buon giorno (bwon joar'• noa) – Good morning/afternoon
Cafone (ka•pho•neh') – A ridiculous but amusing person/clown
Capisce (kah•pee'•shay) – Do you understand
Chooch (chooch) – Dummy, jackass
E Madonne (ee ma•dahn'•neh) – Oh Mother of God
Famiglia (fah•mee'•lyah) – Family
Figlio (fee'•lyoa) – Son
Gabagool (ga•ba•gool') – Capicola, an Italian pork cold cut
Gagootz (ga•gootz') – Insane
Grazie (graa'•tsee•ay) – Thank you
Malocchio (mal•oik') – The evil eye
Mangia (mahn'•jah) – Eat
Morra (moar'•rah) – Italian hand game
Nonna (non'•nah) – Grandmother
Padre (paa'•dray) – Father
Paesans (pie•zonz') – Fellow countrymen/people like me
Pallino (pahl•lee'•noa) – Small target ball in bocce
Pazzo/pazza (paz'•zo/za) – Crazy in the head
Pescatori (pay•skah•toa'•ree) – Fishermen
Pezza di merda (peht'•soa de mayr'da) – Piece of sh*t
Prego (pray'•goa) – You're welcome
Puttana (pu•tah'•nah) – A prostitute
Salute (sa•lute') – Health/Cheers
Schifosa (skee•foe'•za) – A lousy, discussing person
Stugots (stew•gots') – Man's body part
Stunad (stew•nod') – Stupid
Sugo (soog) – Sauce
Tante (tahn'•tay) – Many
Taralli (tah•ral'•lee) – Italian pretzels
Tranquillo (tran•quil'•lo)– Quiet, tranquil
Va bene (va• beh'•nay) – All right
Voglio – (vo'•lyoa) – I want
Ringraziarti – (rin•graz•e•ar'•tee) – To say thank you

Summer of '70

3 older sisters
Mid-1950s

West Technical
Senior Button

Dad with uncle Rico

Nana and Papa 2020

Anne's Kitchen

1971 VW Bus

Our Wedding Tarantella

TOSRV '79

Grandfather Pasquale (left)
and Pop

Granddad Carl Ruff

Maid of the Mist

Socrates Cave T-Shirt

Big Jerry & Annie

Sweet Judi

The Rock & the Vase

State Tournament

Scale Model Design

Cousin Frank